ISBN 978-0-331-67832-1
PIBN 11067567

1 MONTH OF
FREE
READING

at

www.ForgottenBooks.com

By purchasing this book you are eligible for one month membership to ForgottenBooks.com, giving you unlimited access to our entire collection of over 1,000,000 titles via our web site and mobile apps.

To claim your free month visit:

www.forgottenbooks.com/free1067567

English
Français
Deutsche
Italiano
Español
Português

www.forgottenbooks.com

Mythology Photography **Fiction**
Fishing Christianity **Art** Cooking
Essays Buddhism Freemasonry
Medicine **Biology** Music **Ancient
Egypt** Evolution Carpentry Physics
Dance Geology **Mathematics** Fitness
Shakespeare **Folklore** Yoga Marketing
Confidence Immortality Biographies
Poetry **Psychology** Witchcraft
Electronics Chemistry History **Law**
Accounting **Philosophy** Anthropology
Alchemy Drama Quantum Mechanics
Atheism Sexual Health **Ancient History**
Entrepreneurship Languages Sport
Paleontology Needlework Islam
Metaphysics Investment Archaeology
Parenting Statistics Criminology
Motivational

FOREIGN RELATIONS

OF THE

UNITED STATES.

ENFORCEMENT OF REGULATIONS

RESPECTING

FUR SEALS.

WASHINGTON:

GOVERNMENT PRINTING OFFICE.

1895.

IN THE SENATE OF THE UNITED STATES.

MESSAGE

FROM THE

PRESIDENT OF THE UNITED STATES,

IN RESPONSE TO

Senate resolution of January 8, 1895, transmitting information relating to the enforcement of the regulations respecting fur seals, adopted by the Governments of the United States and Great Britain in accordance with the decision of the Tribunal of Arbitration convened at Paris, with other information called for by said resolution.

FEBRUARY 11, 1895.—Read, referred to the Committee on Foreign Relations, and ordered to be printed.

To the Senate:

On the 8th day of January I received a copy of the following Senate resolution:

Resolved, That the President be requested, if not incompatible with the public interests, to communicate to the Senate all reports, documents, and other papers, including logs of vessels, relating to the enforcement of the regulations respecting fur seals adopted by the Governments of the United States and Great Britain in accordance with the decision of the Tribunal of Arbitration convened in Paris and the resolution (regulations?) under which said reports are required to be made, as well as relating to the number of seals taken during the season of 1894, by pelagic hunters and by the lessees of the Pribilof and Commander islands; also, relating to the steps which may have been taken to extend the said regulations to the Asiatic waters of the North Pacific Ocean and Bering Sea, and to secure the concurrence of other nations in said regulations; and further, all papers not heretofore published, including communications of the agent of the United States before said tribunal at Paris, relating to the claims of the British Government on account of the seizure of the sealing vessels in Bering Sea.

In compliance with said request I herewith transmit sundry papers, documents, and reports which have been returned to me by the Secretary of State, the Secretary of the Treasury, and the Secretary of the Navy, to whom said resolution was referred. I am not in possession of any further information touching the various subjects embodied in such resolution.

It will be seen from a letter of the Secretary of the Navy, accompanying the papers and documents sent from his Department, that it is impossible to furnish at this time the complete log books of some of the naval vessels referred to in the resolution; but I venture to express the hope that the reports of the commanders of such vessels herewith submitted will be found to contain in substance so much of the matters recorded in said log books as are important in answering the inquiries addressed to me by the Senate.

GROVER CLEVELAND.

EXECUTIVE MANSION,
February 11, 1895.

To the PRESIDENT:

The Secretary of State, to whom was referred the resolution adopted by the Senate on the 8th ultimo, requesting the President,

if not incompatible with the public interests, to communicate to the Senate all reports, documents, and other papers, including logs of vessels, relating to the enforcement of the regulations respecting fur seals adopted by the Governments of the United States and Great Britain, in accordance with the decision of the Tribunal of Arbitration convened at Paris, and the resolution (regulations ?) under which said reports are required to be made, as well as relating to the number of seals taken during the season of 1894 by pelagic hunters and by the lessees of the Pribilof and Commander islands; also relating to the steps which may have been taken to extend the said regulations to the Asiatic waters of the North Pacific Ocean and Bering Sea, and to secure the concurrence of other nations in said regulations; and further, all papers not heretofore published, including communications of the agent of the United States before said tribunal at Paris, relating to the claims of the British Government on account of the seizure of the sealing vessels in Bering Sea,

has the honor to lay before the President copies of all reports, documents, and other papers found of record in the Department of State relating to the subjects embraced in the resolution.

Respectfully submitted.

W. Q. GRESHAM.

DEPARTMENT OF STATE,
Washington, February 6, 1895.

CORRESPONDENCE OF DEPARTMENT OF STATE.

TABLE OF CONTENTS.

Table of contents—Continued.

Table of contents—continued.

Table of contents—Continued.

Table of contents—Continued.

Table of contents—Continued.

Table of contents—Continued.

No. 1.

Sir Julian Pauncefote to ·Mr. Gresham.

[Telegram.]

NEWPORT, R. I., *August 22, 1893.*

Lord Rosebery proposes to lay before Parliament at once Bering Sea award. He presumes your Government have no objection. Can I reply in that sense?

No. 2.

Mr. Gresham to Sir Julian Pauncefote.

[Telegram.]

DEPARTMENT OF STATE,
Washington, August 22, 1893.

I see no reason why Bering Sea award should not be laid before Parliament, although we have received no official copy.

No. 3.

Mr. Gresham to Mr. Bayard.

[Telegram.]

WASHINGTON, *September 12, 1893.*

The two powers should, without delay, come to an understanding which will make the regulations found to be necessary by the Paris Tribunal of Arbitration practically effective before the next sealing season.

Concurrent legislation and supplemental regulations seem indispensable. You are instructed to inform the British minister that the United States desire to take the matter up at once with the ambassador here, or in some other way satisfactory to both Governments. Efforts to obtain adhesion of other powers to the regulations should be promptly made. The arbitrators recommend that no fur seal be killed on land or sea for one, two, or three years. If this suggestion is adopted the concurrence of Russia should be had, if possible.

No. 4.

Mr. Bayard to Mr. Gresham.

EMBASSY OF THE UNITED STATES,
London, September 13, 1893. (Received September 21.)

SIR: I avail myself of the mail pouch, which closes to-day, to send you two pamphlets on the Bering Sea question and the award thereon of the tribunal at Paris.

I have written to the secretary of state for foreign affairs asking an interview, in order to lay before him the purport of your instruction in relation to proceeding, without delay, to agree upon the regulations in fur sealing, made necessary to effectuate the award of the arbitrators.

I shall communicate to you as soon as possible the result of the interview with Lord Rosebery on the subject.

I have, etc.,   T. F. BAYARD.

No. 5.

Mr. Bayard to Mr. Gresham.

EMBASSY OF THE UNITED STATES,
London, September 13, 1893. (Received September 21.)

SIR: Referring to my previous dispatch of this date, I have now the honor to inform you that I have just had an interview with Her Majesty's secretary of state for foreign affairs in which I acquainted him with the purport of your instruction of to-day by cable in relation to the expediency of the two Governments coming at once to an understanding under which the award of the Paris Tribunal of Arbitration upon the Bering Sea questions would be rendered practically effective before the next sealing season.

His Lordship expressed his willingness to act promptly, and also the opinion that the arrangements for that purpose would be wisely made at Washington, and that the British ambassador, Sir Julian Pauncefote, would be eminently qualified to conduct them in behalf of his Government. But Lord Rosebery told me that he was awaiting a note upon the subject of the award from Sir Charles Tupper, high commissioner for Canada, who has just gone hence to Canada, and was, therefore, not prepared to discuss the matter further until he had heard from him.

I suggested the expediency of the two Governments acting promptly, in which his Lordship expressed his full concurrence, and said he would telegraph Sir Charles Tupper this afternoon and acquaint me with the nature of his reply as soon as it was received.

His Lordship concurred also in my suggestion that it would be highly expedient that no intimation of delay or obstruction should be attributable to Canada, and said in substance that there could be none.

I had a long interview with Sir Charles Tupper on the 12th of August on the general subject of Canadian relations with the United States, which I propose to make the subject of a separate dispatch, in which he expressed the strongest desire to strengthen amicable relations between the United States and Canada; so that I apprehend a ready and willing cooperation in the the arrangements suggested by your cable instruction looking to the effective execution of the award of the Paris Tribunal.

I have, etc.,　　　　　　　　　　　　　　　T. F. BAYARD.

No. 6.

Mr. Gresham to Mr. Bayard.

DEPARTMENT OF STATE,
Washington, September 13, 1893.

SIR: Any benefit that this Government derives from the action of the Paris Tribunal of Arbitration will depend upon the regulations and the willingness of Great Britain to cooperate with us in making them practically effective. Concurrent legislation should be obtained and supplemental rules or orders agreed upon and published before the next sealing season begins. Owners of sealing vessels should know in advance the restriction under which they will have to act.

＊　　＊　　＊　　＊　　＊　　＊　　＊

I fear that whatever is done Canadians, and perhaps Americans, will transfer the ownership of their sealing vessels to citizens or subjects of other powers, thus avoiding the effect of the regulations. It remains to be seen whether other powers will now give their adhesion to the regulations. It would seem that the situation calls for both legislation and another treaty, and perhaps you had better sound Lord Rosebery on that point; also, as to how other powers are to be approached for their adhesion to the regulations.

＊　　＊　　＊　　－　　－　　－　　＊

I am, etc.,

W. Q. GRESHAM.

No. 7.

Mr. Gresham to Mr. Bayard.

[Telegram.]

WASHINGTON, *September 16, 1893.*

Your familiarity with the Bering Sea controversy, the treaty and award, suggests the propriety of intrusting to you the effort to obtain from Great Britain an agreement for the adoption of appropriate means for carrying into effect the regulations, and the President directs me to instruct you to exert yourself in that behalf. It is earnestly hoped that the British Government realizes the importance of prompt action and that it will speedily come to an understanding upon the subject of concurrent legislation, supplemental regulations, and joint effort for obtaining adhesion of other nations.

No. 8.

Mr. Gresham to Mr. Bayard.

DEPARTMENT OF STATE,
Washington, September 19, 1893.

SIR: Referring to my telegram of the 16th instant instructing you in regard to the framing of regulations and legislation on the part of the United States and Great Britain to govern sealing in Bering Sea, I send you for your further information copies of the final decision of the Tribunal of Arbitration with the recommendations made by the tribunal to the two Governments.

I am, etc.,   W. Q. GRESHAM.

[Inclosure 1 in No. 8.]

[English version.]

Award of the Tribunal of Arbitration constituted under the treaty concluded at Washington, the 29th of February, 1892, between the United States of America and Her Majesty the Queen of the United Kingdom of Great Britain and Ireland.

Whereas by a treaty between the United States of America and Great Britain, signed at Washington, February 29, 1892, the ratifications of which by the Governments of the two countries were exchanged at London on May 7, 1892, it was, amongst other things, agreed and concluded that the questions which had arisen between the Government of the United States of America and the Government of Her Britannic Majesty, concerning the jurisdictional rights of the United States in the waters of Bering Sea, and concerning also the preservation of the fur seal in or habitually resorting to the said sea, and the rights of the citizens and subjects of either country as regards the taking of fur seals in or habitually resorting to the said waters, should be submitted to a Tribunal of Arbitration to be composed of seven arbitrators, who should be appointed in the following manner, that is to say: two should be named by the President of the United States; two should be named by Her Britannic Majesty; His Excellency the President of the French Republic should be jointly requested by the high contracting parties to name one; His Majesty the King of Italy should be so requested to name one; His Majesty the King of Sweden and Norway should be so requested to name one; the seven arbitrators to be so named should be jurists of distinguished reputation in their respective countries, and the selecting powers should be requested to choose, if possible, jurists who are acquainted with the English language;

And whereas it was further agreed by Article II of the said treaty that the arbitrators should meet at Paris within twenty days after the delivery of the counter cases mentioned in Article IV, and should proceed impartially and carefully to examine and decide the questions. which had been or should be laid before them as in the said treaty provided on the part of the Governments of the United States and of Her Britannic Majesty respectively, and that all questions considered by the tribunal, including the final decision, should be determined by a majority of all the arbitrators;

And whereas by Article VI of the said treaty, it was further provided as follows:

In deciding the matters submitted to the said arbitrators, it is agreed that the following five points shall be submitted to them in order that their award shall embrace a distinct decision upon each of said five points, to wit:

1. What exclusive jurisdiction in the sea now known as the Bering Sea, and what exclusive rights in the seal fisheries therein, did Russia assert and exercise prior and up to the time of the cession of Alaska to the United States?

2. How far were these claims of jurisdiction as to the seal fisheries recognized and conceded by Great Britain?

3. Was the body of water now known as the Bering Sea included in the phrase, Pacific Ocean, as used in the treaty of 1825 between Great Britain and Russia; and what rights, if any, in the Bering Sea were held and exclusively exercised by Russia after said treaty?

4 Did not all the rights of Russia as to jurisdiction and as to the seal fisheries in Bering Sea east of the water boundary, in the treaty between the United States and Russia, of the 30th of March, 1867, pass unimpaired to the United States under that treaty?

5. Has the United States any right, and if so, what right of protection or property in the fur seals frequenting the islands of the United States in Bering Sea when such seals are found outside the ordinary three-mile limit?

And whereas, by Article VII of the said treaty, it was further agreed as follows:

If the determination of the foregoing questions as to the exclusive jurisdiction of the United States shall leave the subject in such position that the concurrence of Great Britain is necessary to the establishment of regulations for the proper protection and preservation of the fur seal in or habitually resorting to the Bering Sea, the arbitrators shall then determine what concurrent regulations, outside the jurisdictional limits of the respective Governments, are necessary, and over what waters such regulations should extend;

The high contracting parties furthermore agree to cooperate in securing the adhesion of other powers to such regulations;

And whereas, by Article VIII of the said treaty, after reciting that. the high contracting parties had found themselves unable to agree upon a reference which should include the question of the liability of each for the injuries alleged to have been sustained by the other, or by its citizens, in connection with the claims presented and urged by it, and that "they were solicitous that this subordinate question should not interrupt or longer delay the submission and determination of the main questions," the high contracting parties agreed that "either of them might submit to the arbitrators any question of fact involved in said claims and ask for a finding thereon, the question of the liability of either Government upon the facts found to be the subject of further negotiation;"

And whereas the President of the United States of America named the Hon. John M. Harlan, justice of the Supreme Court of the United States, and the Hon. John T. Morgan, Senator of the United States, to be two of the said arbitrators, and Her Britannic Majesty named the Right Hon. Lord Hannen and the Hon. Sir John Thompson, minister of justice and attorney-general for Canada, to be two of the said arbitrators, and His Excellency, the President of the French Republic, named the Baron de Courcel, senator, ambassador of France, to be one of the said arbitrators, and His Majesty, the King of Italy, named the

Marquis Emilio Visconti Venosta, former minister of foreign affairs and senator of the Kingdom of Italy, to be one of the said arbitrators, and His Majesty, the King of Sweden and Norway, named Mr. Gregers Gram, minister of state, to be one of the said arbitrators:

And whereas we, the said arbitrators, so named and appointed, having taken upon ourselves the burden of the said arbitration, and having duly met at Paris, proceeded impartially and carefully to examine and decide all the questions submitted to us, the said arbitrators under the said treaty, or laid before us as provided in the said treaty on the part of the Governments of Her Britannic Majesty and the United States, respectively;

Now we, the said arbitrators, having impartially and carefully examined the said questions, do in like manner by this our award decide and determine the said questions in manner following, that is to say, we decide and determine as to the five points mentioned in Article VI as to which our award is to embrace a distinct decision upon each of them:

As to the first of the said five points, we, the said Baron de Courcel, Mr. Justice Harlan, Lord Hannen, Sir John Thompson, Marquis Visconti Venosta, and Mr. Gregers Gram, being a majority of the said arbitrators, do decide and determine as follows:

By the ukase of 1821, Russia claimed jurisdiction in the sea now known as the Bering's Sea, to the extent of 100 Italian miles from the coasts and islands belonging to her, but, in the course of the negotiations which led to the conclusion of the treaties of 1824 with the United States and of 1825 with Great Britain, Russia admitted that her jurisdiction in the said sea should be restricted to the reach of cannon shot from shore, and it appears that, from that time up to the time of the cession of Alaska to the United States, Russia never asserted in fact or exercised any exclusive jurisdiction in Bering's Sea or any exclusive rights in the seal fisheries therein beyond the ordinary limit of territorial waters.

As to the second of the said five points, we, the said Baron de Courcel, Mr. Justice Harlan, Lord Hannen, Sir John Thompson, Marquis Visconti Venosta, and Mr. Gregers Gram, being a majority of the said arbitrators, do decide and determine that Great Britain did not recognize or concede any claim upon the part of Russia to exclusive jurisdiction as to the seal fisheries in Bering Sea outside of ordinary territorial waters.

As to the third of the said five points, as to so much thereof as requires us to decide whether the body of water now known as the Bering Sea was included in the phrase "Pacific Ocean" as used in the treaty of 1825 between Great Britain and Russia, we, the said arbitrators, do unanimously decide and determine that the body of water now known as the Bering Sea was included in the phrase "Pacific Ocean," as used in the said treaty.

And as to so much of the said third point as requires us to decide what rights, if any, in the Bering Sea were held and exclusively exercised by Russia after the said treaty of 1825, we, the said Baron de Courcel, Mr. Justice Harlan, Lord Hannen, Sir John Thompson, Marquis Visconti Venosta, and Mr. Gregers Gram, being a majority of the said arbitrators, do decide and determine that no exclusive rights of jurisdiction in Bering Sea and no exclusive rights as to the seal fisheries therein were held or exercised by Russia outside of ordinary territorial waters after the treaty of 1825.

As to the fourth of the said five points, we, the said arbitrators, do unanimously decide and determine that all the rights of Russia as to jurisdiction and as to the seal fisheries in Bering Sea east of the water boundary, in the treaty between the United States and Russia of the 30th March, 1867, did pass unimpaired to the United States under the said treaty.

As to the fifth of the said five points, we, the said Baron de Courcel, Lord Hannen, Sir John Thompson, Marquis Viscouti Venosta and Mr. Gregers Gram, being a majority of the said arbitrators, do decide and determine that the United States has not any right of protection or property in the fur seals frequenting the islands of the United States in Bering Sea, when such seals are found outside the ordinary three-mile limit.

And whereas the aforesaid determination of the foregoing questions as to the exclusive jurisdiction of the United States mentioned in Article VI leaves the subject in such a position that the concurrence of Great Britain is necessary to the establishment of regulations for the proper protection and preservation of the fur seal in or habitually resorting to the Bering Sea, the tribunal having decided by a majority as to each article of the following regulations, we, the said Baron de Courcel, Lord Hannen, Marquis Visconti Venosta, and Mr. Gregers Gram, assenting to the whole of the nine articles of the following regulations, and being a majority of the said arbitrators, do decide and determine in the mode provided by the treaty, that the following concurrent regulations outside the jurisdictional limits of the respective Governments are necessary and that they should extend over the waters hereinafter mentioned, that is to say:

ARTICLE 1.

The Governments of the United States and of Great Britain shall forbid their citizens and subjects, respectively, to kill, capture, or pursue at any time and in any manner whatever, the animals commonly called fur seals, within a zone of sixty miles around the Pribilov Islands, inclusive of the territorial waters.

The miles mentioned in the preceding paragraph are geographical miles of sixty to a degree of latitude.

ARTICLE 2.

The two Governments shall forbid their citizens and subjects, respectively, to kill, capture, or pursue, in any manner whatever, during the season extending, each year, from the 1st of May to the 31st of July, both inclusive, the fur seals on the high sea, in the part of the Pacific Ocean, inclusive of the Behring Sea, which is situated to the north of the 35th degree of north latitude, and eastward of the 180th degree of longitude from Greenwich till it strikes the water boundary described in article 1 of the treaty of 1867 between the United States and Russia, and following that line up to Behring Straits.

ARTICLE 3.

During the period of time and in the waters in which the fur-seal fishing is allowed, only sailing vessels shall be permitted to carry on or take part in fur-seal fishing operations. They will, however, be at liberty to avail themselves of the use of such canoes or undecked boats, propelled by paddles, oars, or sails, as are in common use as fishing boats.

ARTICLE 4.

Each sailing vessel authorised to fish for fur seals must be provided with a special license issued for that purpose by its Government and shall be required to carry a distinguishing flag, to be prescribed by its Government.

ARTICLE 5.

The masters of the vessels engaged in fur-seal fishing shall enter accurately in their official log book the date and place of each fur-seal fishing operation, and also the number and sex of the seals captured upon each day. These entries shall be communicated by each of the two Governments to the other at the end of each fishing season.

ARTICLE 6.

The use of nets, fire arms and explosives shall be forbidden in the fur-seal fishing. This restriction shall not apply to shotguns when such fishing takes place outside of Behring's Sea during the season when it may be lawfully carried on.

ARTICLE 7.

The two Governments shall take measures to control the fitness of the men authorized to engage in fur-seal fishing; these men shall have been proved fit to handle with sufficient skill the weapons by means of which this fishing may be carried on.

ARTICLE 8.

The regulations contained in the preceding articles shall not apply to Indians dwelling on the coasts of the territory of the United States or of Great Britain, and carrying on fur-seal fishing in canoes or undecked boats not transported by or used in connection with other vessels and propelled wholly by paddles, oars, or sails, and manned by not more than five persons each in the way hitherto practised by the Indians, provided such Indians are not in the employment of other persons, and provided that, when so hunting in canoes or undecked boats, they shall not hunt fur seals outside of territorial waters under contract for the delivery of the skins to any person.

This exemption shall not be construed to affect the municipal law of either country, nor shall it extend to the waters of Behring Sea or the waters of the Aleutian Passes.

Nothing herein contained is intended to interfere with the employment of Indians as hunters or otherwise in connection with fur-sealing vessels as heretofore.

ARTICLE 9.

The concurrent regulations hereby determined with a view to the protection and preservation of the fur seals shall remain in force, until they have been, in whole or in part, abolished or modified by common agreement between the Governments of the United States and of Great Britain.

The said concurrent regulations shall be submitted every five years to a new examination, so as to enable both interested Governments to consider whether, in the light of past experience, there is occasion for any modification thereof.

And whereas the Government of Her Britannic Majesty did submit to the Tribunal of Arbitration by Article VIII of the said treaty certain questions of fact involved in the claims referred to in the said Article VIII, and did also submit to us, the said tribunal, a statement of the said facts, as follows, that is to say:

FINDINGS OF FACT PROPOSED BY THE AGENT OF GREAT BRITAIN AND AGREED TO AS PROVED BY THE AGENT FOR THE UNITED STATES, AND SUBMITTED TO THE TRIBUNAL OF ARBITRATION FOR ITS CONSIDERATION.

1. That the several searches and seizures, whether of ships or goods, and the several arrests of masters and crews, respectively mentioned in the schedule to the British case, pages 1 to 60, inclusive, were made by the authority of the United States Government. The questions as to the value of the said vessels or their contents, or either of them, and the question as to whether the vessels mentioned in the schedule to the British case, or any of them, were wholly or in part the actual property of citizens of the United States, have been withdrawn from and have not been considered by the tribunal, it being understood that it is open to the United States to raise these questions or any of them, if they think fit, in any future negotiations as to the liability of the United States Government to pay the amounts mentioned in the schedule to the British case.

2. That the seizures aforesaid, with the exception of the *Pathfinder* seized at Neah-Bay, were made in Bering Sea at the distances from shore mentioned in the schedule annexed hereto, marked C.

3. That the said several searches and seizures of vessels were made by public armed vessels of the United States, the commanders of which had, at the several times when they were made, from the Executive Department of the Government of the United States, instructions, a copy of one of which is annexed hereto, marked A, and that the others were, in all substantial respects, the same; that in all the instances in which proceedings were had in the district courts of the United States resulting in condemnation, such proceedings were begun by the filing of libels, a copy of one of which is annexed hereto, marked B, and that the libels in the other proceedings were in all substantial respects the same; that the alleged acts or offenses for which said several searches and seizures were made were in each case done or committed in Bering Sea at the distances from shore aforesaid; and that in each case in which sentence of condemnation was passed, except in those cases when the vessels were released after condemnation, the seizure was adopted by the Government of the United States; and in those cases in which the vessels were released the seizure was made by the authority of the United States; that the said fines and imprisonments were for alleged breaches of the municipal laws of the United States, which alleged breaches were wholly committed in Bering Sea at the distances from the shore aforesaid.

4. That the several orders mentioned in the schedule annexed hereto and marked C, warning vessels to leave or not to enter Bering Sea were made by public armed vessels of the United States, the commanders of which had, at the several times when they were given, like instructions as mentioned in finding 3, and that the vessels so warned were engaged in sealing or prosecuting voyages for that purpose, and that such action was adopted by the Government of the United States.

5. That the district courts of the United States in which any proceedings were had or taken for the purpose of condemning any vessel seized as mentioned in the schedule to the case of Great Britain, pages 1 to 60, inclusive, had all the jurisdiction and powers of courts of admiralty, including the prize jurisdiction, but that in each case the sentence pronounced by the court was based upon the grounds set forth in the libel.

ANNEX A.

TREASURY DEPARTMENT, OFFICE OF THE SECRETARY,
Washington, April 21, 1886.

SIR: Referring to Department letter of this date, directing you to proceed with the revenue steamer *Bear*, under your command, to the seal islands, etc., you are hereby clothed with full power to enforce the law contained in the provisions of section 1956 of the United States Revised Statutes, and directed to seize all vessels, and arrest and deliver to the proper authorities any or all persons whom you may detect violating the law referred to, after due notice shall have been given.

S. Ex. 67——2

You will also seize any liquors or firearms attempted to be introduced into the country without proper permit, under the provisions of section 1955 of the Revised Statutes, and the proclamation of the President, dated 4th February, 1870.

Respectfully, yours,

C. S. FAIRCHILD, *Acting Secretary.*

Capt. M. A. HEALY,
Commanding revenue steamer Bear, San Francisco, Cal.

ANNEX B.

In the district court of the United States for the district of Alaska—August special term, 1886.

Hon. LAFAYETTE DAWSON,
Judge of said District Court:

The libel of information of M. D. Ball, attorney for the United States for the district of Alaska, who prosecutes on behalf of said United States, and being present here in court in his proper person, in the name and on behalf of the said United States, against the schooner *Thornton,* her tackle, apparel, boats, cargo, and furniture, and against all persons intervening for their interest therein, in a cause of forfeiture, alleges and informs as follows:

That Charles A. Abbey, an officer in the Revenue-Marine Service of the United States, and on special duty in the waters of the district of Alaska, heretofore, to wit, on the 1st day of August, 1886, within the limits of Alaska Territory, and in the waters thereof, and within the civil and judicial district of Alaska, to wit, within the waters of that portion of Bering Sea belonging to the said district, on waters navigable from the sea by vessels of 10 or more tons burden, seized the ship or vessel commonly called a schooner, the *Thornton,* her tackle, apparel, boats, cargo, and furniture, being the property of some person or persons to the said attorney unknown, as forfeited to the United States, for the following causes:

That the said vessel or schooner was found engaged in killing fur seal within the limits of Alaska Territory, and in the waters thereof, in violation of section 1956 of the Revised Statutes of the United States.

And the said attorney saith that all and singular the premises are and were true, and within the admiralty and maritime jurisdiction of this court, and that by reason thereof, and by force of the Statutes of the United States in such cases made and provided, the afore-mentioned and described schooner or vessel, being a vessel of over 20 tons burden, her tackle, apparel, boats, cargo, and furniture, became and are forfeited to the use of the said United States, and that said schooner is now within the district aforesaid.

Wherefore the said attorney prays the usual process and monition of this honorable court issue in this behalf, and that all persons interested in the before-mentioned and described schooner or vessel may be cited in general and special to answer the premises, and all due proceedings being had, that the said schooner or vessel, her tackle, apparel, boats, cargo, and furniture may, for the cause aforesaid, and others appearing, be condemned by the definite sentence and decree of this honorable court, as forfeited to the use of the said United States, according to the form of the statute of the said United States in such cases made and provided.

M. D. BALL,
United States District Attorney for the District of Alaska.

ANNEX C.

The following table shows the names of the British sealing vessels seized or warned by United States revenue cruisers, 1886–1890, and the approximate distance from land when seized. The distances assigned in the cases of the *Carolena, Thornton,* and *Onward* are on the authority of United States Naval Commander Abbey. (See Fiftieth Congress, second session, Senate Ex. Doc. No. 106, pp. 20, 30, 40.) The distances assigned in the cases of the *Anna Beck, W. P. Sayward, Dolphin* and *Grace* are on the authority of Captain Shepard, U. S. R. M. (Blue Book, United States, No. 2, 1890, pp. 80–82. See Appendix, Vol. III.)

Name of vessel.	Date of seizure.	Approximate distance from land when seized	United States vessel making seizure.
Carolena..............	Aug. 1, 1886	75 miles	Corwin.
Thornton	....do	70 miles	Corwin.
Onward	Aug. 2, 1886	115 miles	Corwin.
Favourite	....do	Warned by Corwin in about same position as Onward.	
Anna Beck	July 2, 1887	66 miles	Rush.
W. P. Sayward	July 9, 1887	59 miles................................. ...	Rush.
Dolphin	July 12, 1887	40 miles	Rush.
Grace...................	July 17, 1887	96 miles	Rush.
Alfred Adams........	Aug. 10, 1887	62 miles	Rush.
Ada	Aug. 25, 1887	15 miles	Bear.
Triumph	Aug. 4, 1887	Warned by Rush not to enter Bering Sea......	
Juanita...	July 31, 1889	66 miles	Rush.
Pathfinder..............	July 29, 1889	50 miles	Rush.
Triumph..............	July 11, 1889	Ordered out of Bering Sea by Rush. (?) As to position when warned.	
Black Diamond........	....do	35 miles	Rush.
Lily	Aug. 6, 1889	66 miles	Rush.
Ariel	July 30, 1889	Ordered out of Bering Sea by Rush...........	
Kate	Aug. 13, 1889	....do......................................	
Minnie	July 15, 1889	65 miles	Rush.
Pathfinder..............	Mar. 27, 1890	Seized in Neab Bay [1].........................	Corwin.

[1] Neah Bay is in the State of Washington, and the *Pathfinder* was seized there on charges made against her in the Bering Sea in the previous year. She was released two days later.

And whereas the Government of Her Britannic Majesty did ask the said arbritrators to find the said facts as set forth in the said statement, and whereas the agent and counsel for the United States Government thereupon in our presence informed us that the said statement of facts was sustained by the evidence, and that they had agreed with the agent and counsel for Her Britannic Majesty that we, the arbitrators, if we should think fit so to do, might find the said statement of facts to be true.

Now, we, the said arbitrators, do unanimously find the facts as set forth in the said statement to be true.

And whereas each and every question which has been considered by the tribunal has been determined by a majority of all the arbitrators;

Now, we, Baron de Courcel, Lord Hannen, Mr. Justice Harlan, Sir John Thompson, Senator Morgan, the Marquis Visconti Venosta, and Mr. Gregers Gram, the respective minorities not withdrawing their votes, do declare this to be the final decision and award in writing of this tribunal in accordance with the treaty.

Made in duplicate at Paris and signed by us the 15th day of August in the year 1893.

And we do certify this English version thereof to be true and accurate.

ALPH. DE COURCEL.
JOHN M. HARLAN.
JOHN T. MORGAN.
HANNEN.
JNO. S. D. THOMPSON.
VISCONTI VENOSTA.
G. GRAM.

[Inclosure 2 in No. 8.]

[English version.]

Declarations made by the Tribunal of Arbitration and referred to the Governments of the United States and Great Britain for their consideration.

I.

The arbitrators declare that the concurrent regulations, as determined upon by the Tribunal of Arbitration, by virtue of Article VII of the treaty of the 29th of February, 1892, being applicable to the high sea only, should, in their opinion, be supplemented by other regulations applicable within the limits of the sovereignty of each of the two Powers interested and to be settled by their common agreement.

II.

In view of the critical condition to which it appears certain that the race of fur seals is now reduced in consequence of circumstances not fully known, the arbitrators think fit to recommend both Governments to come to an understanding in order to prohibit any killing of fur seals, either on land or at sea, for a period of two or three years, or at least one year, subject to such exceptions as the two Governments might think proper to admit of.

Such a measure might be recurred to at occasional intervals if found beneficial.

III.

The arbitrators declare, moreover, that, in their opinion, the carrying out of the regulations determined upon by the Tribunal of Arbitration, should be assured by a system of stipulations and measures to be enacted by the two Powers; and that the tribunal must, in consequence, leave it to the two Powers to decide upon the means for giving effect to the regulations determined upon by it.

We do certify this English version to be true and accurate and have signed the same at Paris this 15th day of August, 1893.

> ALPH DE COURCEL.
> JOHN M. HARLAN.

I approve Declarations I and III.

> HANNEN.

I approve Declarations I and III.

> JNO. S. D. THOMPSON.
> JOHN T. MORGAN.
> VISCONTI VENOSTA.
> G. GRAM.

No. 9.

Mr. Bayard to Mr. Gresham.

EMBASSY OF THE UNITED STATES,
London, September 19, 1893. (Received September 30.)

SIR: * * * I have to-day received a note from the foreign office informing me that a letter has just been received at the colonial office from Sir Charles Tupper, in Canada, stating that he and the prime minister had been engrossed by arrears of business since their return, but that he was preparing a memorandum on the award in the Bering Sea Arbitration; and I am further informed that Lord Ripon has already telegraphed to Canada to expedite the memorandum in question and its receipt at the colonial office here.

I have every confidence that an effective execution of the award will be agreed upon in as short a time as the complexity and magnitude of the subject, and the somewhat undefined nature of the regulations and recommendations of the Tribunal of Arbitration, will admit.

I have, etc.,

`   T. F. BAYARD.

No. 10.

Mr. Bayard to Mr. Gresham.

[Telegram.]

LONDON, *September 20, 1893.*

Your instructions by cable duly followed. In an interview to-day secretary of state for foreign affairs fully responds to President's wishes for prompt action in executing Bering Sea award.

No. 11.

Mr. Bayard to Mr. Gresham.

EMBASSY OF THE UNITED STATES,
London, September 20, 1893. (Received September 30.)

SIR: I have the honor to acknowledge the receipt of your telegram of the 16th instant, with reference to the negotiation here of a convention to carry out the recommendations accompanying the award in the Bering Sea Arbitration.

Lord Rosebery's absence from town until to-day prevented my seeing him until 4 p. m. I made known to him the purport of your last instruction by cable, and pressed upon him the importance of prompt and active cooperation by the United States and Great Britain to give effective and executive force to the Paris award. He instantly expressed his desire to do so, and said he had no doubt whatever of a similar intent and feeling on the part of Canada.

While expressing this ready concurrence, he pressed me to convey his desire that, as the facts to be dealt with were all in America, Sir Julian Pauncefote, from his full knowledge of the whole business, should be employed on behalf of Great Britain in carrying out the decisions and recommendations of the tribunal.

There is not time before this mail leaves for me to state with more fullness his remarks, which, however, I will do by the next mail; and have just telegraphed you to acknowledge your telegram and state the interview directed by it had been held.

I have, etc.,   T. F. BAYARD.

No. 12.

Mr. Bayard to Mr. Gresham.

EMBASSY OF THE UNITED STATES,
London, September 30, 1893. (Received October 9.)

SIR: I have now the honor to acknowledge your letter of the 13th instant, stating the present condition of affairs arising out of the results of the Paris Arbitration in relation to our interests in Bering Sea and the fur-seal fisheries therein. And, as connected with the same subject, I have also the honor to acknowledge your letter of the 19th instant, inclosing copies of the final award and decision of the same tribunal.

The contents of both these communications have received the careful consideration which their importance demands.

My dispatches of September 19 and of September 30 can both be properly referred to in this communication as bearing upon the relations of the United States with the Dominion of Canada, in which the interests are conducted under the name (*nominis umbra*) of Great Britain, and which in a large degree, but not wholly, include the business of fur sealing, and although the capture of the fur seal (in the high seas) is chiefly carried on by Canadians, yet the dressing of the skins is almost entirely a London industry, and it is said that some ten thousand people are here engaged therein.

Lord Rosebery left London to be in attendance upon the Queen at Balmoral on the day I last had an interview with him, as reported to you, and is expected to return to London next week.

I shall without delay seek another interview with Lord Rosebsry upon his return to London, and endeavor to come to a distinct understanding on the subject under consideration, in order to proceed promptly to carry into practical effect the award and the recommendations with which it is accompanied.

To suspend wholly, even for a single year, the seal catch on the islands might be highly prejudicial to the United States, or their lessees, and as in the provisional or temporary arrangement of May, 1893, between Russia and Great Britain, a limit of 30,000 seals on the Russian islands was agreed to, it would seem a very reasonable figure to adopt for the catch on the Pribilof islands, whose product has been supposed to be about double that of the Russian islands.

I would respectfully ask for an expression of your views on this subject and how far we ought to go in restricting the seal catch on these islands. The mail closes in an hour and I will withhold other comments until I may have had some communication from the foreign office, and received some intimation of the Canadian views.

I have, etc.,

T. F. BAYARD.

No. 13.

Mr. Gresham to Mr. Bayard.

[Telegram.]

DEPARTMENT OF STATE,
Washington, October 3, 1893.

Yours of September 20 received. Lord Rosebery's suggestion has *been* carefully considered, and the President still prefers that all *negotiations for concurrent* action by the two Governments necessary to make the award and recommendations of the Bering Sea Tribunal effective be conducted by you at London, and my instructions cabled September 16 are repeated.

No. 14.

Mr. Gresham to Mr. Bayard.

DEPARTMENT OF STATE,
Washington, October 6, 1893.

SIR: Referring to my telegrams to you of the 16th ultimo and the 3d instant, relative to negotiations for carrying into effect the regulations proposed by the Bering Sea Arbitration Tribunal, I inclose, as of probable use to you in conducting the business, a copy of a letter, dated the 4th ultimo, from the Hon. E. J. Phelps, commenting on the award made by the arbitrators; also a copy of suggestions by Mr. James C. Carter on certain branches of the subject.

I am, etc.,

W. Q. GRESHAM.

[Inclosure 1 in No. 14.]

Mr. Phelps to Mr. Gresham.

BURLINGTON, VT., *September 4, 1893.*

SIR: Having been engaged as counsel for the United States before the Tribunal of Arbitration recently convened at Paris, under the treaty with Great Britain of 1892, in reference to the preservation of the fur seals frequenting the Pribilof Islands in Bering Sea, I deem it proper to place before the Department my views in respect to the award that has been made by the arbitrators.

I regard the regulations which it establishes as amply sufficient, if properly carried into effect, for the preservation of the herd of seals resorting to those islands.

The only months in which pelagic sealing is or can be carried on to any considerable extent are May and June in the North Pacific and July and August, and perhaps the first half of September, in the Bering Sea. A small number of seals may be taken in the North Pacific earlier, and possibly later, than those months, but not large enough to warrant the fitting out of vessels for that purpose, if the pursuit during the months named is prohibited. The business must therefore, in that event, cease, because it will become unprofitable.

Nor would the number that could be taken outside of those months be great enough to endanger the existence of the herd or seriously to interfere with the profits of the industry on the Pribilof Islands.

The award prohibits altogether the killing of the seals in the water, either in the North Pacific or in Bering Sea, during the months of May, June, and July, and prohibits during the remainder of the season in Bering Sea the use of firearms, nets, or explosives, or the taking of seals at all within sixty miles of the Pribilof Islands. This is practically a prohibition of pelagic sealing during the whole season in Bering Sea, because without firearms the seals can not be taken. The Indians manage to secure a few near the shores with spears; but the number that can be so taken is insignificant, especially in the open sea. Pelagic sealing has never been prosecuted in that way, nor could it be made to pay expenses.

The result of the award is therefore a virtual prohibition of pelagic sealing in Bering Sea, and to any very injurious extent in the North Pacific.

A copy of a paper prepared by one of the counsel in the case has been sent me, which, I am informed, has been transmitted to the Department. In this paper it is assumed that 20,000 female seals can be annually destroyed in the water consistently with the observance of the regulations established by the award. In this assumption I do not concur. It is, in my judgment, in conflict with all the evidence in the case on that point, as will be seen by a reference to it.

The sealing season at sea is divided into two periods, the "coast catch," consisting of those taken in the North Pacific prior to July 1 (by which time all the seals have entered the Bering Sea), and the Bering Sea catch, taken between July 1 and September 15. The latter, as has been pointed out, is totally prohibited. Of the former, tables prepared on the basis of the best information attainable show that 72 per cent are taken in the months of May and June, during which sealing in the North Pacific is forbidden by the award. More than seven-eighths of the entire business of pelagic sealing thus comes to an end, and it is obvious that the remainder can not pay for the expeditions necessary to prosecute it, nor be seriously detrimental, if prosecuted, to the existence of the herd.

It is further suggested in the same paper that as the proposed regulations affect only American and British vessels, poachers from those countries can avail themselves of the flag of some other nation to continue their depredations. I regard this apprehension as groundless.

No country, except the United States and Canada, has ever engaged in the pursuit of pelagic sealing in the North Pacific or in Bering Sea. The distance of these waters from all other maritime nations, except Russia and Japan, is so great that they can not engage in it with profit. Russia and Japan are interested to preserve the seal, as both possess seal islands, and their laws therefore protect seal life. This was pointed out by Mr. Blaine in the course of the diplomatic correspondence, when it was suggested by Great Britain that such regulations as might be fixed by the arbitrators should be dependent on the assent of other nations.

If, therefore, Canadian sealers should propose to avail themselves of the protection of the flags of other governments to prosecute a business in which the subjects of such governments are not engaged, it could only be accomplished by obtaining fraudulent registrations of their vessels in those countries, so as to evade the laws of their own. This would involve a connivance on the part of the nations allowing such registrations, which is not to be presumed of any sovereign power.

Nor could they possibly escape detection. If the crews of vessels so registered were composed, as they must be, of Canadians or Americans, and the employment was one, as it would be, in which the citizens of the country of registration were not engaged, it would be impossible for them to avoid exposure. And certainly when that took place no nation would attempt to afford protection to vessels not really their own, but which had been imposed upon them by fraud for the purpose of violating the laws of the nation to which their owners belonged.

I do not conceive, therefore, that the assent of other nations to these *regulations* would be at all necessary. So far as they can be obtained *they may no doubt* be desirable.

It appears to me, and I therefore respectfully submit that the first duty of the United States Government is to pass such laws as will effectually prohibit pelagic sealing by their own citizens under any flag, either in the North Pacific or in Bering Sea, during the close time fixed by these regulations, or in any manner which their terms forbid. This we have solemnly agreed to do by the treaty with Great Britain. Failing to do it, we can not expect them to be adopted by Great Britain. And we should convict ourselves before the world of a want of good faith in our previous diplomatic claims and in those urged before the arbitration. We should next firmly insist upon the enforcement of the regulations by all proper legislation on the part of Great Britain and Canada.

When that is accomplished on both sides, the valuable interest in question will be preserved from the destruction that would otherwise await it.

I venture to suggest further, for the consideration of the Department, that regard should be had by the United States Government to the recommendations of the tribunal relative to the restriction for some limited time of the number of seals to be killed on the Pribilof Islands.

There can be no doubt that these recommendations are judicious, and that a compliance with them would be most beneficial to the industry. They are made in the light of much evidence and unwearied investigations, in furtherance of the object which both nations had in. view, the preservation of the last remnant of this valuable race of animals. A proper respect for the tribunal which has at great personal inconvenience rendered us so great a service would seem to require that their suggestions should be attended to.

In respect of the claim of property in the seals made before the tribunal by the United States Government and disallowed by a majority vote little need be added. That we were right in this assertion I fully and firmly believe, and I am confirmed on this point not only by the views of my associates, but by the dissenting opinions of the eminent and learned members of the tribunal appointed by the United States.

I do not attempt to rehearse the many disadvantages we were placed under in the assertion of this claim by the composition of the tribunal, the terms of the treaty, the grounds previously taken by our Government, and by various other unfavorable circumstances.

Not the least of these was the extraordinary and unexpected action taken by Russia while the hearing before the tribunal was going on, in coming to an agreement with Great Britain in reference to their own seal islands, in which the right for which we contended and for which Russia had previously contended was given up, the vessels seized by Russia in the assertion of that right paid for, and regulations as to the killing of Russian seals provided, which are totally inadequate for their preservation.

Russia was on this question in the same interest with the United States. She had participated with us in the previous negotiations with Great Britain, in which protection for the seals was sought. The agreement made in 1887 between the United States and Great Britain for such protection, and which failed to be carried out in consequence of the objections of Canada, was made upon consultation with and with the concurrence of Russia, and was extended at her request so as to embrace her seal islands. Yet while the hearing before the tribunal was progressing, without any notice to or knowledge of the United States, with a haste for which in any event there could be no conceivable necessity, she permitted herself to,be drawn into an agreement so seriously prejudical to the contention of the United States. If our case had not been a very strong one, this very adroit and successful diplomacy on the part of Great Britain, announced to the tribunal near the close of the hearing, would have been fatal, as it was intended to be.

I can not take leave of this subject, in terminating my connection with the public service in respect to it, without expressing my deep sense of the great ability and learning of the distinguished gentlemen who consented to act as arbitrators, of their unfailing courtesy and patience, and of their earnest efforts to reach a just conclusion. The nations concerned owe them a debt of gratitude which should be suitably acknowledged, since it can not be discharged.

And I desire also to express my appreciation of the thorough and efficient manner in which the case of the United States was prepared and presented by the agent of the Government, and of the very valuable services in its conduct of all the counsel with whom I had the pleasure of being associated.

I have, etc., E. J. PHELPS.

———

[Inclosure 2 in No 14.]

Suggestions by Mr. Carter.

PART I.—THE MATTER OF OBTAINING THE ASSENT OF OTHER NATIONS TO REGULATIONS.

This is a subject of the highest importance, and is not unlikely to result in the greatest difficulty. It is one of the points in which the result of the arbitration may be to hasten the event which the neutral arbitrators fondly supposed they had prevented—the extermination of the seals as a commercial factor.

If it should turn out that the regulations have destroyed the profits of pelagic sealing, or reduced them to so low a point as to afford little temptation for the Canadian and American vessels to engage in it, their first resort will be to seek the protection of another flag; and this may easily be obtained, unless all the maritime powers should be induced to adopt and enforce the regulations.

Before the arbitration, while the United States could take the ground that the seals were its property, and consequently that it had the right to protect the herd everywhere against depredation, it would have been an easy thing to enforce that protection against the vessels of any weak state; but there was never any occasion to take such action, for the reason that none but Canadians and Americans engaged in the business.

Now, however, we may be soon confronted with the situation that vessels carrying, for instance, the flag of Chile, will appear in the sealing waters at prohibited times and in prohibited places. What shall the United States do? How can it now assert a right of property after it has been decided by an international court, in a proceeding to which it was a party, that no such right exists? True, it may say to other powers that they can not plead the judgment in their favor, because they were not parties, and that the United States still continues to assert its claim of property against all nations who were not parties to the proceeding. This course might be strictly just and consistent in the United States. They might insist that the important legal question of the right of property had not been finally settled; that the tribunal was not well constituted to decide it; that the United States would not be satisfied until a tribunal of independent jurists—not including representatives of the interested parties, and having no other questions to consider but this claim of right—had determined that it did not exist. This would be a consistent and honorable attitude in the United States, which would deserve the applause of the world. But the danger would be that the world at large, unacquainted with the real facts in the case, and consequently unacquainted with the real nature of the question, would view such conduct by the United States as a willful and unjustifiable effort to disregard the decision.

In the eyes of the world the judgment of the tribunal would, or might be, regarded as a final decision which ought to put an end to the question; and that inasmuch as it had determined that the seals were wild animals open to pursuit by all, all must be permitted to enjoy the right unless they voluntarily chose to give it up; and that if such a view should result in a destruction of the seals, that consequences must be accepted in preference to a disturbance of the peace of the world.

But another possible consequence of such an attitude by the United States must be contemplated. If they should capture a vessel of Chile or Peru, no critical condition could be brought on, although this is not certain. But suppose they had done this, and then a sealer should appear bearing the flag of some great naval power other than Great Britain? The United States would be utterly disgraced unless they also captured the trespasser, and this would present a very critical situation.

All this makes more apparent the absurd result of the arbitration. Sincerely desiring to protect the seals, but seeking to accomplish this object without wholly humiliating Great Britain, they reject the claim of right in order to reach the subject of regulations, that they may accommodate the difficulty by a dealing with that subject. They thus throw away the only means by which the herd can certainly be preserved, for they declare that all nations have a right to engage in the destructive work, thus making any system of repression ineffective unless the whole world choose to accede to it.

But the effort should be made to induce acquiescence on the part of other maritime powers, and it is to be hoped it may be successful.

PART II.—WHAT POSITION SHOULD THE UNITED STATES TAKE IN RELATION TO PELAGIC SEALING BY ITS OWN CITIZENS DURING THE OPEN SEASON?

This subject is another which the decision of the tribunal makes it exceedingly difficult to deal with.

There has always been a certain measure of inconsistency in the action of the United States in relation to this matter. We insisted before the tribunal that pelagic sealing was a barbarous and inhuman practice, a crime against the law of nature, and which, if it were carried on within the limits of a civilized state, would be stamped as a crime by the laws, and be punished as such; and that its character was not changed by the circumstance that it was carried on beyond the limits of municipal law. Of course we were obliged to meet the suggestion that our conduct was not consistent with this view, inasmuch as we ourselves permitted it, at least in the North Atlantic Ocean. To this we answered that Congress was a popular body, all the members of which could not be supposed to be familiar with the subject; that when our legislation was enacted it was not perceived, as we now clearly perceive, that the whole benefit of the herd of seals could be reaped by the selective killing carried on upon the Pribilof Islands without diminishing the herd, and consequently it was not then clearly perceived that pelagic sealing was an absolutely needless, and therefore an absolutely unjustifiable destruction of a bounty of nature; that, at the same time, many supposed (a wholly erroneous view) that an attempt by us to prevent pelagic sealing was an assertion of dominion over the seas, and that we could not exercise this outside of the waters of Behring Sea, even if we could there; that between these doubts and the hesitancy to prohibit our own citizens from doing what we allowed the citizens of other nations to do, our legislation had, undoubtedly, not proceeded upon views entirely consistent with our propositions as urged upon the tribunal. We asserted, however, that the moment the tribunal established our rights as claimed we should at once shape our legislation in accordance with the decree and absolutely prohibit our own citizens from engaging in pelagic sealing anywhere.

But what shall we do now? Shall we courageously say that the decision settles only the difficulty between the contending parties, but has not in any manner changed our views concerning the principles involved? That we still think that we have a right of property in the seals, and that the slaughter of female seals is barbarous, inhuman, and a crime against nature? Or shall we swallow all our protestations and accept the conclusion that this wretched work is a legitimate employment of human labor? If we take the former course we must prohibit pelagic sealing by our own citizens everywhere, precluding them from trespassing upon the property of our neighbors, the Russians, as well as upon our own, and leave to other nations the glory or the infamy, as well as the profits of this pursuit. If we take the latter we shall reap our part of the profits, if there be any, and occupy the miserable position of engaging in employments which we really believe to be immoral and criminal. I hope, for one, that our country will take the first attitude and persist in it. And my reasons are these:

First. Because we have been wholly right in our contention and the decision is wholly wrong. Nothing can ever be settled in international law until it is settled right. Fundamental truths may be discovered and declared, but they can not be manufactured or annulled. This decision should be viewed, not as discreditable to the tribunal, but as the best result which good men could reach who were, at the start, put in chains by our own action in making up the tribunal. The decision of a tribunal made up in part of representatives of the interested parties, and with laymen for the neutral members, and, moreover, irresistibly tempted to decide adversely to the claim of property in order to be able to settle the difficulty without injuring the susceptibilities of their associates, or of the two nations, can never set at rest any substantial controversy in international law. It will not settle this one. The decision will be challenged by the jurists of the world and will not endure their scrutiny. It proceeds upon a most degraded conception of international law which the enlightened opinion of the world will repudiate.

I would proudly reserve for the United States the glory of persisting in its own conceptions of the true principles of international law, until they shall ultimately triumph.

Those conceptions are that what the laws of God and nature declare to be right must be admitted to be right in international law, and that a decision to the contrary is not only criminal but will bring its *own* punishment along with it.

Our main proposition in harmony with this principle, upon the question of property, was this: "That wherever a useful thing is dependent for its existence and enjoyment by society upon the care and industry of man, those who exercise that care and industry have a right of property in the thing." This is, indeed, a self-evident proposition, for every one must immediately perceive that the care and industry will not be exercised, unless those who would exercise them are assured of their reward. And no one doubts, if the United States should cease its care and industry in and around the Pribilof Islands, the seals would at once be swept from existence.

The above proposition is the foundation upon which the right of property stands, from a shovel to a swarm of bees. No property would exist, and mankind would sink into barbarism and internecine war, each against the other, were it not true. I hope the United States will stand by that proposition and leave to Great Britain the consequences which flow from a denial of it.

Second. Because we shall lose nothing whatever by taking this honorable course. The regulations either leave pelagic sealing as a profitable pursuit, or they do not. If they do, even though the profit be small, the pursuit will be extensively carried on, and the herd will be destroyed as a commercial factor, and pelagic sealing itself must cease. The gain to our citizens would therefore be trifling and not worth any considerable effort, still less worth a sacrifice of our present honorable attitude. If, on the other hand, the regulations shall make pelagic sealing unprofitable it will not be carried on, in which event we shall lose nothing by compelling an abstention from a pursuit which would not be carried on, even if permitted.

Third. The probabilities are that the regulations will leave pelagic sealing a profitable pursuit, although the profits will be very much cut down. It will, therefore, be pursued. At least 20,000 females will be annually taken, and this will result in a speedy reduction of the herd to a point where it will be burdensome expense to the United States to maintain its guard over the islands, and that guard will be removed, and the remnant of the race will be swept away. I apprehend that if the question be put to our commissioners, Messrs. Mendenhall and Merriam, whether the herd can stand an annual draft of 20,000 females by pelagic sealers, the answer will be promptly in the negative. On this supposition, therefore, we should lose nothing by taking the honorable course and the one consistent with our uniform attitude.

On the other hand, let it be supposed that the regulations leave no profit and therefore no temptation to pelagic sealing, and are thus prohibitive of it; in such case also we should lose nothing, but rather gain.

Nor should we omit to hold in contemplation the contingency, quite possible, that pelagic sealing should continue to be prosecuted, but with unsatisfactory results to the sealers, so that they would become dissatisfied with it and, at the end of five years press, under one of the declarations of the tribunal, for a larger privilege, and that Great Britain should be convinced that a larger privilege would result in the destruction of the herd and would not ask for it; in short, that all parties should finally become convinced of what we now know to be the truth, that pelagic sealing and the preservation of the seals are absolutely irreconcilable. Under such circumstances, after the spirit of national jealousy and contention have passed away and Canada comes to see that pelagic sealing is a worthless bauble, I can not help thinking that Great Britain would be willing to concede to us our property claim, and, if necessary, treat this award as the sentence of a tribunal ill constituted to determine the juridical question, and consent to its resubmission to an independent body of jurists under circumstances which would insure a correct determination.   We might thus restore the herd and hold it by a firm title against the world.

Fourth. The United States, by holding this consistent and honorable attitude, would, as above shown, lose nothing, and might, under the favorable circumstances supposed, rehabilitate itself as the sole owner of the seals.   But if they are destined to be swept away I would have the hands of the United States unstained by any participation in the destruction and leave to Great Britain the gathering infamy sure to be visited in the end upon a nation which openly struggles to sweep, and finally succeeds in sweeping, from the face of the earth a bounty of nature designed to be a perpetual benefit to man.

Certainly no one will deny that the seals ought to be preserved. Those who deny that it is our peculiar duty to preserve them will also admit that it is the duty of all nations to preserve them.   The consequence and the infamy must rest upon those who willfully violate this plain duty.

No. 15.

Sir Julian Pauncefote to Mr. Gresham.

NEWPORT, *October 11, 1893.*

SIR: I have the honor to inform you that I have received a dispatch from the Earl of Rosebery recording a conversation with his excellency the United States ambassador in London respecting the negotiations for carrying out the Bering Sea award, in which his Lordship expressed himself as being most anxious that those negotiations should take place at Washington through me, as I have been conversant with the matter from the beginning.   Mr. Bayard has probably reported that conversation to you, and I should be gratified to learn that the wishes expressed by Lord Rosebery to his excellency respecting the negotiation in question are agreeable to your Government.

1 have, etc.,

JULIAN PAUNCEFOTE.

No. 16.

Mr. Gresham to Mr. Bayard.

DEPARTMENT OF STATE,
Washington, October 18, 1893.

SIR: I have to acknowledge receipt of your dispatch of the 30th of September, in reply to letters I addressed to you on the 13th and 19th of the same month, in which you say that on Lord Rosebery's return to London you will continue your effort to obtain adequate action on the award of the Paris Tribunal.

I have had an interview with the President and the Secretary of the Treasury on that part of your letter in which you state:

"To suspend wholly, even for a single year, the seal catch on the islands might be highly prejudicial to the United States or their lessees, *and as in* the provisional or temporary arrangement of May, 1893, between Russia and Great Britain, a limit òf 30,000 seals on the Russian islands was agreed to, it would seem a very reasonable figure to adopt for the catch on the Pribilof Islands, whose product has been supposed to be about double that of the Russian islands. I would respectfully ask for an expression of your views on this subject, and how far we ought to go in restricting the seal catch on these islands."

After again consulting with the President and Secretary Carlisle upon this subject to-morrow the desired instructions will be sent to you.

I inclose herewith, for your information, copy of a note which I sent to the British ambassador at Newport, on the 13th instant, informing him that the President would adhere to his purpose of having you conduct the negotiations at London for concurrent action to make the award and recommendations of the Paris Tribunal effective.

I am, etc.,

W. Q. GRESHAM.

No. 17.

Mr. Gresham to Mr. Bayard.

DEPARTMENT OF STATE,
Washington, October 24, 1893.

SIR: In a recent conversation with the Japanese minister I brought to his attention the regulations recommended by the Paris Tribunal of Arbitration, and inquired whether his Government was willing to take advantage of the opportunity afforded it to give its adhesion to them.

The minister said that Japan, having extensive coasts and islands facing the sealing areas, had an interest in the preservation of seal life, and that his Government would gladly come to an understanding with the United States, Great Britain, and Russia for protecting the seal in the Pacific Ocean north of the thirty-fifth degree of north latitude, between California and Japan.

Mr. Tateno expressed the opinion that his Government could not fairly be expected to give its adhesion to the regulations recommended by the arbitrators, and thus prohibit Japanese subjects from taking seal during the months of May, June, and July of each year "in the part of the Pacific Ocean, inclusive of the Bering Sea, which is situated to the north of the thirty-fifth degree of north latitude and eastward of the one hundred and eightieth degree of longitude from Greenwich, till it strikes the water boundary described in article 1 of the treaty of 1867 between the United States and Russia, and following that line up to Bering Straits," while citizens of the United States and subjects of Great Britain, as well as subjects of all the other powers, are permitted to engage in pelagic sealing between these protected waters and Japan.

A glance at any map on an enlarged scale will enable you to more fully understand the minister's position. He expects shortly to receive precise instructions on this point, looking to an international agreement between the four powers for the preservation, for their common benfit, of fur seals between the two continents and north of the thirty-fifth degree of north latitude.

At the conclusion of an interview with the British ambassador on another subject, I informed him what the Japanese minister had said when asked if his Government would give its adhesion to the regulations recommended by the Tribunal of Arbitration. Sir Julian said he recognized the force of the Japanese position, and that the situation seemed to suggest the propriety of such a treaty between the four powers.

In view of the geographical position of Japan, and her interests in the fur-sealing industry, it is not surprising that that Government should assume this position. If the four chiefly interested powers should come to an understanding of the nature indicated, other commercial nations for obvious reasons would likely respect it.

I send you for your information copy of a letter addressed to me under date of October 10, 1893, by Mr. J. Stanley Brown, on the subject of fur sealing and the regulations recommended by the tribunal for the protection of the seal herd. Should you desire the presence of experts to aid you in your negotiations they will be sent to London.

I am, etc.,

W. Q. GRESHAM.

[Inclosure 1 in No. 17.]

Mr. Brown to Mr. Gresham.

1318 MASSACHUSETTS AVENUE,
Washington, D. C., October 10, 1893. (Received October 17.)

SIR: Prompted by my deep interest in the fur-seal question, acquired through more than two years' close study of it, at the Pribilof Islands and in connection with the arbitration, I beg leave to lay before you briefly certain facts and suggestions bearing thereon.

On the occasion of Sir Richard Webster's recent visit to the city I had a conversation with him of some length on the general subject of the regulations formulated by the Paris Tribunal of Arbitration, and the concurrent action of the two Governments yet to be taken to put them into effective operation. As Sir Richard Webster was counsel for Great Britain, it is not improbable that his statements reflect in some measure the views and purposes held by the present officers of the Crown.

There were three points dwelt upon by Sir Richard:

(a) He insisted, despite the overwhelming evidence to the contrary, that the diminution of the seal herd was due to excessive killing on the Pribilof Islands, and that pelagic sealing could never destroy the seal herd, but on the contrary, the seals were increasing in numbers in the face of it.

(b) He expressed the opinion, with a fine show of earnestness, that the spring catch was peculiarly injurious in its effect upon the herd, and that the two Governments should modify the regulations upon that point by increasing the closed time in the North Pacific and decreasing it in the Bering Sea.

(c) He took the ground that it is unfair to make regulations limiting the rights of the pelagic sealer, while no restrictions were placed upon the Government's management of the Pribilof Islands. He contended that not only should the terms of the regulations be made conditional upon the number of seals annually taken upon the islands, but that the carrying out of these regulations should be made contingent upon a formal statement by the United States of its purposes with regard to the management of the islands, for unless such conditions were imposed there was no guarantee that the alleged improprieties on the islands *would not be continued*, and thus the interests of pelagic sealing suffer.

Sir Richard thought there need be no difficulty in the representatives of the two Governments reaching common ground of agreement as to these suggested changes.

The position (a) taken as to the cause of the decadence of the seals is so untenable and so completely refuted by established facts that it would be idle to waste time in considering it.

The pretense (b) that the spring catch is peculiarly injurious, and that therefore the closed time should be increased in the North Pacific and correspondingly shortened in Bering Sea, is a most ingenious attempt to weaken the efficiency of the regulations by transferring sealing from the region of least danger to that of the greatest. It forms part and parcel of Canada's purpose, manifested from the beginning, to transfer the pelagic sealing to the focal point—the massing ground of seal life—Bering Sea. The relative degree of injuriousness is clearly shown by a few illustrations.

On page 20 of the little brochure prepared in Paris and entitled Pelagic Sealing in the North Pacific Most Destructive in May and June, is a compilation from the British records, which shows that nineteen Canadian vessels captured in the North Pacific in—

	Seals.
January	28
February	835
March	991
April	1,938
May	8,260
June	1,438

The May and June catch are cut off by the present regulations.

During the three years ending with and including 1891 the Canadian fleet took in five months, in the North Pacific, an average of 567 skins per vessel. With ten vessels less they took in Bering Sea 727 skins per vessel in about two and one-half months.

In 1891 the catch of the Canadian fleet in the North Pacific was a little over 21,000 seals, and before the modus vivendi could be enforced a portion of the fleet sealed from three to five weeks in Bering Sea, and with fewer vessels and fewer small boats they took over 28,000 seals in that time.

When a seal mother is killed in the North Pacific it involves her death and that of her unborn offspring, but as the period of gestation is nearly twelve months, and that of nursing from four to five, the killing of a mother in Bering Sea means that three seal lives pay the penalty.

The claim (c) urged, that it would be but just to make the terms an [of ?] execution of the regulations dependent upon the conduct of affairs on the islands, is but a renewal of the attempt made before the Paris Tribunal to exercise a certain control over American territory and minimize the advantages which the United States would receive from its possessions. It will be a long time, even under more favorable conditions than are likely to obtain, before the Pribilof rookeries can contribute a large annual quota; but there is a certain proportion of the young, immature male seals that could with entire safety be taken, and it is not apparent why the United States should be debarred from receiving the income from this source as an offset to the expenditures that will be required to carry out the regulations, to say nothing of the necessity of maintaining the natives on the islands. For four years the United States has had a closed time on the islands, and has submitted itself not only to a loss of revenue, but great expense, in its earnest endeavor to save the seal herd. During that same period pelagic sealing has had full swing, and there is now no good reason why the United States should longer practice self-denial for the benefit of Canadian sealers.

The suggestion that the United States will not properly care for its rookeries in the future is mere pretense. At the last session of Congress I secured the introduction of a clause into the appropriation of the Fish Commission, requiring that Bureau to make an annual inspection of, and to report upon, the condition of the rookeries. This, in addition to the continuous presence of Treasury officials, should surely secure proper management.

There will be no modification offered by Great Britain which will be on the side of increased protection. The general impression given me by Sir Richard's remarks was that England, having won upon the legal points, would now attempt, in the adoption of " concurrent measures," to so modify these regulations that they would bear less heavily upon pelagic sealers.

In conclusion, and aside from the foregoing, I beg leave to add a word as to the general question of the "system of stipulations and measures to be enacted by the two powers," for putting into effect the regulations. As that is a very practical question, before final action is taken upon the contemplated measures, I would earnestly urge that they be submitted to some of the gentlemen here well qualified by experience in the Bering Sea, pelagic sealing, and the practical phases of the question, to pass upon their merits.

Very respectfully,

J. STANLEY BROWN.

No. 18.

Mr. Gresham to Mr. Bayard.

DEPARTMENT OF STATE,
Washington, October 26, 1893.

SIR: I inclose for your information a copy of the contract between the United States and the North American Commercial Company, which enjoys the exclusive right of taking fur seals upon the Pribilof Islands; also extracts from the instructions, dated May 2, 1892, and April 22, 1893, sent to the special agent in charge of the islands, in relation to the number of seals to be taken under the modus vivendi between the United States and Great Britain.

I am, etc.,   W. Q. GRESHAM.

[Inclosure 1 in No. 18.]

Copy of contract between the United States and the North American Commercial Company, under which said company is granted the exclusive right of taking fur seals upon the Pribilof Islands in Alaska.

This indenture, made in duplicate this twelfth day of March, 1890, by and between William Windom, Secretary of the Treasury of the United States, in pursuance of chapter 3 of title 23, Revised Statutes, and the North American Commercial Company, a corporation duly established under the laws of the State of California, and acting by

I. Liebes, its president, in accordance with a resolution of said corporation adopted at a meeting of its board of directors held January 4, 1890:

Witnesseth: That the said Secretary of the Treasury, in consideration of the agreements hereinafter stated, hereby leases to the said North American Commercial Company for a term of twenty years, from the first day of May, 1890, the exclusive right to engage in the business of taking fur seals on the Islands of St. George and St. Paul in the Territory of Alaska, and to send a vessel or vessels to said islands for the skins of such seals.

The said North American Commercial Company, in consideration of the rights secured to it under this lease above stated, on its part covenants and agrees to do the things following, that is to say:

To pay to the Treasurer of the United States each year during the said term of twenty years, as annual rental, the sum of sixty thousand dollars, and in addition thereto agrees to pay the revenue tax, or duty, of two dollars laid upon each fur-seal skin taken and shipped by it from said Islands of St. George and St. Paul, and also to pay to said Treasurer the further sum of seven dollars sixty-two and one-half cents apiece for each and every fur-seal skin taken and shipped from said islands, and also to pay the sum of fifty cents per gallon for each gallon of oil sold by it made from seals that may be taken on said islands during the said period of twenty years, and to secure the prompt payment of the sixty thousand dollars rental above referred to, the said company agrees to deposit with the Secretary of the Treasury bonds of the United States to the amount of fifty thousand dollars, face value, to be held as a guarantee for the annual payment of said sixty thousand dollars rental, the interest thereon when due to be collected and paid to the North American Commercial Company, provided the said company is not in default of payment of any part of the said sixty thousand·dollars rental.

That it will furnish to the native inhabitants of said Islands of St. George and St. Paul annually such quantity or number of dried salmon, and such quantity of salt and such number of salt barrels for preserving their necessary supply of meat as the Secretary of the Treasury shall from time to time determine.

That it will also furnish to the said inhabitants eighty tons of coal annually, and a sufficient number of comfortable dwellings in which said native inhabitants may reside; and will keep said dwellings in proper repair; and will also provide and keep in repair such suitable schoolhouses as may be necessary, and will establish and maintain during eight months of each year proper schools for the education of the children on said islands; the same to be taught by competent teachers, who shall be paid by the company a fair compensation, all to the satisfaction of the Secretary of the Treasury; and will also provide and maintain a suitable house for religious worship; and will also provide a competent physician or physicians, and necessary and proper medicines and medical supplies; and will also provide the necessaries of life for the widows and orphans and aged and infirm inhabitants of said islands who are unable to provide for themselves; all of which foregoing agreements will be done and performed by the said company free of all costs and charges to said native inhabitants of said islands or to the United States.

The annual rental, together with all other payments to the United States, provided for in this lease, shall be made and paid on or before the first day of April of each and every year during the existence of this lease, beginning with the first day of April, 1891.

The said company further agrees to employ the native inhabitants of said islands to perform such labor upon the islands as they are fitted to perform, and to pay therefor a fair and just compensation, such as may be fixed by the Secretary of the Treasury; and also agrees to contribute, as far as in its power, all reasonable efforts to secure the comfort, health, education, and promote the morals and civilization of said native inhabitants.

The said company also agrees faithfully to obey and abide by all rules and regulations that the Secretary of the Treasury has heretofore or may hereafter establish or make in pursuance of law concerning the taking of seals on said islands, and concerning the comfort, morals, and other interests of said inhabitants, and all matters pertaining to said islands and the taking of seals within the possession of the United States. It also agrees to obey and abide by any restrictions or limitations upon the right to kill seals that the Secretary of the Treasury shall judge necessary, under the law, for the preservation of the seal fisheries of the United States; and it agrees that it will not kill, or permit to be killed, so far as it can prevent, in any year a greater number of seals than is authorized by the Secretary of the Treasury.

The said company further agrees that it will not permit any of its agents to keep, sell, give, or dispose of any distilled spirits or spirituous liquors or opium on either of said islands or the waters adjacent thereto to any of the native inhabitants of said islands, such person not being a physician and furnishing the same for use as a medicine.

It is understood and agreed that the number of fur seals to be taken and killed for their skins upon said islands by the North American Commercial Company during the year ending May 1st, 1891, shall not exceed sixty thousand.

The Secretary of the Treasury reserves the right to terminate this lease and all rights of the North American Commercial Company under the same at any time on full and satisfactory proof that the said company has violated any of the provisions and agreements of this lease, or in any of the laws of the United States, or any Treasury regulation respecting the taking of fur seals or concerning the Islands of St. George and St. Paul or the inhabitants thereof.

In witness whereof, the parties hereto have set their hands and seals the day and year above written.

WILLIAM WINDOM,
Secretary of the Treasury.

NORTH AMERICAN COMMERCIAL COMPANY.
By I. LIEBES,   .
President of the North American Commercial Company.

{ North American Commercial
  Company, incorporated
  December, 1889. }

Attest:
H. B. PARSONS, *Assistant Secretary.*

[Inclosure 2, in No. 18.]

Treasury instructions to agents in charge of Seal Islands.

TREASURY DEPARTMENT,
OFFICE OF THE SECRETARY,
Washington, D. C., May 2, 1892.
[Extract.]

SIR: As already advised by telegram, you will proceed at once to the Seal Islands as "Treasury agent in charge," taking passage for that purpose either on the U. S. revenue steamer *Bear*, which leaves Port Townsend on or about May 7, or the Alaska Commercial Company's steamer *Bertha*, which leaves San Francisco about the same date.

Upon your arrival at the islands you will assume charge of the interests and property of the Government, and as its representative you will see to it that the authority with which you are invested is respected in all quarters.

* * * * * * *

Modus vivendi.—You will find inclosed a copy of the modus vivendi between the United States and Great Britain, which you will see goes into force May 1, 1892, and continues while the arbitration is pending, unless otherwise provided for after October 31, 1893.

Foreign agents.—You will observe that the modus (Art. IV) permits the landing on the islands of British agents. In accordance with the international agreement you will permit such duly accredited persons to land for the purposes indicated in the modus.

Your attention is called to the unfortunate representations made to Lord Salisbury last year by the British commissioners. Their statements concerning the alleged violation of the modus in the matter of seal killing were based upon their misinterpretation of the terms of the modus and their misunderstanding of the facts. Especial effort should be made, therefore, to present with exceeding clearness any fact that you may deem necessary or proper to communicate to any British official visiting either island. All affidavits obtained by such agents from the natives or other persons on the island must be taken in the presence of a Government officer, and the foreign agents must conform to such rules of conduct concerning the rookeries as are required of citizens of the United States.

Seal quota.—It is essential to the carrying out of the modus that all seals taken for their skins be killed under the direction of the Government agent. No quota has therefore been assigned the North American Commercial Company. As the limit to be killed for all purposes during the season of 1892 is fixed by international agreement at 7,500, you will so adjust the killing as to provide for a fresh-meat supply for the natives throughout the season. As under the terms of the lease all skins taken will ultimately be turned over to the North American Commercial Company, you will confer with the agent of the lessees as to the kind of skins desired, and request his cooperation in selecting them.

The number of seals to be killed on each island will be in about the proportion of former years, unless, in your judgment, there should be made some modification of the ratio.

Killing season.—The killing season will begin as soon after your arrival as in your judgment the rookeries are in proper condition for driving, and the period for taking seals is left entirely to your discretion, with the exception that no seals are to be taken during the stagy season, which embraces the time between August 10 and September 30.

Driving of seals.—As the perpetuation of seal life has always been and is now the paramount concern of the Government, and is also of the greatest interest to all persons connected with the seal industry, you will take especial care that no methods are permitted in the driving, killing, or general handling of the seals which in your opinion would directly or remotely be injurious to them or in any way jeopardize even in the slightest degree the increase of the seal herd.

Killing of pups.—It was the custom in former years to permit the killing in the fall of a certain number of young seals for the natives' food and clothing. As the skins are not now used for the latter purpose, and as the carcass furnishes not more than 8 pounds of meat when dressed, the value of the food supply thus contributed is not commensurate with the destructive effect which the killing of pups has upon the seal herd. No killing of pups during the coming year will therefore be permitted.

*   *   *

Respectfully, yours,

CHARLES FOSTER, *Secretary.*

Maj. W. H. WILLIAMS,
United States Treasury Agent.

———

TREASURY DEPARTMENT,
OFFICE OF THE SECRETARY,
Washington, D. C., April 26, 1893.

[Extract.]

SIR: Having been appointed Treasury agent in charge of the Seal Islands in Alaska, you are directed to proceed to San Francisco, Cal., so as to arrive there as early as the 10th proximo, and to take passage on the first available conveyance to the islands.

*   *   *   *   *   *   *

Copy of the modus vivendi between the United States and Great Britain is also inclosed for your information, which you will observe continues in force pending the arbitration of the Bering Sea question, unless otherwise provided for after October 31, 1893.

In accordance with the provisions of the modus vivendi the number of seals to be taken during the season of 1893 will be limited to 7,500. In taking this number you will permit no seals to be killed except those yielding good merchantable skins. The killing of pup seals for food for the natives or any purpose will not be permitted.

The killing season will begin as soon after your arrival as in your judgment the rookeries are in proper condition for driving, and the time for taking seals is left to your discretion, with the exception that no seals are to be taken during the stagy period, which is understood to be the period between the 10th of August and the 30th of September. It is believed that if the killing should be confined between the 1st of June and the 10th of August a better quality of skins would be obtained, and less injury would be done to the rookeries. This matter is, however, left, as above stated, to your discretion, and in reference thereto you will confer fully with the representative of the company, its interests and those of the Government in the preservation of the fur seal industry being indentical.

*   *   *   *

Respectfully, yours,

C. S. HAMLIN, *Acting Secretary.*

Mr. JOSEPH B. CROWLEY,
    Special Agent in Charge of Seal Islands,
       Washington, D. C.

No. 19.

Mr. Gresham to Mr. Bayard.

DEPARTMENT OF STATE,
Washington, October 27, 1893.

SIR: I have the honor to acknowledge your dispatch of the 30th ultimo, in which you state that, on Lord Rosebery's return to London from Balmoral, you will continue your efforts for adequate and concurrent action on the award of the Paris Tribunal. You also say:

To suspend wholly, even for a single year, the seal catch on the islands might be highly prejudicial to the United States or their lessees, and, as in the provisional or temporary arrangement of May, 1893, between Russia and Great Britain, a limit of 30,000 seals on the Russian islands was agreed to, it would seem a very reasonable figure to adopt for the catch on the Pribilof Islands, whose product has been supposed to be about double that of the Russian islands. I would respectfully ask for an expression of your views on this subject, and how far we ought to go in restricting the seal catch on these islands.

I sent you yesterday copy of the contract which secures to the North American Commercial Company the exclusive right to take seal on the Pribilof Islands, thinking it advisable that you should know the precise relations between the United States and that company. The President is not now prepared to say how far we ought to go in limiting the seal catch should Great Britain make a demand of that kind. You are well informed on the subject of the seal industry and all matters relating to it, and we rely with confidence upon your judgment in dealing with Lord Rosebery. If Great Britain firmly insists that only a limited number of seals shall be taken on the islands, and you must yield or fail in the effort to obtain a satisfactory understanding for concurrent action, you can report the fact to me, and I will communicate it to the President for his direction.

I have no doubt you will be impressed by the reply of the Japanese minister when I asked him, in an informal conversation, if his Government was willing to give its adhesion to the regulations recommended by the arbitrators. You have the substance of that conversation in my instructions of the 24th instant. I must say that the position of Japan seems to be reasonable. An agreement between the United States, Great Britain, Russia, and Japan, of the character suggested by the minister of the latter country, for the protection of the seal north of a line reaching from California to Japan, along the thirty-fifth degree of north latitude, would likely be respected by other powers. It is very important that the two Governments should come to an understanding which will secure the desired result before the next sealing season begins, and it is not doubted here that you are striving to accomplish that end.

The Russian minister told me a day or two ago that, when informed of the means adopted by the United States and Great Britain to give practical effect to the regulations, his Government would without delay determine whether or not it could give its adhesion, as requested. It may be that other powers will not be willing to be bound by the regulations recommended by the tribunal without knowing what means will be employed by the two Governments for their enforcement.

I am, etc.,

W. Q. GRESHAM.

No. 20.

Mr. Bayard to Mr. Gresham.

EMBASSY OF THE UNITED STATES,
London, November 1, 1893. (Received November 11.)

SIR: I have the honor to state that, pursuant to your directions, the copies of the protocols of the arbitration in the Bering Sea question have just been sent to me from the embassy of the United States at Paris.

The oral arguments of counsel, save and except that of James O. Carter, esq., have not yet been published, as I am as yet informed, and I would like to receive them as soon as they are in print.

As attendant upon framing legislation and coming to an international agreement to carry out the decisions and recommendations of the Paris Tribunal in their award upon the business of fur-seal fishing in Bering Sea, I have also the honor to inclose herewith a copy of a telegram which appeared yesterday in the London newspapers, which indicates the extent to which "pelagic" sealing was carried on in the present season, and likewise suggests a method by which it is proposed to evade the duties and obligations imposed by the treaty and the award of the arbitrators, only upon the Governments of the United States and Great Britain, leaving depredation upon seal life under other flags not only unchecked, but in effect affirmatively legalized by the text of the award and decisions.

Up to this date "pelagic" sealing has been carried on only under the flags of Great Britain and the United States, but what may be done under the flags of other nationalities hereafter can not be definitely anticipated. Therefore, as at present instructed, and in anticipation of cooperative penal enactments by the United States and Great Britain against killing seal in the sea, in violation of the award, it would seem highly expedient to caution the Governments of Japan and Korea, as well as the Sandwich Islands, against attempts which may be made to carry on under their flags, fur seal fishing, contrary to the letter and intent of the Paris decision and recommendations. In this connection I take leave to remark that the avowed reason for the contention against pelagic sealing on the part of the United States has always been the preservation of the seal species for the use of civilized mankind, and the gist of the argument against killing seal in the water has been the impossibility of discrimination between sexes and ages, as well as the insecurity of capture of a large proportion of the seals when so killed.

This rule is not local, but necessarily applies to the fur-seal species everywhere; so that the Government of the United States, in order to be consistent, should be prepared to show its unwillingness to kill seal in the water anywhere, and at all seasons; that is to say, "pelagic" sealing is destructive to the species, and it is only on land that proper discrimination can be exercised.

Therefore, in asking the adhesion of other nations to the regulations prescribed, and recommendations suggested by the arbitrators at Paris, as is stipulated by Article VII of the treaty of February 1892, between the United States and Great Britain, the United States should be prepared to extend the proposed rules into those regions of the high seas adjacent to the sealing islands and sealing resorts of other nations.

The interests of Russia and Japan are almost identical with those of the United States, and what is desirable for one is so alike to all. Each of these powers possesses territory to which the fur seal resort when breeding, and equally with the United States need protective regulation.

I venture therefore, to submit to your judgment the advisability of instructing the representatives of the United States in Japan, Korea, and the Sandwich Islands, to intimate confidentially to those Governments the present condition of affairs, and that the United States and Great Britain are about unitedly to enforce protective measures, by the establishment of a zone of interdiction around the Pribilof group, and a close season from May 1, to July 31, in the Pacific Ocean north of the thirty-fifth degree of north latitude and invite their adhesion to the regulations proposed by the award as published.

You will observe that I have not referred to the fact that, by article 2, of the Paris award, the water boundary described in article 1, of the treaty of 1867 (Alaskan purchase), between the United States and Russia, is the limit in Bering Sea within which the interdiction is to be enforced, but it seems very clear that justice and self-consistency demand of the United States that this interdiction against killing seal at sea would extend to all waters, including those adjacent to the territorial possessions of other countries, and to which the seal resort. Russia and Japan are the two nations territorially interested, and the Sandwich Islands and Korea can justly be appealed to not to allow their flags to be used for purposes unfriendly to the United States.

Of course by the treaty of February, 1892 (Article VII), Great Britain is bound to cooperate with the United States in securing adhesion to the regulations, and it is assumed that of course (it) will do so.

And at the proper time, and in such mode as may be deemed most advisable, such cooperation will be claimed by the United States; but at the present writing the point I desire to make is the word of friendly notification and caution to Japan, Korea, and the Sandwich Islands, lest the use of their flags might be obtained by the solicitation of fur-seal hunters from the United States or Great Britain and her colonies.

The interests of Russia are so entirely similar to those of the United States and so involved in a similar fate that I can not imagine any such warning would be requisite in that quarter.

The participation of Sweden and Norway, France and Italy in the composition of the Paris Tribunal and framing its decrees would seem to render it impossible that those Governments would permit their flags to be used as a cover of depredations against the interests which they themselves had so benevolently adjudicated. So that I think all that need be done in the light of the enormous extent of pelagic sealing during the current year, as shown by the inclosed telegram, and the suggestion of a transfer of the sealing fleet to Japanese waters, and possibly under the Japanese flag, will be a notification and warning by our representative to that Government of the possibility of such attempt and the necessity of preventing its success. You may possibly think it worth while, informally, and in conversation at Washington, to broach the subject to the Japanese minister,

I shall proceed as speedily as possibly in the duty assigned me of coming to such an agreement of cooperation with Her Majesty's Government as will give efficient force to the award of the Paris Tribunal.

I have the honor, etc.,

T. F. BAYARD.

_____

[Inclosure in No. 20.—Press telegram.]

THE BERING SEA FISHERIES,
Victoria, British Columbia, October 25.

The British Columbia sealing catch, including the take of two American vessels, amounts to 70,000 skins. Many of the schooners will go to Japan next season, about half their number setting out before Christmas. It is stated that some of these vessels are likely to transfer their allegiance to another flag.

_____

No. 21.

Mr. Bayard to Mr. Gresham.

EMBASSY OF THE UNITED STATES,
London, November 11, 1893. (Received November 20.)

· SIR: Referring to my dispatch of November 1, I have now the honor to acknowledge your several instructions of October 18, 24, 26, and 27, all having relation to the fur-seal fishery in Bering Sea, and all of which have been perused with great interest.

My dispatch above referred to was mailed just in advance of the arrival of the several instructions above alluded to, but it gave me no little satisfaction to discover that the expression of views I had the honor of submitting therein to you were quite in line with your own, and that in fact you had anticipated certain suggestions I had made therein.

It was quite important for me to possess copies of the contracts of the United States with the lessees of the Pribilof group, and also copies of the Treasury instructions, in 1890 and 1892, to the general and special agents in charge of the Seal Islands.

The report of your conversations with the representatives of Japan, Russia, and Great Britain is impressive and valuable, and I quite concur in the views, as conveyed, of the President and yourself as to the necessity for a general plan of international arrangement in order to give substantial efficacy and value to the regulations and recommendations of the Tribunal of Arbitration.

I venture to draw your attention to the terms of these Treasury Department instructions relating to the number of seal (7,500) which may be taken on the islands under the modus vivendi, which continued in force "pending the arbitration of the Bering Sea question, unless otherwise provided for after October 31, 1893."

The arbitration having now closed, and a decision having been reached, there does not appear to be any provision whatever now in force limiting the number of seals which may be taken on the Seal

Islands of the United States; but by the contract of March 12, 1890, between the United States and the North American Commercial Company it is expressly stipulated that during the year ending May 1, 1891, "the number of fur seals to be taken and killed for their skins shall not exceed 60,000."

With this exception, as to the single year 1891, the Secretary of the Treasury is vested with sole discretion and authority to impose restrictions or limitations upon the seal catch on these islands.

I assume that the Secretary of the Treasury will not fix the number of seals which may be taken in the islands during the next season until the desired international arrangement shall have been made.

May I ask to have obtained for me, at the Treasury Department, a summarized statement of the number of seals taken in the Pribilof Islands in each year since 1871.

I suppose no seals have at any time been taken by the lessees of the United States, excepting on those islands, and that no other leases or licenses were ever granted by the United States for sealing elsewhere.

The fact, however, might as well be stated authoritatively by the Treasury Department in connection with the number of seals taken annually since 1871.

I have, etc.,   T. F. BAYARD.

No. 22.

Mr. Gresham to Mr. Bayard.

[Telegram.]

DEPARTMENT OF STATE,
Washington, November 17, 1893.

The President is anxious that an agreement should speedily be reached for carrying out the decision and recommendations of the Paris Tribunal. If Lord Rosebery has met you in a proper spirit we do not doubt results. Are you hopeful?

No. 23.

Mr. Bayard to Mr. Gresham.

[Telegram.]

LONDON, *November 18, 1893.*

Assure President commencement formal negotiations hitherto prevented by circumstances beyond my control. Secretary of state for foreign affairs just returned. Shall proceed promptly as possible. Good reason to expect efficient cooperation.

No. 24.

Mr. Gresham to Mr. Bayard.

DEPARTMENT OF STATE,
Washington, November 20, 1893.

SIR: I have received and considered your dispatch of the 1st instant, relative to the necessity of obtaining the adhesion and cooperation of other nations, and notably of Japan, Hawaii, Korea, and Russia, to the award and regulations submitted by the Paris Tribunal of Arbitration.

My instructions of the 24th ultimo, which you had apparently not received at the date of writing, anticipates to some extent specific response to your suggestions, at least so far as showing the desire of Japan to become a party to some protective arrangement embracing the entire waters above the thirty-fifth degree of north latitude and between the American and Japanese coasts.

As you remark, the interests of Russia, like those of Japan, are almost identical with those of the United States—what is desirable for one being alike so for all. The concurrence of Russia in any appropriate scheme of protection by the United States and Great Britain may reasonably be expected, and the concurrence of Japan is promised if all the waters above the thirty-fifth degree of north latitude be protected.

The exigencies of the case, however, preclude any delay in reaching the necessary arrangements between the United States and Great Britain as the two parties primarily interested in giving immediate and positive effect to the award and proposals of the Paris Tribunal; and the negotiations to that end should not be made dependent on the acquiescence of other powers.

The President does not doubt that you will press with all urgency negotiations for an agreement upon measures which will be efficient in carrying out the submitted regulations. This is of primary importance.

I am, etc.,

W. Q. GRESHAM.

———

No. 25.

Mr. Gresham to Mr. Bayard.

DEPARTMENT OF STATE,
Washington, November 21, 1893.

SIR: I received late yesterday your dispatch of November 11, and at once addressed a letter to the Secretary of the Treasury requesting the information called for. It may take a few days to make up a statement which will be satisfactory, but it will be forwarded to you as soon as it is received.

I inclose copy of a note received yesterday from the Japanese minister at this capital.* It will gratify you, no doubt, to know that the Japanese Government is willing to give its adhesion to the regulations recommended by the Paris Tribunal of Arbitration on the condition named.

The President thinks it important that Great Britain and the United States should come to an understanding which will make the regulations practically effective before beginning negotiations for an international

———
* Not printed.

agreement between those Governments, Russia and Japan, for the protection of fur seals in the Pacific Ocean north of the thirty-fifth degree of north latitude.

Your dispatch, by telegraph, of the 18th, indicated your belief that Great Britain was meeting you in a proper spirit in your negotiations. This is very encouraging as it is important that an agreement should speedily be reached and announced.

On a visit to the Department yesterday the British ambassador expressed the hope that you and Lord Rosebery would speedily agree upon concurrent action for the protection of the waters embraced within the reported regulations, and that negotiations would immediately follow for an international agreement of the character suggested between the four powers.

I am, etc.,   W. Q. GRESHAM.

No. 26.

Mr. Gresham to Mr. Dun.

[Telegram.]

DEPARTMENT OF STATE,
Washington, November 22, 1893.

It is reported that American and Canadian seal fishery vessels may be placed under the Japanese flag next season. Comity will naturally counsel Japanese Government to defeat any such attempted abuse of friendly flag to evade results of Paris Arbitration.

No. 27.

Mr. Bayard to Mr. Gresham.

[Telegram.]

LONDON, *November 23, 1893.*

Secretary of state for foreign affairs has presented impressive reasons for not withdrawing seal fishery negotiations from British ambassador at Washington. Satisfactory explanation by cable impracticable. Will communicate immediately.

No. 28.

Mr. Uhl to Mr. Bayard.

DEPARTMENT OF STATE,
Washington, November 24, 1893.

SIR: Referring to the Department's reply of the 21st of this month to your dispatch of the 11th instant, relative to the Bering Sea seal question, I enclose for your information a copy of a letter from the Acting Secretary of the Treasury, furnishing the information requested by you regarding the number of seals taken on the Pribilof Islands.

I am, etc.,

EDWIN F. UHL, *Acting Secretary.*

[Inclosure in No. 28.]

Mr. Curtis to Mr. Gresham.

TREASURY DEPARTMENT,
OFFICE OF THE SECRETARY,
Washington, D. C., November 22, 1893.

SIR: I have the honor to acknowledge the receipt of your communication of the 21st instant, wherein request is made for certain information regarding the number of seals taken on the Pribilof Islands, and in reply to inclose herewith a statement showing the number of seals killed on the islands of St. Paul and St. George, for all purposes, from 1870 to 1892, both inclusive. Seals have not been taken by the lessees elsewhere than on the islands of St. Paul and St. George, and no other companies than the North American Commercial Company and its predecessor, as lessees of the islands (the Alaska Commercial Company), have been granted licenses or leases by the United States for sealing on the islands or elsewhere.

With reference to the number of seals taken in 1891 and to note 2 on the inclosed statement, I refer you for full information on the subject to the report of Special Agent W. H. Williams, dated October 10, 1891, a printed copy of which is herewith inclosed.

Respectfully, yours,

W. E. CURTIS, *Acting Secretary.*

Number of fur seals killed on islands of St. Paul and St. George, Alaska, for all purposes from 1870 to 1892, both inclusive.

Year.	Killed on St. Paul.	Killed on St. George.	Total killed on both islands.
1870	15,314	8,459	23,773
1871	81,803	21,157	102,960
1872	81,819	27,000	108,819
1873	81,987	27,190	109,177
1874	98,139	12,446	110,585
1875	94,960	11,500	106,460
1876	83,157	11,500	94,657
1877	67,810	16,500	84,310
1878	88,519	20,804	109,323
1879	80,321	22,190	110,511
1880	84,779	20,939	105,718
1881	83,774	21,289	105,063
1882	79,834	19,978	99,812
1883	63,295	16,214	79,509
1884	88,861	16,573	105,434
1885	88,880	16,144	105,024
1886	88,085	16,436	104,521
1887	89,092	16,668	105,760
1888	86,270	17,034	103,304
1889	87,392	15,225	102,617
1890			21,000
1891			13,482
1892			7,549
Total	1,622,091	355,246	2,010,368

NOTE 1.—The above statement for 1870 to 1889, both inclusive, includes all seals killed from all causes, either intentional or accidental. incident to the taking of sealskins on the two islands. The statement for 1890, 1891, and 1892, represents only those skins taken and which were received by the company as part of their quota. The stagy or defective skins are not included in 1890, 1891, and 1892.

NOTE 2.—The total for 1891 is made up as follows: 7,215 skins taken prior to signing of modus vivendi and issuance of President's proclamation. The remainder, 6,267, were taken after signing of modus as part of the 7,500 allowed them under the agreement.

No. 29.

Mr. Dun to Mr. Gresham.

[Telegram.]

TOKYO, *November 27, 1893.*

Japanese Government agrees to take measures to prevent foreign vessels using the flag of Japan to evade seal fisheries regulations, but declines to require bona fide Japanese vessels to observe regulations unless protection asked for should be given Japanese seal fisheries.

No. 30.

Mr. Dun to Mr. Gresham.

LEGATION OF THE UNITED STATES,
Tokyo, Japan, December 1, 1893.

SIR: On the 24th ultimo, the day following the receipt of your telegraphic instruction dated November 22, 1893, I sought an interview with Mr. Mutsu, His Imperial Japanese Majesty's minister for foreign affairs.

Owing to the illness of Mr. Mutsu, I was received by Mr. Tadasu Hayashi, vice-minister of foreign affairs, to whom I communicated the reading of your telegram and expressed the hope that Japan, in the spirit of friendship that has always governed the relations between the two countries, would meet the wishes of my Government in respect of requiring the observance by vessels flying the Japanese flag of the regulations proposed by the Paris Tribunal.

I said to Mr. Hayashi that this action on the part of Japan would not in my opinion, weaken her claim for protection for her own seal fisheries; that the regulations of the Paris Tribunal could not be extended to the waters near the Japanese islands except by special arrangements between Japan and foreign powers; that, although I was not authorized to say what position my Government would take in the premises, I felt confident that the United States was favorably disposed to meet Japan's wishes in regard to reasonable proposals for the protection of her seal fisheries; but that however well disposed the other great powers might be toward Japan's proposals for the extension of the principle of protection to her seal fisheries, it would necessarily take time to complete the negotiations and determine upon a reasonable zone within which that principle should apply; that in the meantime the regulations of the Paris Tribunal of Arbitration had been announced to the world and it was the intention of the United States and Great Britain to put them into operation next season; that Japan was invited, as a matter of comity and good neighborhood, to adhere to those regulations in order that her flag might not be used to evade them.

I also pointed out to Mr. Hayashi that Japan had not yet submitted to the United States and Great Britain definite proposals for the protection of her seal fisheries; that no zone had been defined within which the taking of seal should be prohibited; that the Paris Tribunal having completed its labors, any arrangement that might hereafter be made for the protection of Japan's seal fisheries must be separate and distinct from the finding of that body; and that such being the case, it appeared to me to be hardly in accord with Japan's well-deserved reputation for fairness that she should make her adhesion to the regulations formulated by an international tribunal of arbitration, for the protection of an American interest, conditional upon the favorable reception by several foreign powers of her proposals not yet sufficiently matured to admit of definite consideration.

At the close of our first interview, Mr. Hayashi said he could not say what action his Government would take in the matter until he had consulted with Mr. Mutsu.

On the 26th ultimo Mr. Hayashi called at this legation and informed me that he was authorized by the minister for foreign affairs to say that the Japanese Government would do everything in its power to prevent the use of the Japanese flag by foreign sailing vessels to evade the regulations of the Paris Tribunal, but that it could not, pending present negotiations, issue an ordinance requiring bona fide Japanese vessels to observe them unless the proposals submitted to the United States and Great Britain for the protection of Japanese interests in the same direction were favorably entertained.

On the 27th ultimo I had the honor to convey to you the substance of this response from the Japanese Government in a telegram.

As a matter of fact, bona fide Japanese vessels have not heretofore been engaged in hunting fur seal beyond the immediate waters of the northern islands of Japan, and the fear of disastrous consequences will, doubtless, prevent this class of vessels extending their operations hereafter to waters where the regulations of the Paris Tribunal apply.

I have, etc.,

EDWIN DUN.

No. 31.

Mr. Gresham to Mr. Bayard.

[Telegram.]

DEPARTMENT OF STATE,
Washington, December 4, 1893.

You will inform Lord Rosebery that, yielding to his desire, this Government consents further negotiations for making the award of the Paris Tribunal effective shall be conducted here with the British ambassador. While your generous offer to visit Washington and aid us is appreciated, the President will not impose the burden upon you.

No. 32.

Mr. Gresham to Mr. Tateno.

DEPARTMENT OF STATE,
Washington, December 5, 1893.

SIR: I have the honor to acknowledge the receipt of your note of the 20th ultimo,* in which you allude to the former correspondence looking to the participation of Japan with the United States, Great Britain, and other powers in an international agreement for the protection of

* Not printed.

fur seals in Bering Sea. In the course of your note you say, by direction of your Government, "that Japan is prepared to become a party to the agreement or regulations for the protection of fur seals, made in pursuance of the Bering Sea award, and to enter upon formal negotiations for that purpose at such time and in such manner as may be deemed suitable." You intimate that as a condition to such future adherence to the agreement or regulations to be made in pursuance of the award, Japan would ask that they "shall be extended to the northernmost portion of the island of Yesso and to the Kurile Islands."

The President is much gratified at the cordial disposition of His Majesty's Government, as elicited by the preliminary inquiry to which your note adverts. The award of the Tribunal of Arbitration at Paris contemplates that the adhesion of other powers to the regulations reported by that high body shall be invited by the parties to the arbitration, and the President is happy to believe that the result of the pending negotiations between the United States and Great Britain for the application of the regulations so reported will be such as to permit the friendly concurrence of other powers toward the common interest involved in the protection of seal life, when formally invited by the two parties.

Accept, etc.,   W. Q. GRESHAM.

No. 33.

Mr. Dun to Mr. Gresham.

LEGATION OF THE UNITED STATES,
Tokyo, Japan, December 13, 1893.

SIR: I have the honor to inclose herewith translation copies of instructions issued by the department for foreign affairs and the department of communications, respectively, to Japanese consuls at San Francisco, Vancouver, and other foreign ports, and to the proper authorities on the seacoast of Japan, to prevent the use of the Japanese flag by foreign vessels for the purpose of evading the regulations of the Paris Tribunal for the protection of fur seal in Bering Sea.

I have, etc.,

EDWIN DUN.

[Inclosure 1 in No. 33.—Translation.]

Caution concerning the granting of temporary certificates of registration.

DEPARTMENT OF FOREIGN AFFAIRS,
Tokyo, December 1, 1893.

To the Consuls at San Francisco, Vancouver, Tientsin, Shanghai, Hongkong, Singapore, Fusan, Ninsen, Korsakoff, and the Commercial Agent at Vladivostock:

Having recently heard that there are certain foreigners abroad who, with the object of carrying on illicit fishing, attempt to make use of the names of Japanese in the sale and purchase of vessels and the transfer of registration of the same to Japan through the recognition at the imperial consulates, and thereupon to proceed directly to the various localities in pursuit of such purpose, you are instructed in the

S. Ex. 67——4

issuance of temporary certificates of registration of vessels to act in the matter with strict caution, so that no certificates shall be granted to parties carrying on such dishonorable business.

HAYASHI TADASU,
Vice-Minister.

[Inclosure 2 in No. 33.—Translation.]

DEPARTMENT OF COMMUNICATIONS,
Tokyo, December   , 1893.

To the Governors of Territories, Imperial Municipalities, and Prefecture upon the Seaboard:

I am instructed to inform you that an agreement has been concluded between Great Britain and the United States concerning fishing in Bering Sea, and that report has reached here that since Japan is not a party thereto, and not bound thereby, some attempts were likely to be made to have vessels belonging to nationals of both countries registered under the names of Japanese and fly the Japanese flag for the purpose of following the pursuit of fishing in Bering Sea.

As the control of fishing by the different countries has become strict, no doubt these designing schemes are contrived to evade the law. In cases, therefore, of the purchase of foreign vessels, if the transfer of registration is requested, you are, upon strict examination, to act in the matter so that no such malfeasance as the above may arise.

SAITO HIDE-AKI,
Chief of the Marine Bureau.

No. 34.

Mr. Bayard to Mr. Gresham.

EMBASSY OF THE UNITED STATES,
London, December 30, 1893. (Received January 9, 1894.)

SIR: Immediately upon receiving your telegraphic instruction to the effect that, yielding to the desire of Her Majesty's Government, the Government of the United States consented to conduct the requisite negotiations at Washington, I addressed a note to Lord Rosebery under date of December 5 and on the 11th received his lordship's reply thereto, and I inclose herewith copies of this correspondence.

Continued reflection upon the situation serves to confirm the opinion I have already had the honor to submit to you—that an agreement that would bind Great Britain (and especially her North American subjects) to a faithful fulfillment of the regulations prescribed by the tribunal at Paris—would under existing circumstances be accomplished with less delay and more conclusively and satisfactorily at Washington than in London.

I have, etc.,   T. F. BAYARD.

[Inclosure 1 in No. 34.]

Mr. Bayard to Lord Rosebery.

EMBASSY OF THE UNITED STATES,
London, December 5, 1893.

MY LORD: Upon receiving your note of November 21, I at once cabled its purport to my Government, and stated at length in a dispatch, your reasons for desiring Sir Julian Pauncefote, the British ambassador, to continue at Washington his connection with the Bering Sea negotiations, and assist in the concluding cooperative action of the two Governments to carry into full effect the treaty of February 29, 1892, the award of the Tribunal of Arbitration at Paris, and the regulations prescribed by that body for the conduct of fur-seal fishing in the waters of Bering Sea and the North Pacific Ocean.

I have now the honor to inform you that I have to-day received by cable from the Secretary of State an instruction to make known to you, that, yielding to your lordship's desire as expressed in conversation and in your note of November 21, the President consents that the negotiations needful to give effect to the decisions of the Tribunal of Arbitration shall be conducted at Washington, and that Her Majesty's Government shall be represented therein by Sir Julian Pauncefote.

Your Lordship will, I am sure, appreciate this evidence on the part of the President to facilitate in every way the accomplishment of the duty yet remaining to be performed by the two Governments, of promptly and thoroughly carrying into effect the decisions of the Tribunal of Arbitration, and the mutual covenant of the two Governments to cooperate in securing the adhesion of other powers to the regulations imposed by the arbitrators.

The rapidly shortening interval before the next sealing season will commence admonishes both Governments entrusted with the duty to expedite the negotiations, and enact, respectively, the legislation needed to execute the decisions of the tribunal, and I shall await with interest your Lordship's communication that Her Majesty's ambassador at Washington has been duly empowered and instructed in the premises.

I have, etc.,

T. F. BAYARD.

[Inclosure 2 in No. 34.]

Lord Rosebery to Mr. Bayard.

FOREIGN OFFICE,
December 11, 1893.

YOUR EXCELLENCY: I have had the honor to receive your note of the 5th instant, stating that your Government had consented that the negotiations for giving effect to the decisions of the Bering Sea Arbitration Tribunal should be conducted at Washington by Sir Julian Pauncefote.

Upon the receipt of your excellency's note, I at once instructed Her Majesty's representative by telegraph to express my acknowledgments to the United States Government for their courteous acquiescence in the views of Her Majesty's Government on this subject, and I avail myself of this opportunity to ask your excellency to accept my best thanks for the trouble which you have also taken in this matter.

I beg to assure you that no time shall be lost in issuing the requisite instructions to Sir Julian Pauncefote with regard to the negotiations. I have, etc.,

ROSEBERY.

No. 35.

Memorandum, British Embassy.

JANUARY 4, 1894.

The existing British legislation does not cover the area to which the regulations prescribed by the award apply.

A draft bill is now being prepared to enforce the provisions of the award, but Her Majesty's Government consider that unless some international agreement can be produced to justify the insertion of fresh provisions, the bill in question must be strictly limited to the terms of the award.

Her Majesty's Government are anxious in the first place to know what action the United States Government are prepared to take respecting the declarations of the arbitrators, which were appended to the award. They consider recommendation No. 1 as specially important, as it will probably affect the accession of other powers to any agreement that may be arrived at.

The Japanese Government have expressed a desire to take part in the discussions respecting the regulations, in order that a general scheme, applicable also to Russian and Japanese waters, may be prepared. Her Majesty's Government would be glad to know whether the United States Government would be disposed to invite the Russian and Japanese Governments to take part in such a discussion at once.

Her Majesty's Government could not consent to the unconditional application of the provisions of the award to other waters than those specified by the arbitrators, but they would be willing to discuss any modifications which would allow of the provisions being so applied.

The Earl of Rosebery considers it necessary that Her Majesty's representative at Washington should be assisted by a delegate from Canada, and thinks it desirable that such a delegate should be accredited as a negotiator. His lordship adds that it is of great importance that Her Majesty's Government and the Government of the United States should exchange drafts of the proposed legislation on each side with as little delay as possible.

J. P.

No. 36.

Mr. Gresham to Mr. Bayard.

[Telegram].

DEPARTMENT OF STATE,
Washington, January 6, 1894.

British ambassador still urges United States agree that a Canadian shall be admitted as negotiator for concurrent action to make regulations reported by Paris Tribunal effective. It is the President's desire that you inform Lord Rosebery this Government will treat with the Imperial Government only.

No. 37.

Mr. Bayard to Mr. Gresham.

[Telegram.]

LONDON, *January 8, 1894.*

Minister for foreign affairs agrees British ambassador, Washington, negotiate execution of 'award alone without Canadian colleague.

No. 38.

Mr. White to Mr. Gresham.

[Telegram.]

LEGATION OF THE UNITED STATES,
Petersburg, January 10, 1894. (Received January 11.)

Russian minister for foreign affairs asks whether the United States is inclined to entertain proposals for modus regarding North Pacific seal fisheries like that now existing between Russia and Great Britain. If so, Russian Government will present such proposal. Dispatch follows.

No. 39.

Mr. White to Mr. Gresham.

LEGATION OF THE UNITED STATES,
St. Petersburg, January 10, 1894. (Received January 22.)

SIR: Count Kapnist, director of the Asiatic department at the imperial foreign office, called upon me yesterday to ask whether the Government of the United States would incline to receive proposals from the Russian Government for a modus vivendi similar to that which now exists between Russia and Great Britain.

He said that Russia had delayed this suggestion until after the close of the Paris Arbitration Conference in order not to complicate matters there, but that his Government would be very glad to submit now the proposal above referred to; he wished, however, that before submitting these proposals the Imperial Government could have some information as to the feeling of our own Government in relation to the matter.

He said that Russia would be very glad to have a more complete, comprehensive, and thorough understanding on the subject, but that until this was reached something provisory in the nature of a modus vivendi was very desirable.

He dwelt especially on the provisional character of any such arrangement, and on the fact that it would not exclude a more complete agreement at any future time.

He also dwelt on the desirability of conforming any such agreement now made to that at present existing between Russia and Great Britain, since any material change would of course necessitate changes in that agreement.

As he showed an especial desire for early information and himself suggested a telegram, I have sent you this day the telegram appended.

I am, etc.,

ANDREW D. WHITE.

No. 40.

Mr. Gresham to Sir Julian Pauncefote.

DEPARTMENT OF STATE,
Washington, January 24, 1894.

EXCELLENCY: When, on the 5th of December last, the President, yielding to the earnestly expressed desire of Her Majesty's Government, consented to transfer from London to this capital the negotiations for the execution of the regulations decided and determined upon by the Tribunal of Arbitration at Paris, for the protection of the fur seal in the Pacific Ocean and Bering Sea outside of territorial waters, it was hoped that the concession to the wishes of Her Majesty's Government would facilitate the adoption of measures necessary for the attainment of that end. This hope was strengthened by the assurance expressed in a note of Lord Rosebery to Mr. Bayard of the 11th of December, that no time should be lost in issuing the requisite instructions to you with regard to the negotiations.

Since the transfer of the negotiations, however, no definite communication in regard to them has been received from Her Majesty's Government, though they have been deferred from day to day to await such a communication. The time thus lost has brought us to the opening of another sealing season without any definite steps having been taken for the execution of the Paris award.

Under these circumstances the President does not think that he would be justified in further awaiting a communication from Her Majesty's Government. The first object to be accomplished is to give immediate effect to the regulations framed by the Tribunal of Arbitration. Those regulations, while general in terms, are designed to attain the principal end which the parties to the arbitration had in view— that of putting an end to the destructive and indiscriminate slaughter of seals on the high seas. It is, therefore, the opinion of this Government that they should be put in force without delay.

Any supplementary rules which may be deemed to be requisite or desirable in order to secure the more efficient execution of the regulations determined upon by the Tribunal of Arbitration as necessary, may form the subject of further negotiation which this Government will be prepared to enter upon without delay. But if something be not done, and speedily done, to give effect to the regulations already determined upon, it is needless to say their object will be defeated. The United States would be glad to prohibit entirely, for a period of three years, or for two years, or for one year, the killing of seals, but unless Her Majesty's Government should be willing to agree to that measure it only remains for the two Governments, at once, to give effect to the regulations determined upon by the tribunal as necessary, in conformity with the treaty.

With a view to facilitate negotiations, I inclose herewith a draft of a convention for the purpose of rendering operative those regulations.

The provisions of this draft are believed to be plain, and do not seem to require extended comment. The first nine articles merely repeat, in identical terms, the corresponding articles of the regulations decided and determined upon by the Tribunal of Arbitration. The other five articles contain stipulations essentially connected with the preceding nine, and intended to secure their execution. They relate merely to the enactment of necessary laws, the policing of the seas, the imposition of penalties, and the identification of vessels, in the manner required by the regulations of the Paris Tribunal, recited in the nine preceding articles.

I inclose herewith a copy of an act of Congress, approved February 21, 1893, which was adopted for the purpose of extending existing statutes to any waters in which the killing of seals might, either as the result of an international arrangement, or of the arbitration under the treaty of February 29, 1892, be forbidden. It is not doubted that Her Majesty's Government will respond to the disposition manifested in this act of Congress to give effect to the results of the arbitration. Such further legislation as may be required on the part of the United States to secure those results this Government binds itself in the convention hereby proposed forthwith to adopt, a like obligation being imposed on Her Majesty's Government to adopt laws necessary on their part.

I have the honor to request that this communication may have your early and most earnest attention.

I have, etc.,   W. Q. GRESHAM.

_____

[Inclosure 1 in No. 40.]

DRAFT MINUTES.

The United States of America and Her Majesty the Queen of the United Kingdom of Great Britain and Ireland, recognizing their obligation under the treaty of February 29, 1892, to consider the award of the Tribunal of Arbitration made under and by virtue of said treaty as a full, perfect, and final settlement of all the questions by said convention submitted to arbitration, including the regulations decided and determined upon by said tribunal as necessary for the protection of the fur seal in the Pacific Ocean and Bering Sea outside of the territorial waters, and to execute and perform the same as such settlement, have appointed as their plenipotentiaries to conclude a convention for that purpose, that is to say:

The President of the United States of America, ——— ———, and Her Majesty the Queen of the United Kingdom of Great Britain and Ireland, ——— ———, who, after having communicated to each other their respective full powers, found in due and good form, have agreed upon and concluded the following articles, to give full effect to the said award and the regulations determined upon by the said tribunal:

ARTICLE 1.

The Governments of the United States and of Great Britain shall forbid their citizens and subjects, respectively, to kill, capture, or pursue, at any time and in any manner whatever, the animals commonly called fur seals, within a zone of sixty miles around the Pribilof Islands, inclusive of the territorial waters.

The miles mentioned in the preceding paragraph are geographical miles, of sixty to a degree of latitude.

ARTICLE 2.

The two Governments shall forbid their citizens and subjects, respectively, to kill, capture, or pursue, in any manner whatever, during the season extending each year from the 1st of May to the 31st of July, both inclusive, the fur seals on the high sea, in the part of the Pacific Ocean, inclusive of the Bering Sea, which is situated to the north of the thirty-fifth degree of north latitude and eastward of the one hundred and eightieth degree of longitude from Greenwich, till it strikes the water boundary described in Article I of the treaty of 1867 between the United States and Russia, and following that line up to Bering Straits.

ARTICLE 3.

During the period of time and in the waters in which the fur-seal fishing is allowed, only sailing vessels shall be permitted to carry on or take part in fur-seal fishing operations. They will, however, be at liberty to avail themselves of the use of such canoes or undecked boats, propelled by paddles, oars, or sails as are in common use as fishing boats.

ARTICLE 4.

Each sailing vessel authorized to fish for fur seals must be provided with a special license issued for that purpose by its Government and shall be required to carry a distinguishing flag to be prescribed by its Government.

ARTICLE 5.

The masters of the vessels engaged in fur-seal fishing shall enter accurately in their official log book the date and place of each fur-seal fishing operation, and also the number and sex of the seals captured upon each day. These entries shall be communicated by each of the two Governments to the other at the end of each fishing season.

ARTICLE 6.

The use of nets, firearms, and explosives shall be forbidden in the fur-seal fishing. This restriction shall not apply to shotguns when such fishing takes place outside of Bering Sea, during the season when it may be lawfully carried on.

ARTICLE 7.

The two Governments shall take measures to control the fitness of the men authorized to engage in fur-seal fishing; these men shall have been proved fit to handle with sufficient skill the weapons by means of which this fishing may be carried on.

ARTICLE 8.

The regulations contained in the preceding articles shall not apply to Indians dwelling on the coasts of the territory of the United States or of Great Britain and carrying on fur-seal fishing in canoes or undecked boats not transported by or used in connection with other vessels and propelled wholly by paddles, oars, or sails, and manned by not more than five persons each in the way hitherto practiced by the Indians, provided such Indians are not in the employment of other persons, and provided that, when so hunting in canoes or undecked boats, they shall not hunt fur seals outside of territorial waters under contract for the delivery of the skins to any person.

This exemption shall not be construed to affect the municipal law of either country, nor shall it extend to the waters of Bering Sea or the waters of the Aleutian Passes.

Nothing herein contained is intended to interfere with the employment of Indians as hunters or otherwise in connection with fur-sealing vessels as heretofore.

ARTICLE 9.

The concurrent regulations hereby determined with a view to the protection and preservation of the fur seals shall remain in force until they have been, in whole or in part, abolished or modified by common agreement between the Governments of the United States and of Great Britain.

The said concurrent regulations shall be submitted every five years to a new examination, so as to enable both interested Governments to consider whether, in the light of past experience, there is occasion for any modification thereof.

ARTICLE 10.

The high contracting parties further agree that they will, respectively, without delay, enact such laws as shall appear requisite to carry into full effect all and every of the foregoing articles, and will from time to time, respectively, enact such further laws as may hereafter appear requisite to the like end.

ARTICLE 11.

The high contracting parties will also proceed to maintain now and hereafter in the waters of Bering Sea and of the North Pacific Ocean, from the —— day of March until the —— day of November in each year, a sufficient force of vessels properly equipped and fitted for the service of enforcing the stipulations herein contained and the laws agreed upon as aforesaid.

ARTICLE 12.

It is further agreed that every vessel, citizen, or subject of the nationality or under the jurisdiction of either of the high contracting parties, offending against the prohibitions recited in any of the foregoing articles, or violating any of the provisions of the laws passed for the enforcement of the said articles, or any of them, may be seized and detained by the naval or other duly commissioned officers of either of the high contracting parties, but they shall in case the seizure be made by one party of the citizens, subjects, or vessels of the other, be handed over for trial as soon as practicable to the authorities of the nation to which they respectively belong. The witnesses and proof necessary to establish the offense shall also be sent with them.

The high contracting parties shall forthwith designate, each to the other, a post or posts as near and convenient as may be to the area of the high sea described in the second above article, at which each party may deliver to the other for trial any vessels or persons seized or detained, and appoint a suitable officer or person to receive the same, together with any proofs of guilt, and shall make due provision for the immediate taking of the depositions of witnesses to be used, so far as the same may be used, at the trial or trials, so that such witnesses may not be long detained.

The penalty for every such offense or violation to be imposed upon any person convicted shall be a fine of not less than ——, nor more than ——, or imprisonment for not more than ——, or both such fine and imprisonment, and all vessels whose crew are found engaged in any such violation, their tackle, apparel, furniture, provisions, and all seal-skins on board, shall be condemned by proceedings in some court of competent jurisdiction and forfeited to the goverpment under whose laws such condemnation and forfeiture shall take place. .

ARTICLE 13.

It is further agreed that the distinguishing flag to be carried by the vessels which may be licensed by either of the high contracting parties under the provisions of article 4, shall be white in color, —— feet long and —— feet wide, and have thereon in black a letter S, as large as the said dimensions will admit, and shall always be conspicuously displayed.

ARTICLE 14.

The present convention shall be duly ratified by the President of the United States, by and with the advice and consent of the Senate thereof, and by Her Britannic Majesty, and the ratification shall be exchanged either at Washington or at London as early as possible.

In faith whereof we, the respective plenipotentiaries, have signed this convention and have hereunto affixed our seals.

No. 41.

Sir Julian Pauncefote to Mr. Gresham.

WASHINGTON, *January 30, 1894.*

SIR: I have the honor to acknowledge the receipt of your note of the 24th instant, inclosing for the consideration of my government the draft of a convention for giving effect (with appropriate legislation) to the award of the Bering Sea Tribunal of Arbitration as regards the regulations therein prescribed for the protection of the fur seal, and applicable to the high seas.

I transmitted a copy of your note and of its inclosures to the Earl of Rosebery by the mail of the 27th instant, and I also telegraphed the substance to him.

On receipt of his Lordship's reply I shall have the honor to address a further communication to you.

I have, etc.,   JULIAN PAUNCEFOTE.

No. 42.

Mr. Bayard to Mr. Gresham.

EMBASSY OF THE UNITED STATES,
London, February 21, 1894. (Received March 2.)

SIR: I have the honor to acknowledge yours of the 26th ultimo,* inclosing a copy of your correspondence with the British Ambassador at Washington, in relation to the enforcement of the award of the tribunal at Paris, and a draft of a proposed convention to effect this purpose.

---

* Not printed.

Reflection but confirms the opinion which I have heretofore communi, cated to you (and in which I am happy to find that you so fully concur)- that the first and essential step is the frank, clear, and explicit accept- ance by the two governments of the letter and spirit of the decrees of the tribunal.

The importance of accepting the award *ipsissimis verbis* is to prevent a new and different treaty from being substituted for the treaty of Feb- ruary, 1892, and its sequel, the award of the tribunal in August. 1893. These two documents must be kept and considered together as essen- tial and inseparable parts of the same transaction; and the award expressly recites the treaty of February, 1892, one feature of which was the distinct covenant to accept whatever decision might be reached by the arbitrators and enact laws to carry it into effect and procure the adhesion of other nations to the result.

But I will not repeat further what I have heretofore in this corre- spondence had the honor to state on this subject.

I inclose herewith copies of a report * just made to Parliament by the British agent at Tokyo (M. de Bunsen), which throws a good deal of light upon the proceedings of the pelagic sealers in the eastern-side of the Pacific Ocean, and which indicates impressively the necessity for prompt action by Great Britain and her North American dependencies and the United States, to compel by adequate and penal legislation obedience by their respective citizens to the regulations decreed by the Tribunal of Arbitration, a duty which can not be honorably avoided or delayed.

I have, etc.,   T. F. BAYARD. ·

No. 43.

Mr. Gresham to Mr. Bayard.

[Telegram.]

DEPARTMENT OF STATE,
Washington, February 22, 1894.

December 4 this Government yielded to the often expressed desire of Great Britain that further negotiations for making effective the award of the Paris Tribunal be conducted here. The British ambassador having since repeatedly informed me that he had not received expected instructions from his Government, the Department, on January 24, addressed him a note formally proposing the immediate conclusion of a convention to put in force the award, including the regulations, but nothing definite has been heard from Sir Julian, although from time to time I have urged that prompt action was necessary. The duty of the two Governments to give effect to the award is plain and simple. This long delay is difficult to understand, and it is the President's desire that you represent the matter impressively to Her Majesty's Government.

---

* Not printed.

No. 44.

Mr. Bayard to Mr. Gresham.

[Telegram.]

LONDON, *February 26, 1894.*

Saw Lord Rosebery to-day. Draft of law to give full effect to the award and regulations mailed to Sir Julian Pauncefote last Saturday. Lord Rosebery assures intent to execute award without evasion or hesitation. Have sent him note deprecating delay and impressively urging immediate conclusion of the convention.

No. 45.

Mr. Bayard to Mr. Gresham.

EMBASSY OF THE UNITED STATES,
London, February 28, 1894. (Received March 12.)

SIR: I have now the honor to acknowledge the receipt of your instruction by telegram of the 22d instant in relation to the necessity of efficacious action upon the award and regulations of the Paris Tribunal of Arbitration.

I applied at the foreign office at once for an interview, but Lord Rosebery left town in the afternoon of the 23d, and my interview with im was consequently delayed until the Monday following.

On receipt of your telegram, I at once prepared a note to Lord Rosebery, in accordance with the desire of the President, as expressed in our telegram, but considered it expedient to have some conversation ith him before placing the note in his hands (which I did, however, efore leaving), a copy of which is herewith inclosed.

In the course of the conversation, after being informed that the draft for an act of Parliament, to give effect to the regulations determined by the arbitrators, had gone forward to Sir Julian Pauncefote at Washington, I expressed my surprise and regret that Sir Julian had not been definitely instructed to sign with you the convention, accepting in full the award of the Paris tribunal and the regulations prescribed by that body, leaving penal legislation, framed with intent to enforce the regulations, to be cooperatively provided in addition by the two powers.

I impressed upon his Lordship the elaborate presentation and prolonged argument of the case on both sides before the arbitrators, with the voluminous testimony which had resulted in a very careful and well considered judgment, which was absolutely binding on the high contracting parties, and must be honorably accepted and obeyed as to every provision, and in the very words employed by them.

This having been done then the proper language to enforce the regulations could readily be agreed upon.

Lord Rosebery did not seem aware of the proposition for a convention, and asked why the cooperative legislation would not be sufficient, adding, with some positiveness, that I might rest assured that it was their purpose to evade nothing, but to join us in giving full effect to the award.

To this last remark I promptly, and of course, assented, but gave my reasons as above stated for believing a convention to be manifestly the most direct and efficient step to attain the end in view.

His Lordship called in one of the under secretaries, to whom I repeated my views, and he promised, after consultation with his law experts, to communicate with me.

I did not desire, however, to press the matter with him so far as to divert the settlement from Washington, or to give warrant for the creation of any delay on this side the Atlantic.

My conviction strengthens that a substantial obedience to the prescribed regulations, especially that feature which forbids at all times the use of firearms in seal hunting in Bering Sea, must render the business of such little profit that it will not be worth pursuing. Nor do I see how the Canadians can, without suicidal discredit, withhold their legislative cooperation.

I have, etc., T. F. BAYARD.

[Inclosure in No. 45.]

Mr. Bayard to Lord Rosebery.

EMBASSY OF THE UNITED STATES,
London, February 23, 1894.

MY LORD: I am to-day instructed by cable to convey to Her Majesty's Government an expression of the disappointment felt by the President in the unexpected and regretted delay in coming to an agreement for the efficient execution of the regulations for the conduct of fur-seal fishing in Bering Sea and the Northern Pacific Ocean, which were determined and established by the Tribunal of Arbitration, and promulgated on August 15 last.

A review of our correspondence will disclose that, as early as the middle of September last, I had the honor to address a note to your lordship, the object of which was to make these regulations practically effective in due anticipation of the sealing season of the present year.

And that it was in consequence of your Lordship's suggestions and urgent representations in your note of November 21, in reply to mine of the day previous, that I became empowered on December 5 to communicate to you that, "yielding to your Lordship's desire, as expressed in conversation and in your note of November 21, the President consents that the negotiations needful to give effect to the decisions of the Tribunal of Arbitration shall be conducted at Washington, and that Her Majesty's Government shall be represented by Sir Julian Pauncefote."

And I would also recall to your Lordship that Washington was expressly proposed by you as the scene of the contemplated negotiation, because of the greater expedition if conducted there.

On the 11th December I had the honor to receive your reply, stating that—

Upon the receipt of your excellency's note I at once instructed Her Majesty's representative, by telegraph, to express my acknowledgments to the United States Government for their courteous acquiescence in the views of Her Majesty's Government on this subject, and I avail myself of this opportunity to ask your excellency to accept my best thanks for the trouble which you have also taken in this matter.

I beg to assure you that no time shall be lost in issuing the necessary instructions to Sir Julian Pauncefote with regard to these negotiations.

The contents of this note were duly communicated to my Government; and since then from time to time I have been informed by the Secretary of State that he had held several interviews on the subject with Sir Julian Pauncefote, who was, however, still awaiting the definite instructions from his Government, which would enable him to join in a convention for effectually executing the apparently plain and simple duty of giving effect to the award and decisions of the Tribunal of Arbitration, according to the terms of the treaty of February 29, 1892, and the concurrent regulations determined and established for the proper protection and preservation of the fur seal in, or habitually resorting to, the Bering Sea, outside the jurisdiction and limits of the respective Governments.

The season of the migration northward of the seal herds is now near at hand, and reports, apparently well founded and most disquieting, are current of extensive preparations of sealing vessels to continue the pelagic and indiscriminate killing and capture of seals, regardless of the regulations determined by the Tribunal of Arbitration as necessary for the proper protection and preservation and the species.

Under these circumstances, I am impelled to apply to your Lordship, in order that no further time may be lost in issuing the requisite instructions to Sir Julian Pauncefote at Washington to proceed, so that the great purposes for which resort was had to the principle of voluntary and amicable arbitration between the two friendly powers may not be deprived of complete success.

I have the honor to be, etc.,   ·   T. F. BAYARD.

No. 46.

Mr. Bayard to Mr. Gresham.

EMBASSY OF THE UNITED STATES,
London, March 7, 1894. (Received March 16.)

SIR: In continuance of the subject of my last dispatch of February 28 and its inclosures, I have now the honor to inclose herewith a copy of a note, dated the 2d instant, which I received on the 3d instant after the departure of the mail to the United States on that day.

By the resignation of Mr. Gladstone, Lord Rosebery has become prime minister in his stead; and although the Earl of Kimberley is gazetted as secretary of state for foreign affairs, yet he has not yet formally been inducted into office, nor have I been notified of his assumption of its duties.

The tenor of Lord Rosebery's note is to me disappointing, and I shall at the earliest possible moment point out to his successor some of the reasons for such a feeling on the part of the Government of the United States. Nevertheless, it is somewhat satisfactory to observe the emphasis with which assurance is given "that the United States Government may rely upon the loyal fulfillment of the obligations imposed (by the decision of the Tribunal of Arbitration at Paris) upon this country.

It is difficult to see why recourse was to be had by Her Majesty's Government to "expert advisers" in regard to concluding a convention for the formal and explicit acceptance by both nations of the determination of a tribunal to which in advance and by formal treaty they had mutually pledged their faith and covenanted to procure the adhesion of the other powers.

If, however, an efficient and plenary execution of the Paris award and the regulations as determined and established for the control of fur-seal hunting in the North Pacific and Bering Sea can be obtained by cooperative statutes, the desired end will have been attained, and I sincerely trust the draft of legislative enactments which Lord Rose bery states went forward ten days ago to Washington may prove satisfactory and competent for the end in view.

For your possible convenience, I inclose copies of the imperial act of 1893, referred to in Lord Rosebery's note, which remains in force till July, 1895, and draw your attention to certain provisions which I have marked in relation to wide powers bestowed upon the Queen in council.

Just so soon as it is practicable I propose to address a note to the new secretary of state for foreign affairs, in order that the averments of intention "to give prompt effect to the regulations framed by the tribunal," contained in Lord Rosebery's note, may not lack a corresponding agreement on the part of the United States, and the substance of a treaty may thus be framed for future use and reference.

I have, etc.,

T. F. BAYARD.

[Inclosure 1 in No. 46.]

Lord Rosebery to Mr. Bayard.

FOREIGN OFFICE, *March 2, 1894.*

YOUR EXCELLENCY: Her Majesty's Government have given due weight to the considerations urged by your excellency at our interview on the 26th ultimo, in support of the proposal of the United States Government that a convention should be concluded at once between Great Britain and the United States for the purpose of giving effect, as soon as possible, to the award of the Tribunal of Arbitration as regards the regulations therein prescribed and applicable to the high seas.

They have also given careful attention to your excellency's note of the 23d instant, which you placed in my hands in the course of our interview.

In that note the disappointment of the United States is expressed at the unexpected and regrettable delay which has occurred in coming to an agreement as to the best means of giving effect to the award.

At the risk of repeating what I said to your excellency on that occasion, I desire to record my emphatic assurance that there is no wish on the part of Her Majesty's Government to evade the decisions or to disregard the recommendations of the arbitrators, and that the United States Government may rely on the loyal fulfillment of the obligations thereby imposed on this country.

Considerable delay has, no doubt, occurred, but on the part of Her Majesty's Government it has been caused by the repeated references which, in view of the magnitude of the Canadian interests involved, it has been incumbent on Her Majesty's Government to make to the Dominion Government.

The first object of both powers is to give prompt effect to the regulations framed by the tribunal. The principal end of these regulations is to control the operations of pelagic sealers on the high seas. The new sealing season is rapidly approaching, and Her Majesty's Government concur with the Government of the United States that unless some steps be taken at once, there is risk that the objects of the award may, during the present year, be defeated, a result which would be equally deplored by both Governments.

The proposal of your Government is to proceed by a convention. This suggestion has been carefully considered by her Majesty's Government in communication with their expert advisers. They do not, however, find themselves able to share the views expressed in Mr. Gresham's note to Sir Julian Pauncefote, of the 24th January, as to the advantage of this mode of proceeding.

I need not trouble your excellency at length with the reasons on which their conclusion is based, as I have instructed Sir Julian Pauncefote to communicate them confidentially to Mr. Gresham; but I may mention that Her Majesty's Government have no power to put into force by order in council, as your excellency thought possible, the provisions of a convention such as is proposed by Mr. Gresham. Their powers in that respect regarding the fur-seal fisheries are limited to those conferred by the imperial act of 1893 (North Pacific seal fisheries act, 1893), which remains in force till July, 1895. For carrying out the award of the tribunal fresh legislative enactments, will, in any case, be required. A bill for that purpose has, as I informed your excellency, been prepared, and I forwarded it to Her Majesty's ambassador at Washington by the mail of the 24th ultimo, and I have instructed his excellency to communicate it confidentially to Mr. Gresham, and to explain and discuss with him the course which Her Majesty's Government think most advisable under the circumstances.

I have, etc.,   ROSEBERY.

[Inclosure 2 in No. 46.]

CHAPTER 23. AN ACT to provide for prohibiting the catching of seals at certain periods in Behring Sea and other parts of the Pacific Ocean adjacent to Behring Sea. [29th June, 1893.]

Whereas it is expedient to extend the sea fishery (Behring Sea) act, 1891, to other waters of the North Pacific Ocean adjacent to Behring Sea, and for that purpose to repeal and reenact that act:

Be it therefore enacted by the Queen's most Excellent Majesty, by and with the advice and consent of the lords spiritual and temporal, and Commons, in this present Parliament assembled, and by the authority of the same, as follows:

1. (1) Her Majesty the Queen may, by order in council, prohibit during the period specified by the order, the catching of seals by British ships in such parts of the seas to which this act applies as are specified by the order.

(2) While an order in council under this act is in force—

(a) a person belonging to a British ship shall not kill, take, or hunt, or attempt to kill or take, any seal during the period and within the seas specified by the order; and

(b) a British ship shall not, nor shall any of the equipment or crew thereof, be used or employed in such killing, taking, hunting, or attempt.

(3.) If there is any contravention of this act, any person committing, procuring, aiding, or abetting such contravention shall be guilty of a misdemeanor within the meaning of the merchant shipping act, 1854, and the ship and her equipment, and everything on board thereof, shall be liable to be forfeited to Her Majesty as if an offence had been committed under section one hundred and three of the said act, and the provisions of sections one hundred and three and one hundred and four and part ten of the said act, and of section thirty-four of the merchant shipping act, 1876 (which are set out in the schedule to this act), shall apply as if they were herein reenacted, and in terms made applicable to an offence and forfeiture under this act, and any commissioned officer on full pay in the naval service of Her Majesty the Queen may seize the ship's certificate of registry.

(4) Any commissioned officer on full pay in the naval service of Her Majesty, the Queen, shall have power, during the period and in the seas specified by the order, to stop and examine any British ship, and to detain her, or any portion of her equipment, or any of her crew, if in his judgment the ship is being or is preparing to be used or employed in contravention of this act.

(5) For carrying into effect an arrangement with any foreign State, an order in council under this act may provide that such officers of that State, as are specified in the order, may exercise the like powers under this act as may be exercised by such a commissioned officer as aforesaid in relation to a British ship, and the equipment and crew and certificate thereof, and that such British officers, as are specified in the order, may exercise, with the necessary mondifications, the powers conferred by this act in relation to a ship of the said foreign State, and the equipment and crew and papers thereof.

(6) If during the period and within the seas specified by the order a British ship is found having on board thereof fishing or shooting implements or seal skins or bodies of seals, it shall lie on the owner or master of such ship to prove that the ship was not used or employed in contravention of this act.

2. (1) Where an officer has power under this act to seize a ship's certificate of registry, he may either retain the certificate and give a provisional certificate in lieu thereof, or return the certificate with an indorsement of the grounds on which it was seized, and in either case may direct the ship, by an addition to the provisional certificate or to the indorsement, to proceed forthwith to a specified port, being a port where there is a British court having authority to adjudicate in the matter, and if this direction is not complied with, the owner and master of the ship shall, without prejudice to any other liability, each be liable to a fine not exceeding one hundred pounds.

(2) Where in pursuance of this section a provisional certificate is given to a ship, or the ship's certificate is indorsed, any officer of customs in Her Majesty's dominions or British consular officer may detain the ship until satisfactory security is given for her appearance in any legal proceedings which may be taken against her in pursuance of this act.

3. (1) A statement in writing, purporting to be signed by an officer having power in pursuance of this act to stop and examine a ship, as to the circumstances under which or grounds on which he stopped and examined the ship, shall be admissible in any proceedings, civil or criminal, as evidence of the facts or matters therein stated.

(2) If evidence contained in any such statement was taken on oath in the presence of the person charged in the evidence, and that person had an opportunity of cross-examining the person giving the evidence and of making his reply to the evidence, the officer making the statement may certify that the evidence was so taken and that there was such opportunity as aforesaid.

4. (1) Her Majesty the Queen in council may make, revoke, and alter orders for the purpose of this act, and every such order shall be forthwith laid before both houses of Parliament and published in the London Gazette.

(2) Any such order may contain any limitations, conditions, qualifications, and exceptions which appear to Her Majesty in council expedient for carrying into effect the object of this act.

5. (1) This act shall apply to the animal known as the fur seal, and to any marine animal specified in that behalf by an order in council under this act, and the expression "seal" in this act shall be construed accordingly.

(2) This act shall apply to the seas within that part of the Pacific Ocean known as Behring's Sea, and within such other parts of the Pacific Ocean as are north of the forty-second parallel of north latitude.

(3) The expression "equipment" in this act includes any boat, tackle, fishing or shooting instruments, and other things belonging to a ship.

(4) This act may be cited as the seal fishery (North Pacific) act, 1893.

(5) The seal fishery (Behring's Sea) act, 1891, is hereby repealed, but any order in council in force under that act shall continue as if it had been made in pursuance of this act.

(6) This act shall be and remain in force until the first day of July, one thousand eight hundred and ninety-five.

SCHEDULE.

ENACTMENTS OF MERCHANT SHIPPING ACT (17 & 18 Vict. c. 104) APPLIED.

Section 103.

*   *   *   *   *   *   *

And in order that the provisions as to forfeitures may be carried into effect, it shall be lawful for any commissioned officer on full pay in the military or naval service of Her Majesty, or any British officer of customs, or any British consular officer, to seize and detain any ship which has, either wholly or as to any share therein, become subject to forfeiture as aforesaid, and to bring her for adjudication before the high court of admiralty in England or Ireland, or any court having admiralty jurisdiction in Her Majesty's dominions; and such court may thereupon make such order in the case as it may think fit, and may award to the officer bringing in the same for adjudication such portion of the proceeds of the sale of any forfeited ship or share as it may think right.

Section 104.

No such officer as aforesaid shall be responsible, either civilly or criminally, to any person whomsoever, in respect of the seizure or detention of any ship that has been seized or detained by him in pursuance of the provisions herein contained, notwithstanding that such ship is not brought in for adjudication, or, if so brought in, is declared not to be liable to forfeiture, if it is shown to the satisfaction of the judge or court before whom any trial relating to such ship or such seizure or detention is held that there were reasonable grounds for such seizure or detention; but if no such grounds are shown such judge or court may award payment of costs and damages to any party aggrieved and make such other order in the premises as it thinks just.

PART X.—LEGAL PROCEDURE.

APPLICATION.

Section 517.

The tenth part of this act shall in all cases where no particular country is mentioned apply to the whole of Her Majesty's dominions.

LEGAL PROCEDURE (GENERAL).

Section 518.

In all places within Her Majesty's dominions, except Scotland, the offences hereinafter mentioned shall be punished and penalties recovered in manner following (that is to say):

(1) Every offence by this act declared to be a misdemeanor shall be punishable by

fine or imprisonment with or without hard labour, and the court before which such offence is tried may in England make the same allowances and order payment of the same costs and expenses as if such misdemeanor had been enumerated in the act passed in the seventh year of His late Majesty King George the Fourth, chapter sixty-four, or any other act that may be passed for the like purpose, and may in any other part of Her Majesty's dominions make such allowances and order payment of such costs and expenses (if any) as are payable or allowable upon the trial of any misdemeanor under any existing act or ordinance, or as may be payable or allowable under any act or law for the time being in force therein.

(2) Every offence declared by this act to be a misdemeanor shall also be deemed to be an offence hereby made punishable by imprisonment for any period not exceeding six months, with or without hard labor, or by a penalty not exceeding one hundred pounds, and may be prosecuted accordingly in a summary manner, instead of being prosecuted as a misdemeanor.

(3) Every offence hereby made punishable by imprisonment for any period not exceeding six months, with or without hard labour, or by any penalty not exceeding one hundred pounds, shall in England and Ireland be prosecuted summarily before any two or more justices, as to England in the manner directed by the act of the eleventh and twelfth years of the reign of Her Majesty Queen Victoria, chapter forty-three, and as to Ireland in the manner directed by the act of the fourteenth and fifteenth years of the reign of Her Majesty Queen Victoria, chapter ninety-three, or in such other manner as may be directed by any act or acts that may be passed for like purposes. And all provisions contained in the said acts shall be applicable to such prosecutions in the same manner as if the offences in respect of which the same are instituted were hereby stated to be offences in respect of which two or more justices have power to convict summarily or to make a summary order.

(4) In all cases of summary convictions in England, where the sum adjudged to be paid exceeds five pounds, or the period of imprisonment adjudged exceeds one month, any person who thinks himself aggrieved by such conviction may appeal to the next court of general or quarter sessions.

(5) All offences under this act shall in any British possession be punishable in any court or by any justice of the peace or magistrate in which or by whom offences of a like character are ordinarily punishable, or in such other manner, or by such other courts, justices, or magistrates, as may from time to time be determined by any act or ordinance duly made in such possession in such manner as acts and ordinances in such possession are required to be made in order to have the force of law.

Section 519.

Any stipendiary magistrate shall have full power to do alone whatever two justices of the peace are by this act authorized to do.

Section 520.

For the purpose of giving jurisdiction under this act, every offence shall be deemed to have been committed, and every cause of complaint to have arisen, either in the place in which the same actually was committed or arose, or in any place in which the offender or person complained against may be.

Section 521.

In all cases where any district within which any court or justice of the peace or other magistrate has jurisdiction, either under this act or under any other act, or at common law, for any purpose whatever, is situate on the coast of any sea, or abutting on or projecting into any bay, channel, lake, river, or other navigable water, every such court, justice of the peace, or magistrate shall have jurisdiction over any ship or boat being on or lying or passing off such coast, or being in or near such bay, channel, lake, river, or navigable water as aforesaid, and over all persons on board such ship or boat or for the time being belonging thereto, in the same manner as if such ship, boat, or persons were within the limits of the original jurisdiction of such court, justice, or magistrate.

Section 522.

Service of any summons or other matter in any legal proceeding under this act shall be good service, if made personally on the person to be served, or at his last place of abode, or if made by leaving such summons for him on board any ship to which he may belong with the person being or appearing to be in command or charge of such ship.

Section 523.

In all cases where any court, justice, or justices of the peace, or other magistrate, has or have power to make an order directing payment to be made of any seaman's wages, penalties, or other sums of money, then, if the party so directed to pay the same is the master or owner of a ship, and the same is not paid at the time and in manner prescribed in the order, the court, justice, or justices, or other magistrate, who made the order, may, in addition to any other powers they or he may have for the purpose of compelling payment, direct the amount remaining unpaid to be levied by distress or poinding and sale of the said ship, her tackle, furniture, and apparel.

Section 524.

Any court justice or magistrate imposing any penalty under this act for which no specific application is herein provided, may, if it or he thinks fit, direct the whole or any part thereof to be applied in compensating any person for any wrong or damage which he may have sustained by the act or default in respect of which such penalty is imposed, or to be applied in or toward payment of the expenses of the proceedings; and, subject to such directions or specific application as aforesaid, all penalties recovered in the United Kingdom shall be paid into the receipt of Her Majesty's exchequer in such manner as the treasury may direct, and shall be carried to and form part of the consolidated fund of the United Kingdom; and all penalties recovered in any British possession shall be paid over into the public treasury of such possession, and form part of the public revenue thereof.

Section 525.

The time for instituting summary proceedings under this act shall be limited as follows (that is to say):

(1) No conviction for any offence shall be made under this act in any summary proceeding instituted in the United Kingdom, unless such proceeding is commenced within six months after the commission of the offence; or, if both or either of the parties to such proceeding happen during such time to be out of the United Kingdom, unless the same is commenced within two months after they both first happen to arrive or to be at one time within the same.

(2) No conviction for any offence shall be made under this act in any proceeding instituted in any British possession, unless such proceeding is commenced within six months after the commission of the offence; or if both or either of the parties to the proceeding happen during such time not to be within the jurisdiction of any court capable of dealing with the case, unless the same is commenced within two months after they both first happen to arrive or to be at one time within such jurisdiction.

(3) No order for the payment of money shall be made under this act in any summary proceeding instituted in the United Kingdom, unless such proceeding is commenced within six months after the cause of complaint arises; or, if both or either of the parties happen during such time to be out of the United Kingdom, unless the same is commenced within six months after they both first happen to arrive or to be at one time within the same.

(4) No order for the payment of money shall be made under this act in any summary proceeding instituted in any British possession, unless such proceeding is commenced within six months after the cause of complaint arises; or, if both or either of the parties to the proceeding happen during such time not to be within the jurisdiction of any court capable of dealing with the case, unless the same is commenced within six months after they both first happen to arrive or be at one time within such jurisdiction.

And no provision contained in any other act or acts, ordinance or ordinances for limiting the time within which summary proceedings may be instituted shall affect any summary proceeding under this act.

Section 526.

Any document required by this act to be executed in the presence of or to be attested by any witness or witnesses may be proved by the evidence of any person who is able to bear witness to the requisite facts, without calling the attesting witness or witnesses or any of them.

Section 527.

Whenever any injury has, in any part of the world, been caused to any property belonging to Her Majesty or to any of Her Majesty's subjects by any foreign ship, if at any time thereafter such ship is found in any port or river of the United Kingdom or within three miles of the coast thereof, it shall be lawful for the judge of any court of record in the United Kingdom or for the judge of the high court of admiralty, or in Scotland the court of session, or the sheriff of the county within whose jurisdiction such ship may be, upon its being shown to him by any person applying summarily that such injury was probably caused by the misconduct or want of skill of the master or mariners of such ship, to issue an order directed to any officer of customs or other officer named by such judge, requiring him to detain such ship until such time as the owner, master, or consignee thereof has made satisfaction in respect of such injury, or has given security, to be approved by the judge, to abide the event of any action, suit, or other legal proceeding that may be instituted in respect of such injury, and to pay all costs and damages that may be awarded thereon; and any officer of customs or other officer to whom such order is directed shall detain such ship accordingly.

Section 528.

In any case where it appears that before any application can be made under the foregoing section such foreign ship shall have departed beyond the limits therein mentioned, it shall be lawful for any commissioned officer on full pay in the military or naval service of Her Majesty; or any British officer of customs, or any British consular officer, to detain such ship until such time as will allow such application to be made and the result thereof to be communicated to him; and no such officer shall be liable for any costs or damages in respect of such detention unless the same is proved to have been made without reasonable grounds.

Section 529.

In any action, suit, or other proceeding in relation to such injury the person so giving security as aforesaid shall be made defendant or defender, and shall be stated to be the owner of the ship that has occasioned such damage; and the production of the order of the judge made in relation to such security shall be conclusive evidence of the liability of such defendant or defender to such action, suit, or other proceeding.

LEGAL PROCEDURE (SCOTLAND).

Section 530.

In Scotland every offence which by this act is described as a felony or misdemeanor may be prosecuted by indictment or criminal letters at the instance of Her Majesty's advocate before the high court of justiciary, or by criminal libel at the instance of the procurator fiscal of the county before the sheriff, and shall be punishable with fine and with imprisonment, with or without hard labour in default of payment, or with imprisonment, with or without hard labour, or with both, as the court may think fit, or in the case of felony with penal servitude, where the court is competent thereto; and such court may also, if it think fit, order payment by the offender of the costs and expenses of the prosecution.

Section 531.

In Scotland, all prosecutions, complaints, actions, or proceedings under this act, other than prosecutions for felonies or misdemeanors, may be brought in a summary form before the sheriff of the county, or before any two justices of the peace of the county or burgh where the cause of such prosecution or action arises, or where the offender or defender may be for the time, and when of a criminal nature or for penalties, at the instance of the procurator fiscal of court, or at the instance of any party aggrieved, with concurrence of the procurator fiscal of court; and the court may, if it think fit, order payment by the offender or defender of the costs of the prosecution or action.

Section 532.

In Scotland all prosecutions, complaints, actions, or other proceedings under this act may be brought either in a written or printed form, or partly written and partly printed, and where such proceedings are brought in a summary form it shall not be necessary in the complaint to recite or set forth the clause or clauses of the act on which such proceeding is founded, but it shall be sufficient to specify or refer to such clause or clauses, and to set forth shortly the cause of complaint or action, and the remedy sought; and when such complaint or action is brought in whole or in part for the enforcement of a pecuniary debt or demand, the complaint may contain a prayer for warrant to arrest upon the dependence.

Section 533.

In Scotland, on any complaint or other proceeding brought in a summary form under this act being presented to the sheriff clerk or clerk of the peace, he shall grant warrant to cite the defender to appear personally before the said sheriff or justices of the peace on a day fixed, and at the same time shall appoint a copy of the same to be delivered to him by a sheriff officer or constable, as the case may be, along with the citation; and such deliverance shall also contain a warrant for citing witnesses and havers to compear at the same time and place to give evidence and produce such writs as may be specified in their citation; and where such warrant has been prayed for in the complaint or other proceeding, the deliverance of the sheriff clerk or clerk of the peace shall also contain warrant to arrest upon the dependence in common form: *Provided always*, That where the apprehension of any party, with or without a warrant, is authorised by this act, such party may be detained in custody until he can be brought at the earliest opportunity before any two justices, or the sheriff who may have jurisdiction in the place, to be dealt with as this act directs, and no citation or induciæ shall in such case be necessary.

Section 534.

When it becomes necessary to execute such arrestment on the dependence against goods or effects of the defender within Scotland, but not locally situated within the jurisdiction of the sheriff or justices of the peace by whom the warrant to arrest has been granted, it shall be competent to carry the warrant into execution on its being indorsed by the sheriff clerk or clerk of the peace of the county or burgh respectively within which such warrant comes to be executed.

Section 535.

In all proceedings under this act in Scotland the sheriff or justices of the peace shall have the same power of compelling attendance of witnesses and havers as in cases falling under their ordinary jurisdiction.

Section 536.

The whole procedure in cases brought in a summary form before the sheriff or justices of the peace in Scotland shall be conducted vivâ voce, without written pleadings, and without taking down the evidence in writing, and no record shall be kept of the proceedings other than the complaint, and the sentence or decree pronounced thereon.

Section 537.

It shall be in the power of the sheriff or justices of the peace in Scotland to adjourn the proceedings from time to time to any day or days to be fixed by them, in the event of absence of witnesses or of any other cause which shall appear to them to render such adjournment necessary.

Section 538.

In Scotland all sentences and decrees to be pronounced by the sheriff or justices of the peace upon such summary complaints shall be in writing; and where there is a decree for payment of any sum or sums of money against a defender, such decree shall contain warrant for arrestment, poinding, and imprisonment in default of payment, such arrestment, poinding, or imprisonment to be carried into effect by sheriffs' officers or constables, as the case may be, in the same manner as in cases arising under the ordinary jurisdiction in the sheriff or justices: *Provided always*, That nothing herein contained shall be taken or construed to repeal or effect an act of the fifth and sixth years of William the Fourth, intituled "An act for abolishing, in Scotland, imprisonment for civil debts of small amount."

Section 539.

In all summary complaints and proceedings for recovery of any penalty or sum of money in Scotland, if a defender who has been duly cited shall not appear at the time and place required by the citation, he shall be held as confessed, and sentence or decree shall be pronounced against him in terms of the complaint, with such costs and expenses as to the court shall seem fit: *Provided always*, That he shall be entitled to obtain himself reponed against any such decree at any time before the same be fully implemented, by lodging with the clerk of court a reponing note, and consigning in his hands the sums decerned for, and the costs which had been awarded by the court, and on the same day delivering or transmitting through the post to the pursuer or his agent a copy of such reponing note; and a certificate by the clerk of court of such note having been lodged shall operate as a sist of diligence till the cause shall have been reheard and finally disposed of, which shall be on the next sitting of the court, or on any day to which the court shall then adjourn it.

Section 540.

In all summary complaints or other proceedings not brought for the recovery of any penalty or sum of money in Scotland, if a defender, being duly cited, shall fail to appear, the sheriff or justices may grant warrant to apprehend and bring him before the court.

Section 541.

In all cases where sentences or decrees of the sheriff or justices require to be enforced within Scotland, but beyond the jurisdiction of the sheriff or justices by whom such sentences or decrees have been pronounced, it shall be competent to carry the same into execution upon the same being indorsed by the sheriff clerk or clerk of the peace of the county or burgh within which such execution is to take place.

Section 542.

No order, decree, or sentence pronounced by any sheriff or justice of the peace in Scotland under the authority of this act shall be quashed or vacated for any misnomer, informality, or defect of form; and all orders, decrees, and sentences so pronounced shall be final and conclusive, and not subject to suspension, advocation, reduction, or to any form of review or stay of execution, except on the ground of corruption or malice on the part of the sheriff or justices, in which case the suspension, advocation, or reduction must be brought within fourteen days of the date of the order, decree, or sentence complained of: *Provided always,* That no stay of execution shall be competent to the effect of preventing immediate execution of such order, decree, or sentence.

Section 543.

Such of the general provisions with respect to jurisdiction, procedure, and penalties contained in this act as are not inconsistent with the special rules hereinbefore laid down for the conduct of legal proceedings and the recovery of penalties in Scotland, shall, so far as the same are applicable, extend to such last-mentioned proceedings and penalties: *Provided always,* That nothing in this act contained shall be held in any way to annul or restrict the common law of Scotland with regard to the prosecution or punishment of offences at the instance or by the direction of the lord advocate, or the rights of owners or creditors in regard to enforcing a judicial sale of any ship and tackle, or to give to the high court of admiralty of England any jurisdiction in respect of salvage in Scotland which it has not heretofore had or exercised.

ENACTMENT OF MERCHANT SHIPPING ACT, 1876 (39 & 40 VICT., c. 80.), APPLIED.

Section 34.

Where under the merchant shipping acts, 1854 to 1876, or any of them, a ship is authorised or ordered to be detained, any commissioned officer on full pay in the naval or military service of Her Majesty, or any officer of the board of trade or customs, or any British consular officer may detain the ship, and if the ship after such detention or after service on the master of any notice of or order for such detention proceeds to sea before it is released by competent authority, the master of the ship, and also the owner, and any person who sends the ship to sea, if such owner or person be party or privy to the offence, shall forfeit and pay to Her Majesty a penalty not exceeding one hundred pounds.

Where a ship so proceeding to sea takes to sea when on board thereof in the execution of his duty any officer authorised to detain the ship, or any surveyor or officer of the board of trade or customs, the owner and master of the ship shall each be liable to pay all expenses of and incidental to the officer or surveyor being so taken to sea, and also a penalty not exceeding one hundred pounds, or, if the offence is not prosecuted in a summary manner, not exceeding ten pounds for every day until the officer or surveyor returns, or until such time as would enable him after leaving the ship to return to the port from which he is taken, and such expenses may be recovered in like manner as the penalty.

No. 47.

Mr. Gresham to Mr. White.

DEPARTMENT OF STATE,
Washington, March 9, 1894.

SIR: I have to acknowledge the receipt of your dispatch of January 10, last, reporting that the imperial foreign office desired to know whether the Government of the United States would be disposed to entertain proposals for a modus vivendi as regards the North Pacific seal fisheries, similar to that now existing between Russia and Great Britain.

A reply has been unavoidably delayed by the failure thus far of the British Government to commence negotiations for the enforcement of the award of the Paris Tribunal of Arbitration. That award constitutes a valid obligation on the contracting parties, and every effort is being made by this Government to give it speedy effect in all its parts.

The award contemplates that the United States and Great Britain shall extend joint invitations to other powers to give their adhesion to such measures as may be agreed upon for the enforcement of the reported regulations, and the cordial character of the proposal of Russia plainly indicates that the adhesion of that Government will not be difficult to obtain.

I am, etc.,

W. Q. GRESHAM.

No. 48.

Mr. Gresham to Mr. Bayard.

[Telegram.]

WASHINGTON, *March 17, 1894.*

Great Britain still objects to a convention, and insists that award can be enforced by legislation. The President thinks convention necessary. The British ambassador suggested, a week ago, continuance of modus vivendi for another year. I replied the modus was only applicable to Bering Sea and suggested its renewal for another year, so enlarged, however, as to protect all the waters embraced in the second regulation, thus affording time for a treaty between United States, Great Britain, Russia, and Japan. The ambassador said he would telegraph this suggestion to his Government. To-day he informed me Great Britain did not favor such a modus, and I suggested a renewal of the existing modus for twelve months, with an added clause protecting the waters in the North Pacific embraced in the second regulation only during the months of May, June, and July, assuring the ambassador this Government could agree to nothing less.

The ambassador said it would be difficult to give notice to sealers which had already left their home ports, and it would be harsh to seize them without notice. I replied such sealers had left with knowledge of the award, and that both Governments were bound to enforce the regulations, and therefore contemplating that the regulations would be enforced; and that we would see to giving our sealers notice, asking no immunity for them, and Great Britain could do the same. The ambassador said he would telegraph at once my last offer to his Government.

But little time remains for concurrent action contemplated by the award. This Government is not responsible for the delay, and if Great Britain declines the last offer of a temporary agreement, the situation will become embarrassing for both Governments.

No. 49.

Mr. Gresham to Mr. Bayard.

DEPARTMENT OF STATE,
Washington, March 17, 1894.

SIR: The British ambassador called at the State Department about noon on the 7th instant and informed me that he had received from his Government a draft of a bill to be introduced into Parliament for putting into force the Bering Sea award, and other papers which he desired to submit for my inspection before a formal interview. I informed him I was ready for the interview whenever it would suit his convenience; that I knew of nothing so important as the Bering Sea award, and the sooner we reached an agreement for making it effective the better it would be for both Governments. Sir Julian stated that at 3 o'clock the next day he would be ready for an interview, at which hour he again arrived at the Department and for the first time handed me the draft. I informed him that I would examine it as speedily as possible, and after conferring with the President I would be ready for another interview, which we agreed should be on the 10th at 11 p. m. Sir Julian appeared at the appointed time, and I called his attention to the following defects in the draft submitted:

Paragraph 1 of section 1 declares that the reported regulations shall have effect as if they were set out in the act, and paragraph 2 declares that any person violating the act shall be deemed guilty of a misdemeanor within the meaning of the merchants' shipping act of 1854, and the ship employed in such contravention, and her equipment and everything on board thereof, shall be liable to be forfeited as if the offense had been committed under another act, "*Provided*, That the court, without prejudice to any other power, may release the ship, equipment, or thing, on payment of a fine not exceeding five hundred pounds." The penalty prescribed in the shipping act for a misdemeanor is a fine not exceeding 100 pounds.

The court is thus given discretion to punish offenders with nominal fines and release ships employed in contravention of the act on payment of like fines.

Paragraph 3 declares that certain sections of British acts shall apply as if they were expressly recited and in terms made applicable to the act, "and any commissioned officer on full pay in the naval service of Her Majesty the Queen may seize the ship's certificate of registry." Neither in this nor other sections of the draft is it made the duty of British officers to arrest offending persons and ships.

Paragraph 2 of Section VII reads:

Where, on any proceeding against a person or ship in respect of any offense under this act, it is proved that the ship sailed from its port of departure before the scheduled provisions were published there, and that such person or the master of the ship did not subsequently and before such alleged offense receive notice of those provisions, such person shall be acquitted and the ship shall be released and not forfeited.

This paragraph is plainly intended to protect Canadian sealers which have already left Victoria to hunt seals in violation of the regulations. Should the bill become a law and a Canadian ship be caught any time taking seals in the waters described in the first regulation, or the waters described in the second regulation, during the months of May, June, and July, it could not be forfeited if it sailed from its port of departure before the scheduled provisions were published at that port and the master did not receive notice of the regulations before the offense was committed. The owners and masters of Canadian sealing schooners or ships were all familiar with the treaty and award of the Paris Tribunal before the ships left their home ports for this season. They knew it was the duty of both Governments to enforce the regulations and protect the inhibited waters; they were bound to contemplate that both Governments would do what the treaty and the award obliged them to do, and they are not, therefore, entitled to the protection contemplated by the seventh section of the draft.

Having urged these objections to the bill, I again informed Sir Julian that a convention such as I had proposed was in the strict line of what the award called for, and that I would like to know what objection his Government had to proceeding in that way. He replied that his Government did not think a convention was necessary; that it was opposed to a convention; that legislation would accomplish all that was needed, and that if a convention should be agreed upon, it would not be operative in his country without Parliamentary action. I replied that a convention would have the force of law in this country, and that I presumed Parliament could speedily give it such force in England. Sir Julian said he had suggested to Lord Rosebery that, owing to the lapse of time and the near approach of the inhibited season (he would not say whether Canada or London was to blame), it would be well for the two Governments to renew the modus vivendi for another year.

I replied that this would not protect the waters of the North Pacific embraced in the second regulation, that the modus was applicable only to the waters of Bering Sea, and asked Sir Julian if he was in favor of extending the existing modus for twelve months so as to embrace all the waters included in the second regulation. He replied that he did not think his Government was willing to go so far; that his idea was simply to close the Bering Sea for another year, leaving the waters of the North Pacific, south of the Aleutian Islands, free, as heretofore, thus giving more time to reach an agreement for the enforcement of the award. I informed the ambassador that this Government was not responsible for the failure thus far to put into force the award, including the regulations; that I would agree to nothing looking to a departure from the award; that I would entertain a proposition for a modus vivendi on the basis of the first and second regulations, to be operative for twelve months, during which time a treaty might be entered into between the United States, Great Britain, Russia, and Japan, settling the entire sealing question. Sir Julian seemed to think there was force in this suggestion, and said he would at once telegraph to London for authority to enter into such an agreement, which he has done, but has as yet received no reply.

Should an arrangement of this kind not be entered into, I fear we will soon be confronted with serious questions.

I am, etc.,

W. Q. GRESHAM.

No. 50.

Mr. Bayard to Mr. Gresham.

[Telegram.]

LONDON, *March 19, 1894.*

Your instructions communicated to the Earl of Kimberley to-day and impressed upon him serious embarrassments which were threatened if your latest proposition to renew and extend operation of modus (vivendi) shall not be accepted. It was readily agreed to between us that failure or delay in faithful execution of award would inflict disastrous blow to principle of arbitration, and I was again assured most emphatically of full intent of British Government to carry out their obligation. I again stated reasons for convention with supplementary legislation as best mode of complying with award. A bill for executing award ready for introduction here and only excluded last week unavoidably. Earl of Kimberley promised further information without delay.

No. 51.

Mr. White to Mr. Gresham.

LEGATION OF THE UNITED STATES,
St. Petersburg, March 21, 1894. (Received April 7.)

SIR: I have the honor to acknowledge the receipt of yours of March 9 last, in relation to an arrangement contemplated by the United States Government between the said Government, Great Britain, and possibly other powers, including Russia, and to say that I have this day advised the Imperial foreign office as to the main points of interest to Russia contained in your said dispatch.

I am, etc., ANDREW D. WHITE.

No. 52.

Mr. Gresham to Mr. Bayard.

[Telegram.]

WASHINGTON, *March 22, 1894.*

Made this proposition to British ambassador yesterday:

Extend existing modus for one year, amended so as to include waters in North Pacific down to forty-second parallel for months May, June, July. If this is not accepted, and ambassador intimated to-day it would not be, it is believed Congress will pass a bill for enforcement of regulations this season on our part.

No. 53.

Mr. Gresham to Mr. White.

[Telegram.]

DEPARTMENT OF STATE,
Washington, March 24, 1894.

United States will agree to prohibit their citizens from taking seals within 10 miles of Russian coast and within zone of 30 miles around Commander and Robbin islands until agreement is terminated by notice.

No. 54.

Mr. Bayard to Mr. Gresham.

[Telegram.]

LONDON, *March 27, 1894.*

At our interview to-day Lord Kimberley gave me a copy of latest proposed agreement between you and British ambassador at Washington as to close season north of 42°, commencing May. As the United States have every possible interest for immediate legislation to enforce award, I would accept Lord Kimberley's amendment suggesting that close season shall cease August 1 as to that power which has then prepared by its legislation to enforce award. Notice has been given last week of introduction of bill next Thursday in the House of Commons by the attorney-general, who drafted it; no opposition anticipated. Am satisfied Lord Kimberley is as anxious as ourselves to secure honorable execution of award.

No. 55.

Mr. Gresham to Mr. Bayard.

[Telegram.]

WASHINGTON, *March 28, 1894.*

The President objects to stipulation proposed to be added by Lord Kimberley, as it implies a possible violation of agreement by United States. This Government can not consent to a modus which does not embrace paragraph 4 of proposition telegraphed by British ambassador. You can assure Lord Kimberley United States will enact legislation to enforce award on their part before August 1, and the President will not doubt Great Britain will do the same; but, if for any unexpected reason award should not be in force on that day, it is not desirable either party should have the right to denounce the treaty.

No. 56.

Mr. Gresham to Mr. White.

[Telegram.]

DEPARTMENT OF STATE,
Washington, March 28, 1894.

United States will agree to prohibit their citizens hunting seal within 10 miles of Russian coasts and within zone of 30 miles around Commander and Robbin islands, annual catch on islands to be limited to 30,000; that Russian officers may seize offending American vessels, turning them over to United States for trial. Agreement to be terminated at will by either party on notice.

No. 57.

Mr. Gresham to Prince Cantacuzene.

DEPARTMENT OF STATE,
Washington, March 28, 1894.

MY DEAR SIR: Referring to a communication of this morning, I inclose herewith for your information draft of a modus vivendi which the United States are willing to enter into with the Imperial Government of Russia for the protection of fur seals on the Russian side of the Bering Sea.

Very truly, yours, W. Q. GRESHAM.

[Inclosure in No. 57.]

Agreement between the Government of the United States and the Imperial Government of Russia for a modus vivendi in relation to the fur-seal fisheries in Behring Sea and the North Pacific Ocean.

For the purpose of avoiding difficulties and disputes in regard to the taking of fur seal in the waters of Bering Sea and the North Pacific Ocean, and to aid in the preservation of seal life, the Government of the United States and the Imperial Government of Russia have entered into the following temporary agreement, with the understanding that it is not to create a precedent for the future, and that the contracting parties mutually reserve entire liberty to make choice hereafter of such measures as may be deemed best adapted for the protection of the fur-seal species, whether by means of prohibitive zones or by the complete prohibition of pelagic sealing, or by appropriate regulation of seal hunting in the high seas.

1. The Government of the United States will prohibit citizens of the United States from hunting fur seal within a zone of ten nautical miles along the Russian coasts of Bering Sea and of the North Pacific Ocean, as well as within a zone of thirty nautical miles around the Komandorsky (Commander) Islands and Tulienew (Robbin) Island, and will promptly use its best efforts to ensure the observance of this prohibition by citizens and vessels of the United States.

2. Vessels of the United States engaged in hunting fur seal in the above-mentioned zones outside of the territorial waters of Russia may be seized and detained by the naval or other duly commissioned officers of Russia; but they shall be handed over as soon as practicable to the naval or other commissioned officers of the United States or to the nearest authorities thereof. In case of impediment or difficulty in so doing, the commander of the Russian cruiser may confine his action to seizing the ship's papers of the offending vessels in order to deliver them to a naval or other commissioned officer of the United States or to communicate them to the nearest authorities of the United States as soon as possible.

3. The Government of the United States agrees to cause to be tried by the ordinary courts, with all due guarantees of defense, such vessels of the United States as may be seized, or the ship's papers of which may be taken, as herein prescribed, by reason of their engaging in the hunting of fur seal within the prohibited zones outside of the territorial waters of Russia aforesaid.

4. The Imperial Russian Government will limit to 30,000 head the number of fur seal to be taken during the year 1894 on the coasts of Komandorsky (Commander) and Tulienew (Robbin) islands.

5. The present agreement shall have no retroactive force as regards the seizuré of any seal-hunting vessel of the United States by the naval or other commissioned officer of Russia prior to the conclusion hereof.

6. The present agreement being intended to serve the purpose of a mere provisional expedient to meet existing circumstances, may be terminated at will by either party upon giving notice to the other.

In witness whereof we, Walter Q. Gresham, Secretary of State of the United States, and Prince Cantacuzene, envoy extraordinary and minister plenipotentiary of His Majesty the Emperor of all the Russias, have, on behalf of our respective Governments, signed and sealed this agreement in duplicate and in the English and French languages, in the city of Washington, this   day   , 1894.

[SEAL.]
[SEAL.]

No. 58.

Mr. Bayard to Mr. Gresham.

[Telegram.]

LONDON, *March 29, 1894.*

Had an interview with minister for foreign affairs. Your instructions by cable communicated. Will reply as soon as possible.

No. 59.

Mr. Bayard to Mr. Gresham.

[Telegram.]

LONDON, *March 30, 1894.*

A bill for executing award and regulations was introduced in the House of Commons by attorney-general yesterday; read for the first time; second reading next Monday. No opposition.

No. 60.

Mr. Bayard to Mr. Gresham.

EMBASSY OF THE UNITED STATES,
London, March 30, 1894. (Received April 9.)

SIR: I have the honor to acknowledge the receipt of your several telegrams of the 17th, 22d, and 28th instant. all in relation to the measures requisite for enforcing the Bering Sea award and regulations.

An interview with Lord Kimberley was instantly sought on the 29th instant, and promptly accorded at his residence, and was followed by a note from me which restated with precision and fullness all that had passed between us on that occasion in relation to the subject matter under consideration, a copy of which note is now herewith inclosed.

When we parted (about 2 p. m.) Lord Kimberley was immediately to meet Sir Charles Russell, the attorney-general, for consultation upon this subject; and, although I have not yet received a reply to my last note, yet the report of the proceedings in the House of Commons yesterday discloses the fact that the attorney-general had introduced the bill to enforce the award and regulations as established by the Tribunal of Arbitration, that it had been read the first time without opposition, and the second reading fixed for Monday next, and to this effect I have to-day telegraphed you.

I am entirely confident of the intention of this Government to live up to their agreement, and provide by law for the full and honorable execution of the decree of the arbitrators.

Under their constitutional arrangements—differing from those of the United States—a treaty has not the force of law, and legislative machinery is requisite to put their conventions in operative force.

Last autumn, and throughout the session, until the recess in March, the Irish home rule bill, and one or two other measures, domestic and political in their nature, completely blocked the way of other business, and excluded all other consideration.

Now and at last the path is clear, and I am not able to doubt that the measure introduced will speedily become the law, and, once under legal control, I believe all international friction will be at least minimized or put an end to in Bering Sea.

I have, etc.,
T. F. BAYARD.

[Inclosure in No. 60.]

Mr. Bayard to Lord Kimberley.

EMBASSY OF THE UNITED STATES,
London, March 29, 1894.

DEAR LORD KIMBERLEY: Referring to our conversation of this morning on the subject of enforcing the award of the Tribunal of Arbitration in the Bering Sea fur sealing case, I beg leave in this note to repeat what I then said.

I am this morning instructed by cable that the President is unable to consent to the emendation suggested by you to paragraph 4 of the Memorandum of Agreement between Sir Julian Pauncefote and Secretary Gresham, at Washington, for the reason that it implies a possibility of violation by the United States of the agreement and also of the stipulations of the convention of February, 1892, and of the award of the Tribunal of Arbitration at Paris. I am instructed to assure your Lordship that the United States Government will enact legislation to enforce the award completely, on its part, before the 1st of August next, and that the President entertains no doubt that Great Britain will equally do the same.

As stated by me in our last interview on this subject, it is the desire, and manifestly it is essential to the interests of the United States, that the results of the arbitration should be completely carried into effect, and without delay; and this has been urged in their behalf ever since the award was promulgated in August last.

The President has great satisfaction in believing that it is the equal purpose of both Governments to carry into effect and enforce the decrees of the Tribunal of Arbitration in letter and spirit; and he is not willing that the force of the treaty which created the arbitration, or any of its results, should be weakened or departed from in any particular.

It was with this purpose that it was proposed by the United States in October last by a convention to accept at once and unqualifiedly the award of the tribunal, and the regulations determined and established by it for fur-seal fishing in the North Pacific Ocean and Bering Sea; but to this mode of action Her Majesty's Government demurred, and therefore they now desire, by cooperative legislation, and with the promptness necessitated by the circumstances of the case, to effectuate the same result.

Moreover, the welcome and hearty concurrence of your Lordship in the solicitude expressed by me that international resort to arbitration should not fail in completeness, nor its success in any degree be impaired, give great confidence that the arrangements as proposed by the two negotiators at Washington will be adopted.

Believe me, etc.,

T. F. BAYARD.

No. 61.

Mr. Gresham to Mr. White.

DEPARTMENT OF STATE,
Washington, March 30, 1894.

SIR: On the 9th instant I answered your dispatch of January 10th, in relation to the suggested Russian-American modus vivendi in regard to the fur-seal fisheries of the North Pacific, and pointed out the necessity of deferring a joint understanding, reciprocally applicable to the waters within the purview of the award of the Paris Tribunal of Arbitration, until the invitation contemplated in that award could be extended by the United States and Great Britian acting in concert.

Since then, as the result of conferences I have had with the Russian minister here, the way has been opened for the adoption of a more limited understanding with the Imperial Government.

I have given to Prince Cantacuzene a draft of a modus vivendi, a copy of which I inclose * in order that you may submit it to the Russian Government for its information as to what the United States are willing to do in this relation.

It will be observed that the modus vivendi is not reciprocal in its application to the eastern waters of the North Pacific and Bering Sea. Our information is that Russian subjects have never taken seal on our side of those waters, and there is no reason to apprehend that they will do so now. For that reason, the United States exact nothing from Russia in the way of reciprocity, relying on the stipulated right to terminate the agreement at will, in the event of Russia permitting her subjects to poach in the waters embraced in the regulations of the Paris award.

My telegram of the 28th instant advised you of the essential features of the proposed modus.

I am, etc.,

W. Q. GRESHAM.

---

* See inclosure in No. 57.

No. 62.

Mr. Gresham to Mr. Bayard.

[Telegram.]

WASHINGTON, *March 31, 1894.*

Proposition British Government communicated by British ambassador to-day not accepted. Delay on the part of Great Britain and apparent unwillingness to protect waters in first and second regulations against Canadian sealers this season have created some feeling of irritation in Congress. Think bill for full enforcement of award will pass Senate Monday and House in a few days thereafter.

No. 63.

Mr. Bayard to Mr. Gresham.

[Telegram.]

LONDON, *April 3, 1894.*

Long interview with the minister for foreign affairs yesterday, and pressed the necessity for prompt action. Bill as now published gives legislative force to all regulations of Paris Arbitration May 1. I consider it highly important that bill before Congress should strictly adhere to phraseology of regulations, and that measures of both Governments should be as nearly as possible identical. Comments of press of both parties favorable.

No. 64.

Mr. White to Mr. Gresham.

LEGATION OF THE UNITED STATES,
St. Petersburg, April 3, 1894. (Received April 19.)

SIR: I inclose a copy of a note just received from the imperial minister of foreign affairs proposing a modus vivendi similar to that now in operation between Russia and Great Britain, which the Imperial Government understands from the recent telegram of the State Department to this legation that our own Government is ready to adopt.

It will be observed that the method of putting the proposed arrangement into force suggested by the imperial minister is very simple, and I may be allowed to suggest that, if our own Government take the same view, a brief dispatch by cable to me to that effect would be well received here by the Imperial Government as showing that we are ready to meet their views with promptness.

I am, etc.,

AND. D. WHITE.

[Inclosure in No. 64—Translation]

Mr. Giers to Mr. White.

MR. MINISTER: The Government of the United States of North America, having agreed to an arrangement concerning fur-seal fishing similar to the one which already exists between us and Great Britain, I consider it my duty to address you the present note on the subject, accompanied by the reservations which we have formulated toward England.

S. Ex. 67——6

1. It is understood, in the first place, that the understanding established between our two Governments leaves unimpaired all the rights of Russia in its territorial waters.

2. In delivering to the authorities of the United States the American ships engaged in hunting fur seals in the prohibited waters, we do not in any way intend to prejudice the question of the rights of maritime power to extend its territorial jurisdiction in certain special cases beyond erritorial waters properly so called.

3. The Imperial Government reserves its entire liberty as to the choice in the future between the two systems of protecting fur seals, either by means of a prohibited zone or by means of complete prohibition of pelagic hunting, or by regulating it on the high seas.

4. The present arrangement shall only be in force until further orders, will only have an essentially provisional character, and shall in no way be used as a precedent.

Under these reservations we consent to the following conditions:

1. The Government of the United States of North America shall forbid its subjects hunting fur seals within a zone of 10 nautical miles along all the Russian coasts of Bering Sea and the Northern Pacific Ocean as well as in a zone of 30 nautical miles around the Commandorski and Tiulenew islands (Robbin Island).

2. Ships belonging to subjects of the United States of North America occupied in fishing fur-seals in the above-mentioned zone outside of the territorial waters of Russia may be seized by Russian ships of war to be delivered over to ships of war of the United States or to the nearest American authorities. In case that this can not be done, or where there arises difficulty in doing so, the commander of the Russian ship may confine himself to seizing the ship's papers of the above-mentioned vessels to the end that they may be handed over to a ship of war of the United States or sent to the nearest American authorities at the earliest opportunity.

3. The Government of the United States agrees to have tried by the ordinary tribunals offering all necessary guarantees American ships which shall have been seized for fishing fur seal in the prohibited zones outside of Russian territorial waters.

4. The Imperial Government will limit the catch of fur seals on the coast of the Commandorski and Tiulenew (Robbin) islands to 30,000 head during the present year.

5. An agent of the Government of the United States may be allowed to land on the above-mentioned Commandorski and Tiulenew islands, so as to collect from the local authorities all necessary information bearing on the working and results of the present agreement, but the local authorities shall be previously informed of the date of his visit which shall not be for a greater length of time than a few weeks.

6. The present agreement shall have no retrospective force as to the seizure of American vessels which may have been previously seized by ships of the imperial navy.

The above-mentioned points being based exactly on the texts of our arrangements with Great Britain to which the Government of the United States of North America has already adhered, we do not doubt that the latter will accept it (i. e., the present agreement). A simple acknowledgement conveying the formal acceptance by your Government would be sufficient in our eyes to establish that the agreement between the two Governments concerning fur-seal fishing is provisionally agreed upon until further order.

Please accept, etc.,   GIERS.

No. 65.

Mr. Bayard to Mr. Gresham.

EMBASSY OF THE UNITED STATES,
London, April 4, 1894. (Received April 13.)

• SIR: I had the honor to address you under date of 30th ultimo, and now inclose copies of your telegram of March 31 and of my telegraphic reply to the same of the 3d instant, both relating to the proposed enforcement of the Bering Sea regulations.

ˈ The sentence of your above telegram, "Proposition British Government communicated by British ambassador to-day not accepted," was not quite clear to me in its meaning, nor was I able in my interview of April 2 with Lord Kimberley to obtain from him an entirely satisfactory explanation.

The action of this Government, however, in fixing May 1 as the date for the operation of the new law for enforcing the fur-sealing regulations, would appear to make unnecessary any ad interim arrangement.

I have the honor to inclose copies of the proposed British act as published here yesterday, and which (as I was informed) was telegraphed verbatim to the United States, with the purpose probably of procuring identity of legislative expression.

Lord Kimberley showed me a copy of the bill introduced by Mr. McCreary in the House of Representatives and referred to the Committee on Foreign Relations, which copy had been much interlined and amended, and as it did not accurately follow the phraseology of the regulations, as "determined and established" by the Tribunal of Arbitration at Paris, I drew your attention in my last telegram to what I conceive to be of great importance—that we should incorporate and adopt in our law to enforce these regulations the full and precise language employed by the arbitrators.

The more I consider the logical and necessary results of a complete enforcement of these regulations as decreed, the more plainly does it appear to me that profitable pelagic fur-seal fishing is inconsistent therewith.

This, of course, is equally obvious to the British-American sealers, and· the strain upon their sense of honorable obligation and legal duty may be estimated by expressions in the parliament at Ottawa, and the departure of there sealing vessels with full knowledge of the regulations of the arbitration and the pendency of legislation to penalize their breach.

The telegraphic reports announce the passage, yesterday, of the bill in the Senate, and I suppose speedy action will similarly follow in the House of Representatives.

I have, etc., T. F. BAYARD.

———

[Inclosure in No. 65.]

BERING SEA AWARD BILL.

ARRANGEMENT OF CLAUSES.

Clause:
1. Enactment of articles of arbitrators' award respecting the fur seal.
2. Provision as to ship's papers.
3. Orders in council.
4. Liabilities of masters to punishment.
5. Definitions.
6. Short title.
7. Commencement of act.
8. Duration of act.
   Schedules.

A BILL to provide for carrying into effect the award of the Tribunal of Arbitration constituted under a treaty between Her Majesty the Queen and the United States of America.

Whereas by a treaty between Her Majesty the Queen and the Government of the United States of America various questions which had arisen respecting the taking and preservation of the fur seal in the North Pacific were referred to arbitrators as mentioned in the treaty;

And whereas the award of such arbitrators (in this act referred to as the Bering Sea Arbitration Award), dated the fifteenth day of August one thousand eight hundred and ninety-three, contained the provisions set out in the first schedule to this act; and it is expedient to provide for carrying the same into effect:

Be it therefore enacted, by the Queen's most Excellent Majesty, by and with the advice and consent of the Lords spiritual and temporal, and Commons, in this present Parliament assembled, and by the authority of the same, as follows:

1. (1) The provisions of the Bering Sea Arbitration Award set out in the first schedule to this act shall have effect as if those provisions (in this act referred to as the scheduled provisions) were enacted by this act, and the acts directed by articles one and two thereof to be forbidden were expressly forbidden by this act.

(2) If there is any contravention of this act, any person committing, procuring, aiding, or abetting such contravention shall be guilty of a misdemeanor within the meaning of the merchant shipping act, 1854, and the ship employed in such contravention and her equipment, and everything on board thereof, shall be liable to be forfeited to Her Majesty as if an offence had been committed under section one hundred and three of the said act; provided that the court, without prejudice to any other power, may release the ship, equipment, or thing on payment of a fine not exceeding *five hundred pounds*.

(2) The provisions of the merchant shipping act, 1854, with respect to official logs (including the penal provisions) shall apply to every vessel engaged in fur-seal fishing.

(3) Every person who forges or fraudulently alters any licence or other document issued for the purpose of article four or of article seven in the first schedule to this act, or who procures any such licence or document to be forged or fraudulently altered, or who knowing any such licence or document to be forged or fraudulently altered uses the same, or who aids in forging or fraudulently altering any such licence or document, shall be guilty of a misdemeanor within the meaning of the merchant shipping act, 1854.

(4) Subject to this act, the provisions of sections one hundred and three and one hundred and four and part ten of the merchant shipping act, 1854, and of section thirty-four of the merchant shipping act, 1876, which are set out in the second schedule to this act, shall apply as if they were herein reenacted, and in terms made applicable to an offence and forfeiture under this act; and any commissioned officer on full pay in the naval service of Her Majesty the Queen may seize the ship's certificate of registry.

2. (1) Where an officer seizes, under this Act, a ship's certificate of registry, he may either retain the certificate and give a provisional certificate in lieu thereof, or return the certificate with an indorsement of the grounds on which it was seized, and in either case may direct the ship, by an addition to the provisional certificate or to the indorsement, to proceed forthwith to a specified port, being a port where there is a British court having authority to adjudicate in the matter, and if this direction is not complied with the owner and master of the ship shall, without prejudice to any other liability, each be liable to a fine not exceeding *one hundred pounds.*

(2) Where in pursuance of this section a provisional certificate is given to a ship, or the ship's certificate is indorsed, any officer of customs in Her Majesty's dominions or British consular officer may detain the ship until satisfactory security is given for her appearance in any legal proceedings which may be taken against her in pursuance of this act.

3. (1) Her Majesty the Queen in council may make, revoke, and alter orders for carrying into effect the scheduled provisions, and this act, and every such order, shall be forthwith laid before both houses of Parliament and published in the London Gazette, and shall have effect as if enacted in this act.

(2) If there is any contravention of any regulation made by any such order, any person committing, procuring, aiding, or abetting such contravention shall be liable to a penalty not exceeding *one hundred pounds.*

(3) An order in council under this act may provide that such officers of the United States of America as are specified in the order may in respect of offences under this act exercise the like powers under this act as may be exercised by a commissioned officer of Her Majesty in relation to a British ship, and the equipment and certificate thereof; and that such British officers as are specified in the order may exercise the powers conferred by this act, with any necessary modifications specified in the order, in relation to a ship of the United States of America, and the equipment and certificate thereof.

4. (1) Where any offence under this act has been committed by some person belonging to a ship, or by means of a ship, or the equipment of a ship, the master of the ship shall be deemed guilty of such offence, and the ship and her equipment shall be liable to forfeiture under this act.

(2) Provided that if it is proved that the master issued proper orders for the observance, and used due diligence to enforce the observance of this act, and the regulations in force thereunder, and that the offence in question was actually committed by some other person without his connivance, and that the actual offender has been convicted, or that he has taken all proper means in his power to prosecute such offender, if alive, to conviction, the master or the ship shall not be liable to any penalty or forfeiture other than such sum as will compensate for any injury caused by the offence, and will prevent any profit accruing by reason of the offence to the master or crew or owner of the ship.

5. (1) The expression "equipment" in this act includes any boat, tackle, fishing or shooting instruments, and other things belonging to a ship.

6. This act may be cited as the Bering Sea award act, 1894.

7. (1) This act shall come into operation on the *first day of May, one thousand eight hundred and ninety-four,* provided that Her Majesty in council, if at any time it appears expedient so to do, having regard to the circumstances which have then arisen in relation to the scheduled provisions or to the enforcement thereof, may suspend the operation of this act or any part thereof during the period mentioned in the order, and the same shall be suspended accordingly.

(2) Where on any proceeding against a person or ship in respect of any offence under this act it is proved that the ship sailed from its port of departure before the scheduled provisions were published there, and

that such person or the master of the ship did not, after such sailing and before the alleged offence, receive notice of those provisions, such person shall be acquitted, and the ship shall be released and not forfeited.

8. This act shall remain in force so long as the scheduled provisions remain in force and no longer.

Provided that if by agreement between Her Majesty the Queen and the Government of the United States of America, the scheduled provisions are modified, then Her Majesty in council may order that this act shall, subject to any modifications, specified in the order, apply, and the same shall accordingly apply, to the modified provisions in like manner as if they were set out in the first schedule to this act.

SCHEDULES.

First Schedule.

Provisions in award of the Tribunal of Arbitration constituted under the treaty concluded at Washington on the 29th of February, 1892, between Her Majesty the Queen and the United States of America.

And whereas the aforesaid determination of the foregoing questions as to the exclusive jurisdiction of the United States mentioned in Article VI leaves the subject in such a position that the concurrence of Great Britain is necessary to the establishment of regulations for the proper protection and preservation of the fur seal in or habitually resorting to the Bering Sea, the tribunal having decided by a majority as to each article of the following regulations, we, the said Baron de Courcel, Lord Hannen, Marquis Visconti Venosta, and Mr. Gregers Gram, assenting to the whole of the nine articles of the following regulations, and being a majority of the said arbitrators, do decide and determine in the mode provided by the treaty that the following concurrent regulations outside the jurisdictional limits of the respective Governments are necessary, and that they should extend over the waters hereinafter mentioned—that is to say:

Article 1. The Governments of the United States and of Great Britain shall forbid their citizens and subjects, respectively, to kill, capture, or pursue at any time and in any manner whatever, the animals commonly called fur seals, within a zone of 60 miles around the Pribiloff Islands, inclusive of the territorial waters.

The miles mentioned in the preceding paragraph are geographical miles, of 60 to a degree of latitude.

Article 2. The two Governments shall forbid their citizens and subjects, respectively, to kill, capture, or pursue in any manner whatever, during the season extending each year from the 1st May to the 31st July, both inclusive, the fur seals on the high sea in the part of the Pacific Ocean, inclusive of the Behring Sea, which is situated to the north of the 35th degree of north latitude, and eastward of the 180th degree of longitude from Greenwich till it strikes the water boundary described in Article I of the treaty of 1867 between the United States and Russia, and following that line up to Behring Straits.

Article 3. During the period of time and in the waters in which the fur-seal fishing is allowed, only sailing vessels shall be permitted to carry on or take part in fur-seal fishing operations. They will, however, be at liberty to avail themselves of the use of such canoes or undecked boats, propelled by paddles, oars, or sails, as are in common use as fishing boats.

Article 4. Each sailing vessel authorised to fish for fur-seals must be provided with a special licence issued for that purpose by its Government, and shall be required to carry a distinguishing flag to be prescribed by its Government.

Article 5. The masters of the vessels engaged in fur-seal fishing shall enter accurately in their official log-book the date and place of each fur-seal fishing operation, and also the number and sex of the seals captured upon each day. These entries shall be communicated by each of the two Governments to the other at the end of each fishing season.

Article 6. The use of nets, fire-arms, and explosives shall be forbidden in the fur-seal fishing. This restriction shall not apply to shot guns when such fishing takes place outside of Behring's Sea during the season when it may be lawfully carried on.

Article 7. The two Governments shall take measures to control the fitness of the men authorised to engage in fur-seal fishing. These men shall have been proved fit to handle with sufficient skill the weapons by means of which this fishing may be carried on.

ARTICLE 8. The regulations contained in the preceding articles shall not apply to Indians dwelling on the coasts of the territory of the United States or of Great Britain, and carrying on fur-seal fishing in canoes or undecked boats not transported by or used in connexion with other vessels and propelled wholly by paddles, oars, or sails, and manned by not more than five persons each in the way hitherto practised by the Indians, provided such Indians are not in the employment of other persons, and provided that, when so hunting in canoes or undecked boats, they shall not hunt fur-seals outside of territorial waters under contract for the delivery of the skins to any person.

This exemption shall not be construed to affect the municipal law of either country, nor shall it extend to the waters of Behring Sea, or the waters of the Aleutian Passes.

Nothing herein contained is intended to interfere with the employment of Indians as hunters or otherwise in connexion with fur-sealing vessels as heretofore.

ARTICLE 9. The concurrent regulations hereby determined with a view to the protection and preservation of the fur-seals, shall remain in force until they have been, in whole or in part, abolished or modified by common agreement between the Governments of the United States and of Great Britain.

The said concurrent regulations shall be submitted every five years to a new examination, so as to enable both interested Governments to consider whether, in the light of past experience, there is occasion for any modification thereof.

SECOND SCHEDULE.

ENACTMENTS OF MERCHANT SHIPPING ACT (17 & 18 VICT., C. 104) APPLIED.

Section 103.

*   *   *   *   *   *   *

And in order that the above provisions as to forfeitures may be carried into effect, it shall be lawful for any commissioned officer on full pay in the military or naval service of Her Majesty, or any British officer of customs, or any British consular officer, to seize and detain any ship which has, either wholly or as to any share therein, become subject to forfeiture as aforesaid, and to bring her for adjudication before the high court of admiralty in England or Ireland, or any court having admiralty jurisdiction in Her Majesty's dominions; and such court may thereupon make such order in the case as it may think fit, and may award to the officer bringing in the same for adjudication such portion of the proceeds of the sale of any forfeited ship or share as it may think right.

Section 104.

No such officer as aforesaid shall be responsible, either civilly or criminally, to any person whomsoever, in respect of the seizure or detention of any ship that has been seized or detained by him in pursuance of the provisions herein contained, notwithstanding that such ship is not brought in for adjudication, or, if so brought in, is declared not to be liable to forfeiture, if it is shown to the satisfaction of the judge or court before whom any trial relating to such ship or such seizure or detention is held that there were reasonable grounds for such seizure or detention; but if no such grounds are shown, such judge or court may award payment of costs and damages to any party aggrieved, and make such other order in the premises as it thinks just.

PART X.—LEGAL PROCEDURE.

APPLICATION.

Section 517.

The tenth part of this act shall in all cases, where no particular country is mentioned, apply to the whole of Her Majesty's dominions.

LEGAL PROCEDURE (GENERAL).

Section 518.

In all places within Her Majesty's dominions except Scotland, the offences hereinafter mentioned shall be punished and penalties recovered in many following; (that is to say)

(1) Every offence by this act declared to be a misdemeanor shall be punishable by fine or imprisonment, with or without hard labour, and the court before which such

offence is tried may, in England, make the same allowances and order payment of the same costs and expenses as if such misdemeanor had been enumerated in the act passed in the seventh year of His late Majesty King George the Fourth, chapter sixty-four, or any other act that may be passed for the like purpose, and may in any other part of Her Majesty's dominions make such allowances and order payment of such costs and expenses (if any) as are payable or allowable upon the trial of any misdemeanor under any existing act or ordinance or as may be payable or allowable under any act or law for the time being in force therein.

(2) Every offence declared by this act to be a misdemeanor shall also be deemed to be an offence hereby made punishable by imprisonment for any period not exceeding six months, with or without hard labour, or by a penalty not exceeding one hundred pounds, and may be prosecuted accordingly in a summary manner, instead of being prosecuted as a misdemeanor.

(3) Every offence hereby made punishable by imprisonment for any period not exceeding six months, with or without hard labour, or by any penalty not exceeding one hundred pounds, shall, in England and Ireland, be prosecuted summarily before any two or more justices; as to England in the manner directed by the act of the eleventh and twelfth years of the reign of Her Majesty Queen Victoria, chapter forty-three, and as to Ireland in the manner directed by the act of the fourteenth and fifteenth years of the reign of Her Majesty Queen Victoria, chapter ninety-three, or in such other manner as may be directed by any act or acts that may be passed for like purposes. And all provisions contained in the said acts shall be applicable to such prosecutions in the same manner as if the offences in respect of which the same are instituted were hereby stated to be offences in respect of which two or more justices have power to convict summarily or to make a summary order.

(4) In all cases of summary convictions in England, where the sum adjudged to be paid exceeds five pounds, or the period of imprisonment adjudged exceeds one month, any person who thinks himself aggrieved by such conviction may appeal to the next court of general or quarter sessions.

(5) All offenses under this act shall in any British possession be punishable in any court or by any justice of the peace or magistrate in which or by whom offences of a like character are ordinarily punishable, or in such other manner, or by such other courts, justices, or magistrates, as may from time to time be determined by any act or ordinance duly made in such possession in such manner as acts and ordinances in such possession are required to be made in order to have the force of law.

Section 519.

Any stipendiary magistrate shall have full power to do alone whatever two justices of the peace are by this act authorised to do.

Section 520.

For the purpose of giving jurisdiction under this act, every offence shall be deemed to have been committed, and every cause of complaint to have arisen, either in the place in which the same actually was committed or arose, or in any place in which the offender or person complained against may be.

Section 521.

In all cases where any district within which any court or justice of the peace or other magistrate has jurisdiction, either under this act or under any other act or at common law, for any purpose whatever, is situate on the coast of any sea, or abutting on or projecting into any bay, channel, lake, river, or other navigable water, every such court, justice of the peace, or magistrate shall have jurisdiction over any ship or boat being on or lying or passing off such coast, or being in or near such bay, channel, lake, river, or navigable water as aforesaid, and over all persons on board such ship or boat, or for the time being belonging thereto, in the same manner as if such ship, boat, or persons were within the limits of the original jurisdiction of such court, justice, or magistrate.

Section 522.

Service of any summons or other matter in any legal proceeding under this act shall be good service, if made personally on the person to be served, or at his last place of abode, or if made by leaving such summons for him on board any ship to which he may belong with the person being or appearing to be in command or charge of such ship.

Section 523.

In all cases where any court, justice or justices of the peace, or other magistrate has or have power to make an order directing payment to be made of any seaman's wages, penalties, or other sums of money, then, if the party so directed to pay the same is the master or owner of a ship, and the same is not paid at the time and in manner prescribed in the order, the court, justice or justices, or other magistrate who made the order, may, in addition to any other powers they or he may have for the purpose of compelling payment, direct the amount remaining unpaid to be levied by distress or poinding and sale of the said ship, her tackle, furniture, and apparel.

Section 524.

Any court, justice, or magistrate imposing any penalty under this act, for which no specific application is herein provided, may, if it or he thinks fit, direct the whole or any part thereof to be applied in compensating any person for any wrong or damage which he may have sustained by the act or default in respect of which such penalty is imposed, or to be applied in or towards payment of the expenses of the proceedings; and, subject to such directions or specific application as aforesaid, all penalties recovered in the United Kingdom shall be paid into the receipt of Her Majesty's exchequer in such manner as the treasury may direct, and shall be carried to and form part of the consolidated fund of the United Kingdom; and all penalties recovered in any British possession shall be paid over into the public treasury of such possession, and form part of the public revenue thereof.

Section 525.

The time for instituting summary proceedings under this act shall be·limited as follows; that is to say:

(1) No conviction for any offence shall be made under this act in any summary proceeding instituted in the United Kingdom, unless such proceeding is commenced within six months after the commission of the offence; or, if both or either of the parties to such proceeding happen during such time to be out of the United Kingdom, unless the same is commenced within two months after they both first happen to arrive, or to be at one time within the same.

(2) No conviction for any offence shall be made under this act in any proceeding instituted in any British possession, unless such proceeding is commenced within ·six months after the commission of the offence; or if both or either of the parties to the proceeding happen during such time not to be within the jurisdiction of any court capable of dealing with the case, unless the same is commenced within two months after they both first happen to arrive or to be at one time within such jurisdiction.

(3) No order for the payment of money shall be made under this act in any summary proceeding instituted in the United Kingdom, unless such proceeding is commenced within six months after the cause of complaint arises; or, if both or either of the parties happen during such time to be out of the United Kingdom, unless the same is commenced within six months after they both first happen to arrive or to be at one time within the same.

(4) No order for the payment of money shall be made under this act in any summary proceeding instituted in any British possession, unless such proceeding is commenced within six months after the cause of complaint arises; or, if both or either of the parties to the proceeding happen during such time not to be within the jurisdiction of any court capable of dealing with the case, unless the same is commenced within six months after they both first happen to arrive or be at one time within such jurisdiction.

And no provision contained in any other act or acts, ordinance or ordinances, for limiting the time within which summary proceedings may be instituted shall affect any summary proceeding under this act.

Section 526.

Any document required by this act to be executed in the presence of or to be attested by any witness or witnesses may be proved by the evidence of any person who is able to bear witness to the requisite facts, without calling the attesting witness or witnesses or any of them.

Section 527.

Whenever any injury has, in any part of the world, been caused to any property belonging to Her Majesty or to any of Her Majesty's subjects by any foreign ship, if at any time thereafter such ship is found in any port or river of the United

Kingdom or within three miles of the coast thereof, it shall be lawful for the judge of any court of record in the United Kingdom or for the judge of the high court of admiralty, or in Scotland the court of session, or the sheriff of the county within whose jurisdiction such ship may be, upon its being shown to him by any person applying summarily that such injury was probably caused by the misconduct or want of skill of the master or mariners of such ship, to issue an order directed to any officer of customs or other officer named by such judge, requiring him to detain such ship until such time as the owner, master, or consignee thereof has made satisfaction in respect of such injury, or has given security, to be approved by the judge, to abide the event of any action, suit, or other legal proceeding that may be instituted in respect of such injury, and to pay all costs and damages that may be awarded thereon; and any officer of customs or other officer to whom such order is directed shall detain such ship accordingly.

Section 528.

In any case where it appears that before any application can be made under the foregoing section such foreign ship will have departed beyond the. limits therein mentioned, it shall be lawful for any commissioned officer on full pay in the military or naval service of Her Majesty, or any British officer of customs, or any British consular officer to detain such ship until such time as will allow such application to be made and the result thereof to be communicated to him; and no such officer shall be liable for any costs or damages in respect of such detention unless the same is proved to have been made without reasonable grounds.

Section 529.

In any action, suit, or other proceeding in relation to such injury, the person so giving security as aforesaid shall be made defendant or defender and shall be stated to be the owner of the ship that has occasioned such damage; and the production of the order of the judge made in relation to such security shall be conclusive evidence of the liability of such defendant or defender to such action, suit, or other proceeding.

LEGAL PROCEDURE (SCOTLAND).

Section 530.

In Scotland every offense which by this act is described as a felony or misdemeanor may be prosecuted by indictment or criminal letters at the instance of Her Majesty's advocate before the high court of justiciary, or by criminal libel at the instance of the procurator fiscal of the county before the sheriff, and shall be punishable with fine and with imprisonment, with or without hard labour in default of payment, or with imprisonment, with or without hard labour, or with both, as the court may think fit, or in the case of felony with penal servitude, where the court is competent thereto; and such court may also, if it think fit, order payment by the offender of the costs and expenses of the prosecution.

Section 531.

In Scotland, all prosecutions, complaints, actions, or proceedings under this act, other than prosecutions for felonies or misdemeanors, may be brought in a summary form before the sheriff of the county, or before any two justices of the peace of the county or burgh where the cause of such prosecution or action arises, or where the offender or defender may be for the time, and when of a criminal nature or for penalties, at the instance of the procurator fiscal of court, or at the instance of any party aggrieved, with concurrence of the procurator fiscal of court; and the court may, if it think fit, order payment by the offender or defender of the costs of the prosecution or action.

Section 532.

In Scotland all prosecutions, complaints, actions, or other proceedings under this act may be brought either in a written or printed form, or partly written and partly printed, and where such proceedings are brought in a summary form it shall not be necessary in the complaint to recite or set forth the clause or clauses of the act on which such proceeding is founded, but it shall be sufficient to specify or refer to such clause or clauses, and to set forth shortly the cause of complaint or action, and the remedy sought; and when such complaint or action is brought in whole or in part for the enforcement of a pecuniary debt or demand, the complaint may contain a prayer for warrant to arrest upon the dependence.

Section 533.

In Scotland, on any complaint or other proceeding brought in a summary form under this act being presented to the sheriff clerk or clerk of the peace, he shall grant warrant to cite the defender to appear personally before the said sheriff or justice of the peace on a day fixed, and at the same time shall appoint a copy of the same to be delivered to him by a sheriff officer or constable, as the case may be, along with the citation; and such deliverance shall also contain a warrant for citing witnesses and havers to compear at the same time and place to give evidence and produce such writs as may be specified in their citation; and where such warrant has been prayed for in the complaint or other proceeding, the deliverance of the sheriff clerk or clerk of the peace shall also contain warrant to arrest upon the dependence in common form: *Provided always*, That where the apprehension of any party, with or without a warrant, is authorized by this act, such party may be detained in custody until he can be brought at the earliest opportunity before any two justices, or the sheriff who may have jurisdiction in the place, to be dealt with as this act directs, and no citation or induciæ shall in such case be necessary.

Section 534.

When it becomes necessary to execute such arrestment on the dependence against goods or effects of the defender within Scotland, but not locally situated within the jurisdiction of the sheriff or justice of the peace by whom the warrant to arrest has been granted, it shall be competent to carry the warrant into execution on its being indorsed by the sheriff clerk or clerk of the peace of the county or burgh respectively within which such warrant comes to be executed.

Section 535.

In all proceedings under this act in Scotland the sheriff or justices of the peace shall have the same power of compelling attendance of witnesses and havers as in cases falling under their ordinary jurisdiction.

Section 536.

The whole procedure in cases brought in a summary form before the sheriff or justices of the peace in Scotland shall be conducted viva voce, without written pleadings, and without taking down the evidence in writing, and no record shall be kept of the proceedings other than the complaint, and the sentence or decree pronounced thereon.

Section 537.

It shall be in the power of the sheriff or justices of the peace in Scotland to adjourn the proceedings from time to time to any day or days to be fixed by them, in the event of absence of witnesses or of any other cause which shall appear to them to render such adjournment necessary.

Section 538.

In Scotland all sentences and decrees to be pronounced by the sheriff or justices of the peace upon such summary complaints shall be in writing; and where there is a decree for payment of any sum or sums of money against a defender, such decree shall contain warrant for arrestment, poinding, and imprisonment in default of payment, such arrestment, poinding, or imprisonment to be carried into effect by sheriffs, officers, or constables, as the case may be, in the same manner as in cases arising under the ordinary jurisdiction in the sheriff or justices: *Provided always*, That nothing herein contained shall be taken or construed to repeal or affect an act of the fifth and sixth years of William the Fourth, intituled "An act for abolishing, in Scotland, imprisonment for civil debts of small amount."

Section 539.

In all summary complaints and proceedings for recovery of any penalty or sum of money in Scotland, if a defender who has been duly cited shall not appear at the time and place required by the citation, he shall be held as confessed, and sentence or decree shall be pronounced against him in terms of the complaint, with such costs and expenses as to the court shall seem fit: *Provided always*, That he shall be entitled to obtain himself reponed against any such decree at any time before the same be fully implemented, by lodging with the clerk of court a reponing note, and consigning in his hands the sum decerned for, and the costs which had been awarded by the court, and on the same day delivering or transmitting through the post to the pursuer or his agent a copy of such reponing note; and a certificate by the clerk of court of such note having been lodged shall operate as a sist of diligence till the cause shall have been reheard and finally disposed of, which shall be on the next sitting of the court, or on any day to which the court shall then adjourn it.

Section 540.

In all summary complaints or other proceedings not brought for the recovery of any penalty or sum of money in Scotland, if a defender, being duly cited, shall fail to appear, the sheriff or justices may grant warrant to apprehend and bring him before the court.

Section 541.

In all cases where sentences or decrees of the sheriff or justices require to be enforced within Scotland, but beyond the jurisdi- tion of the sheriff or justices by whom such sentences or decrees have been pronounced, it shall be competent to carry the same into execution upon the same being indorsed by the sheriff clerk or clerk of the peace of the county or burgh within which such execution is to take place.

Section 542.

No order, decree, or sentence pronounced by any sheriff or justice of the peace in Scotland under the authority of this act shall be quashed or vacated for any misnomer, informality, or defect of form; and all orders, decrees, and sentences so pronounced shall be final and conclusive, and not subject to suspension, advocation, reduction, or to any form of review or stay of execution, except on the ground of corruption or malice on the part of the sheriff or justices, in which case the suspension, advocation, or reduction must be brought within fourteen days of the date of the order, decree, or sentence complained of: *Provided always*, That no stay of execution shall be competent to the effect of preventing immediate execution of such order, decree, or sentence.

Section 543.

Such of the general provisions with respect to jurisdiction, precedure, and penalties contained in this act as are not inconsistent with the special rules hereinbefore laid down for the conduct of legal proceedings and the recovery of penalties in Scotland, shall, so far as the same are applicable, extend to such last-mentioned proceedings and penalties: *Provided always*, That nothing in this act contained shall be held in any way to annul or restrict the common law of Scotland with regard to the prosecution or punishment of offences at the instance or by the direction of the lord advocate, or the rights of owners or creditors in regard to enforcing a judicial sale of any ship and tackle, or to give to the high court of admiralty of England any jurisdiction in respect of salvage in Scotland which it has not heretofore had or, exercised.

ENACTMENT OF MERCHANT SHIPPING ACT, 1876 (39 AND 40 VICT., C. 80.), APPLIED.

Section 34.

Where under the merchant shipping acts, 1854 to 1876, or any of them, a ship is authorised or ordered to be detained, any commissioned officer on full pay in the naval or military service of Her Majesty, or any officer of the board of trade or customs, or any British consular officer may detain the ship, and if the ship after such detention or after service on the master of any notice of or order for such detention proceeds to sea before it is released by competent authority, the master of the ship, and also the owner, and any person who sends the ship to sea, if such owner or person be party or privy to the offence, shall forfeit and pay to Her Majesty a penalty not exceeding one hundred pounds.

Where a ship so proceeding to sea takes to sea when on board thereof in the execution of his duty any officer authorised to detain the ship, or any surveyor or officer of the board of trade or customs, the owner and master of the ship shall each be liable to pay all expenses of and incidental to the officer or surveyor being so taken to sea, and also a penalty not exceeding one hundred pounds, or, if the offence is not prosecuted in a summary manner, not exceeding ten pounds for every day until the officer or surveyor returns, or until such time as would enable him after leaving the ship to return to the port from which he is taken, and such expenses may be recovered in like manner as the penalty.

No. 66.

Mr. Gresham to Mr. Bayard.

[Telegram.]

DEPARTMENT OF STATE,
Washington, April 4, 1894.

Bill which passed Senate yesterday contains nothing but provisions for enforcement of regulations. House committee unanimously instructed its chairman to move suspension of rules and pass bill immediately. At all events, bill will be a law this week.

No. 67.

Mr. Gresham to Mr. Bayard.

[Telegram.]

DEPARTMENT OF STATE,
Washington, April 5, 1894.

Bill for enforcing Bering Sea award has passed both Houses.

No. 68.

Sir Julian Pauncefote to Mr. Gresham.

WASHINGTON, *April 5, 1894.*

SIR: On the 8th ultimo I had the honor to place in your hands confidentially, by desire of Her Majesty's principal secretary of state for foreign affairs, a draft of a bill which Her Majesty's Government proposed to introduce into Parliament to give effect to the fur-seal fishery regulations prescribed by the award of the Bering Sea Tribunal of Arbitration. Since that date negotiations have been proceeding with reference, first, to the adoption of a modus vivendi during the present year in order to give longer time to elaborate and complete the necessary legislation in both countries; secondly, to the settlement of the Bering Sea claims which were laid before the Tribunal of Arbitration; and thirdly, to a proposed conference of the four powers mostly interested in the fur-seal fishery to consider what regulations, applicable not only on the high seas but within the sovereignty of each power, it might be expedient to adopt in accordance with the first declaration appended to the award.

Those negotiations continued up to the 2d instant, when you informed me that the President had arrived at the conclusion that it would be better to abandon the proposed modus vivendi, as he now believed that both Governments would be able to complete their legislation before the commencement of the close season prescribed by the award, namely the 1st of May; you added that a bill would be pressed through Congress at once for that purpose. I accordingly informed the Earl of Kimberley of the President's views and I learned that the British legislation is proceeding with the utmost rapidity with a view to its coming into force on the 1st of May.

I have now received instructions from Lord Kimberley to propose to you that we should at once proceed to discuss the best mode of carrying out articles 4 and 7 of the regulations prescribed by the award.

A delegate from Canada, as previously arranged, is prepared to come to Washington to assist me in the discussion of the details in question, which are now very pressing, and as to which it is manifestly desirable that the two Governments should secure as much similarity of treatment as possible.

I should be much obliged therefore if you would kindly inform me whether this proposal is agreeable to you, and if so on what date it will be convenient to you to hold our first meeting.

I have, etc.,

JULIAN PAUNCEFOTE.

No. 69.

Mr. Bayard to Mr. Gresham.

[Telegram.]

LONDON, *April 6, 1894.*

Everything indicates early passage bill to enforce award. Please send copies United States statutes upon the subject.

No. 70.

Mr. Bayard to Mr. Gresham.

EMBASSY OF THE UNITED STATES,
London, April 6, 1894. (Received April 16.)

SIR: Referring to my dispatch of the 4th instant, I have now the honor to acknowledge your telegram of the 5th (which was delivered to-day), relating to the legislative enforcement of the Bering Sea award.

In connection with the subject, I inclose the copy of the note I received from Lord Kimberley on the night of the 4th instant and of my reply on the day following.

The indications now are that the measure will be acted on on Monday next, and probably with no further opposition, although they are awaiting "points" expecting to be made by the Canadian government, whose efforts in the matter would not seem to be dictated by any strong desire to carry out the obligations under which the arbitration came into being.

I have, etc.,

T. F. BAYARD.

[Inclosure 1 in No. 70.]

Lord Kimberley to Mr. Bayard.

FOREIGN OFFICE, *April 4, 1894.*

DEAR MR. BAYARD: I find from an interchange of telegrams with Sir Julian Pauncefote that he misled me as to the amendments in the United States bill for carrying out the Bering Sea award, to which I *referred* at my interview with you on the 2d instant.

I inclose for your information the United States bill as I understand it now to stand passed, and I also send you a copy of our bill as to-day amended.

You will see that in section 2, paragraph (1), one of the "mays" to which you objected has been taken out and a " shall" has been substituted with other words, and an amendment has been inserted in section 3, paragraph (3).

Believe, me, etc., KIMBERLEY.

[Inclosure 2 in No. 70.]

Mr. Bayard to Lord Kimberley.

EMBASSY OF THE UNITED STATES,
London, April 5, 1894.

DEAR LORD KIMBERLEY: Let me thank you for your note of last night, and the copies of the British measure, and that of the United States, to'put in operative force the regulations determined and established by the Paris Tribunal of Arbitration.

I have just been informed by my Government of the passage by the Senate, on the day before yesterday, of a bill for the plenary enforcement of these regulations, and that the bill will, by the concurrence of the House of Representatives, become a law before this week expires.

From such examination as I have been enabled to bestow, since your kindness permitted me to compare the provisions of the proposed measures of the respective Governments, I am disposed to believe that these two measures will, when carried out in that good faith which has animated both the high contracting parties in this important transaction, secure full and faithful compliance with the award of the Tribunal of Arbitration.

Of course time is now the essence of the transaction, as the sealing season has already opened and the proposed close season is but three weeks off, so that every opportunity for friction or misapprehension should be carefully guarded against.

Let us hope the legislative action of the two Governments will proceed pari passu, and with that promptitude and absence of delay which should accompany the abitrament to its close.

Believe me, etc., T. F. BAYARD.

No. 71.

Sir Julian Pauncefote to Mr. Gresham.

WASHINGTON, *April 9, 1894.*

DEAR MR. GRESHAM: With reference to our conversation of this morning respecting section 7 of the British act to give effect to the Bering Sea award, I have much pleasure in informing you that I have just received a telegram from the Earl of Kimberley which will, I trust, remove all misapprehension as 'to the meaning and effect of that provision.

Lord Kimberley desires me to give you the assurance that the clause in question will not prevent the seizure of British sealers violating the regulations of the award, and that the question of notice will only arise at the trial. In fact such sealers will be dealt with by the British cruisers as if they had received notice of the regulations, and it will be left to the court to decide the question of notice as affecting only the liability of the defendants to penalties. I am to add that the instructions to the British cruisers will be explicit in the above sense.

I remain, etc.,

JULIAN PAUNCEFOTE.

No. 72.

Mr. Gresham to Mr. Bayard.

[Telegram.]

DEPARTMENT OF STATE,
Washington, April 9, 1894.

Omitting the preamble in which the reported regulations are set out literally, the following is the bill to give effect to the award of the Paris Tribunal as passed and approved:

That no citizen of the United States, or person owing the duty of obedience to the laws or the treaties of the United States, nor any person belonging to or on board of a vessel of the United States, shall kill, capture, or pursue, at any time, or in any manner whatever, outside of territorial waters, any fur seal in the waters surrounding Pribilov Islands within a zone of sixty geographical miles (sixty to a degree of latitude) around said islands, exclusive of the territorial waters.

SEC. 2. That no citizen of the United States, or person above described in section one of this act, nor any person belonging to or on board of a vessel of the United States, shall kill, capture, or pursue, in any manner whatever, during the season extending from the first day of May to the thirty-first day of July, both inclusive, in each year, any fur seal on the high seas outside of the zone mentioned in section one and in that part of the Pacific Ocean, including Behring Sea, which is situated to the north of the thirty-fifth degree of north latitude and to the east of the one hundred and eightieth degree of longitude from Greenwich until it strikes the water boundary described in article one of the treaty of eighteen hundred and sixty-seven, between the United States and Russia, and following that line up to Behring Straits.

SEC. 3. No citizen of the United States or person above described, in the first section of this Act, shall, during the period and in the waters in which by section two of this Act the killing of fur-seals is not prohibited, use or employ any vessel, nor shall any vessel of the United States be used or employed, in carrying on or taking part in fur-seal fishing operations, other than a sailing vessel propelled by sails exclusively, and such canoes or undecked boats, propelled by paddles, oars, or sails as may belong to, and be used in connection with, such sailing vessel; nor shall any sailing vessel carry on or take part in such operations without a special license obtained from the Government for that purpose, and without carrying a distinctive flag prescribed by the Government for the same purpose.

SEC. 4. That every master of a vessel licensed under this act to engage in fur-seal fishing operations shall accurately enter in his official log book the date and place of every such operation, and also the number and sex of the seals captured each day; and on coming into port, and before landing cargo, the master shall verify, on oath, such official log book as containing a full and true statement of the number and character of his fur-seal fishing operations, including the number and sex of seals captured; and for any false statement willfully made by a person so licensed by the United States in this behalf he shall be subject to the penalties of perjury; and any seal skins found in excess of the statement in the official log book shall be forfeited to the United States.

SEC. 5. That no person or vessel engaging in fur-seal fishing operations under this Act shall use or employ in any such operations, any net, firearm, airgun, or explosive: *Provided however,* That this prohibition shall not apply to the use of shotguns in such operations outside of Behring Sea during the season when the killing of fur seals is not there prohibited by this Act.

SEC. 6. That the foregoing sections of this act shall not apply to Indians dwelling on the coast of the United States, and taking fur seals in canoes or undecked boats propelled wholly by paddles, oars, or sails, and not transported by or used in connection with other vessels, or manned by more than five persons, in the manner *heretofore* practiced by the said Indians: *Provided, however,* That the exception made in this section shall not apply to Indians in the employment of other persons, or who shall kill, capture, or pursue fur seals outside of territorial waters under contract to deliver the skins to other persons, nor to the waters of Behring Sea or of the passes between the Aleutian Islands.

Sec. 7. That the President shall have power to make regulations respecting the special license and the distinctive flag mentioned in this Act and regulations otherwise suitable to secure the due execution of the provisions of this act, and from time to time to add to, modify, amend, or revoke such regulations, as in his judgment may seem expedient.

Sec. 8. That, except in the case of a master making a false statement under oath in violation of the provisions of the fourth section of this Act, every person guilty of a violation of the provisions of this Act, or of the regulations made thereunder, shall for each offense be fined not less than two hundred dollars, or imprisoned not more than six months, or both; and all vessels, their tackle, apparel, furniture, and cargo, at any time used or employed in violation of this Act, or of the regulations made thereunder, shall be forfeited to the United States.

Sec. 9. That any violation of this Act, or of the regulations made thereunder, may be prosecuted either in the district court of Alaska or in any district court of the United States in California, Oregon, or Washington.

Sec. 10. That if any unlicensed vessel of the United States shall be found within the waters to which this Act applies, and at a time when the killing of fur seals is by this Act there prohibited, having on board seal skins or bodies of seals, or apparatus or implements suitable for killing or taking seals; or if any licensed vessel shall be found in the waters to which this Act applies, having on board apparatus or implements suitable for taking seals, but forbidden then and there to be used, it shall be presumed that the vessel in the one case and the apparatus or implements in the other was or were used in violation of this Act until it is otherwise sufficiently proved.

Sec. 11. That it shall be the duty of the President to cause a sufficient naval force to cruise in the waters to which this Act is applicable to enforce its provisions, and it shall be the duty of the commanding officer of any vessel belonging to the naval or revenue service of the United States, when so instructed by the President, to seize and arrest all vessels of the United States found by him to be engaged, used, or employed in the waters last aforesaid in violation of any of the prohibitions of this Act, or of any regulations made thereunder, and to take the same, with all persons on board thereof, to the most convenient port in any district of the United States mentioned in this Act, there to be dealt with according to law.

Sec. 12. That any vessel or citizen of the United States, or person described in the first section of this Act, offending against the prohibitions of this Act or the regulations thereunder, may be seized and detained by the naval or other duly commissioned officers of Her Majesty the Queen of Great Britain, but when so seized and detained they shall be delivered as soon as practicable, with any witnesses and proofs on board, to any naval or revenue officer or other authorities of the United States, whose courts alone shall have jurisdiction to try the offense and impose the penalties for the same: *Provided, however,* That British officers shall arrest and detain vessels and persons as in this section specified only after, by appropriate legislation, Great Britain shall have authorized officers of the United States duly commissioned and instructed by the President to that end to arrest, detain, and deliver to the authorities of Great Britain vessels and subjects of that Government offending against statutes or regulations of Great Britain enacted or made to enforce the award of the treaty mentioned in the title of this Act.

Approved, April 6, 1894.

No. 73.

Mr. Gresham to Sir Julian Pauncefote.

DEPARTMENT OF STATE,
Washington, April 10, 1894.

EXCELLENCY: Owing to illness, from which I have not fully recovered, I shall at this time content myself with a partial reply to your note of the 5th instant.

It was after Her Majesty's Government had refused its assent to one or more offers of this Government to enter into a modus vivendi (the terms of which seemed not unfair to you) for the protection for one year of the waters described in the first and second regulations reported by the Tribunal of Arbitration, thus affording the two Governments more time for the enforcement of the award by appropriate legislation or otherwise, that I informed you on the 2d instant the President, in view of the near approach of the close season, had arrived at the conclusion that negotiations for a temporary agreement had better be abandoned and our efforts directed to obtaining the requisite legislation before the first of May.

I also informed you at the same time of my confident belief that a bill fully satisfying the requirements of the award on the part of the United States would speedily pass Congress, and that the President would not permit himself to doubt Her Majesty's Government would be equally prompt in obtaining similar legislation from Parliament.

The bill, a copy of which I inclose herewith, passed the Senate on the 3d instant, the House of Representatives two days later, and on the 6th instant was approved by the President.*

Her Majesty's Government will not fail to see in its provisions evidence of an earnest desire and fixed determination on the part of this Government to observe and enforce the treaty and award in letter and spirit, and I need hardly say the President heard with satisfaction your assurance that British legislation of a similar character was proceeding with the utmost rapidity, with the view of having it in force before the beginning of the close season. In this connection I venture to repeat some of the observations which I made in one of our interviews a few days after you unofficially placed in my hands, on the 8th ultimo, a draft of a bill which you informed me Her Majesty's Government proposed to introduce into Parliament to give effect to the Paris award.

After providing that the regulations shall have the same force and effect as if therein set out, the first section declares that any person violating its provisions shall be deemed guilty of a misdemeanor within the meaning of the merchant's shipping act of 1854, and the ship employed in such contravention, and her equipment, and everything on board thereof, shall be liable to be forfeited as if the offense had been committed under another merchant act, "provided that the court, without prejudice to any other power, may release the ship, equipment, or thing on payment of a fine not exceeding five hundred pounds." The penalty prescribed in the shipping act for a misdemeanor is a fine not exceeding one hundred pounds.

Should this bill become a law, the court will have discretion to punish offenders with nominal fines, and release ships employed in contravention of the act on payment of like fine. In the opinion of this Government these penalties are not sufficiently severe to deter lawless men from trespassing upon the inhabited waters, and you will observe that the act of Congress referred to provides for the absolute forfeiture of ships employed in taking or hunting seals in violation of the award.

In reply to my statement that, while the draft authorized any commissioned officer on full pay in the naval service of Her Majesty to seize offending ships, it nowhere made it the duty of such officers to do so. You stated that, although you did not think the draft was fairly open to this objection, orders in council and instructions which would be issued to the proper officers would impose that duty upon them.

---

* See inclosure in No. 72.

Subsection 2 of section 7 reads:

Where, on any proceeding against a person or ship in respect of any offense under this act, it is proved that the ship sailed from its port of departure before the scheduled provisions were published there, and that such person, or the master of the ship, did not subsequently and before such alleged offense receive notice of these provisions, such person shall be acquitted and the ship shall be released and not forfeited.

This provision is doubtless intended to protect against loss Canadians who may engage in sealing in the inhibited waters during the approaching close season, and when I informed you it was for that reason disappointing to this Government, you stated that it would be unfair to forfeit ships for violating a law which their owners and masters did not know was in force, and that you thought each Government was at liberty to enact such legislation as in its judgment would fully execute the award. 1 replied that when the Canadian sealers left their home ports their masters were not ignorant of the provisions of the treaty and the award; that they then knew both Governments were bound to adopt measures for the enforcement of the regulations before the first of May; that they no doubt departed contemplating this would be done; that this Government would provide no immunity for its citizens during the approaching close season, and that Her Majesty's Government should seek none for her subjects. I remarked further that the two Governments were alike bound to give effect to the award; that each was interested in the means employed by the other for that purpose, and you expressed, as you had on former occasions, the gratifying assurance that Great Britain would not fail to enact a law for due and timely execution of both the treaty and the award.

In your note you say you are instructed by Lord Kimberley to propose that we at once proceed to discuss the best mode of carrying out articles 4 and 7 of the regulations prescribed by the award, and request that I name a day for that purpose, as you desire a Canadian shall come to Washington to assist in the details in question, which are now very pressing, and as to which it is manifestly desirable the two Governments should secure as much similarity of treatment as possible.

In reply to your request I am instructed by the President to suggest that the proposed negotiations can be entered upon to so much better advantage when the statutes of both Governments are before us, that it is advisable to postpone the conference until the bill now pending in Parliament has become a law, and its exact provisions have been ascertained.

I do not anticipate difficulty in then reaching an understanding alike satisfactory to both Governments upon any remaining questions growing out of the treaty and award or properly related to them.

I have the honor to be, with the highest consideration, Mr. Ambassador,

Your obedient servant, W. Q. GRESHAM.

No. 74.

Mr. Bayard to Mr. Gresham.

[Telegram.]

LONDON, *April 10, 1894.*

Yesterday I again impressed upon British minister for foreign affairs injustice and objectionable nature of provision requiring previous notice to sealing vessels. Last night in debate attorney-general said clause had been entirely misunderstood in the United States, and declared imperial obligation was imposed on Great Britain, and if Canada should not consent still Imperial Government would loyally carry award into effect. Leaders of opposition join with Government in declaring honor of the country involved in carrying out award. The text of the act of Congress has been received.

No. 75.

Sir Julian Pauncefote to Mr. Gresham.

BRITISH EMBASSY,
Washington, April 11, 1894.

SIR: I have the honor to acknowledge the receipt of your note of yesterday's date and to express my regret at the cause which, as you inform me, prevents you from entering more fully at present into the subject of my note to you of the 5th instant.

I have acquainted my Government by telegram with the grounds on which the President suggests that the proposed discussion as to the best mode of carrying out the fourth and seventh articles of the Bering Sea award should be deferred.

I desire to take this opportunity of correcting a misapprehension which appears to have arisen as regards the abandonment of the proposals for a modus vivendi.

1 have no recollection of Her Majesty's Government having refused to assent to any reasonable proposal on the subject.

They originally expressed their willingness to agree to a renewal for one year of the existing modus vivendi, which closes up the whole of Bering Sea, but your Government thought this proposal insufficient, and desired that the whole of the waters covered by the award should be similarly closed. Her Majesty's Government considered so great an extension of the present modus vivendi unnecessary, and, as the result of further negotiations, an arrangement was drawn up under which the close season of three months prescribed by the award (from May 1 to July 31) should be put in force under the existing legislation in both countries, as far south as the forty-second degree, that being the limit of the British statutory power, and no seals being found after the 1st of May below that degree. This was tantamount to the enforcement of the close season prescribed by the award. It was also provided that if the two powers should not have completed the necessary legislation before the 1st of August, the close season should continue for such further period as the powers should think necessary for that purpose.

The above modus vivendi (which was part of a larger arrangement embracing other matters) was accepted by both powers, but Her Majesty's Government, in order to obviate any future misunderstanding, desired to stipulate that if the British legislation should be completed by the 1st of August the seas should be open to British sealers whether, at that date, the legislation of the United States was complete or not.

This stipulation was objected to by the President on the ground, as I understood, that it implied a possible tardiness on the part of the United States Government in perfecting its legislation. I offered, therefore, to substitute a clause providing that the close season should continue, as regards the vessels, subjects, or citizens of either power, whose legislation might not have been completed by that date, until such power should have carried out its obligations in that respect.

But these suggestions were of no avail, and on the 2d instant you informed me that the President had decided to abandon the modus vivendi, and to proceed with legislation to enforce the whole award.

I am unable, therefore, to concur in the statement at the commencement of your note that Her Majesty's Government refused their assent to one or more offers of your Government to enter into a modus vivendi.

At the same time I did not intend to complain of the action of your Government in abandoning the the modus vivendi, as it has been found practicable by both powers to dispense with it by timely legislation.

Turning now to the objections stated in your note to certain provisions of the British bill to carry out the award, I beg leave to make the following observations:

. As regards the penalties proposed by the bill, I remember your pointing out to me that they were less deterrent than those imposed by the legislation of the United States, which gave no discretion to the courts but enacted absolute forfeiture of the vessel for breach of the regulations and "minimum" fines. This led to an academic discussion on the system of "minimum" punishments, which, I observed, was not favored in British legislation. I certainly understood your remarks in the light of mere criticism and not of serious objection, as it must be assumed that the British courts would not do otherwise than impose adequate punishments.

As regards the objection to the phraseology of section 1, relating to the seizure of ships, I observed that in my opinion the word "may" would be construed as imperative, and that, in any case, the instructions to the naval officers would probably remove all doubt on the point.

As regards the seventh section, which relates to the question of notice to the sealers of the regulations having been put into force, I trust that the assurances contained in my semiofficial communication of the 9th instant will have disposed of the objection to that provision, as they were evidently based on a misapprehension of its meaning and effect.

I beg to thank you, in conclusion, for the copies of the United States act to give effect to the award, which are transmitted in your note.

I have, etc.,

JULIAN PAUNCEFOTE.

No. 76.

Mr. Gresham to Mr. Bayard.

[Telegram]

DEPARTMENT OF STATE,
Washington, April 11, 1894.

Secretary of the Navy will need copy of British act before preparing his instructions. As soon as it passes you will please telegraph full text, or so much as corresponds with section 12 of our act.

No. 77.

Mr. Bayard to Mr. Gresham.

EMBASSY OF THE UNITED STATES,
London, April 11, 1894. (Received April 23.)

SIR: The last dispatch I had the honor to address to you on the subject of the legislation to enforce the Bering Sea award and regulations was dated the 6th instant, and beg I leave now to inclose herewith a copy of a telegram I had the honor to send you on the same subject on the 10th instant.

Your telegram, transmitting the text of the act of Congress to enforce the award and regulations of the Paris Tribunal, commenced to reach me on Monday evening last and was completed that night, and I herewith inclose a full copy thereof.

I beg to draw your attention to the word "exclusive," in the last line of section 2, which purports to follow the phraseology of article 1 of the regulations, which, according to your telegram. are set out literally in the preamble to the act of Congress to enforce those regulations.

I presume "exclusive" is an error arising in the telegraphic transmission, and that in the text of the statute it is "inclusive," and in accordance with the regulations recited in the preamble.

While I have confidence that it is the full intention of this Government to carry out in equality of force and good faith the letter and spirit of their treaty stipulations, yet I have thought it best to supplement my personal conversation with Lord Kimberley by a note, which I have written him to-day, and a copy of which I herewith inclose.

I have, etc.,

T. F. BAYARD.

———

[Inclosure in No. 77.]

Mr. Bayard to Lord Kimberley.

APRIL 11, 1894.

DEAR LORD KIMBERLEY: The full text of the United States statute carrying into effect the award and regulations of the Tribunal of Arbitration at Paris has been telegraphed to me, and I find (that as I had supposed) no exemption from the penalties prescribed therein is made in favor of any vessel or citizen of the United States who may have departed on a sealing voyage in the North Pacific or Bering Sea at any time since the award of the tribunal was announced at Paris on August 15 last, without further notification of the measures to put the award and regulations into operation.

As I have heretofore had the honor to bring to the attention of your lordship, no individuals are entitled to so little consideration by either of the two Governments, and none assuredly should be more swiftly visited with punishment than those who, from the nature of their occupation, had the fullest knowledge, and means of knowledge, of the public and careful stipulations of the two Governments in their convention of February, 1892.

The expressions in debate by the attorney-general and of leading members on both sides of the House give me great confidence that the Government of Her Majesty will equally and explicitly enforce the award, as that of the United States has already done, so that no pretext can be left for reflection upon the practice of arbitration or its unimpeachable execution in the present important case.

Believe me, etc.,

T. F. BAYARD.

No. 78.

Sir Julian Pauncefote to Mr. Gresham.

WASHINGTON, *April 12, 1894.*

DEAR MR. GRESHAM: With reference to my previous letter of the 5th instant respecting the meaning and effect of section 7 (2) of the bill now before Parliament in England, to carry out the Bering Sea award, I beg to inform you that I have received a telegram from the Earl of Kimberley in which he inquired whether you are aware that the publication of the schedule provisions mentioned in that clause means the publication of the provisions of the award and not the publication of the act of Parliament to give effect to them.

This further explanation will, I should think, dispose of all objections to the phraseology of the clause.

I am, etc.,   JULIAN PAUNCEFOTE.

[Inclosure in No. 78.]

In clause 7, subclause 2, of the British bill the following phrase occurs:

"Where * * * it is proved that the ship sailed from its port of departure before the scheduled provisions were published there," etc. The publication referred to is that of the provisions of the award, not that of the bill.

No. 79.

Mr. Gresham to Mr. Bayard.

[Telegram.]

WASHINGTON, *April 13, 1894.*

British ambassador informs me he has telegram from Earl of Kimberley saying the words "scheduled provisions," mentioned in seventh section of pending British bill, mean the regulations of the award, and not the act to give effect to them.   Doubt is entertained here of the correctness of this interpretation.   When Sir Julian gave me copy of the bill I informed him that I did not think the seventh section would meet the just expectations of this Government.   He replied the award was not self-executing; that it had not been put in force, and it would be unfair to forfeit ships which left their home ports when the regulations were not in force.   The British Government seems to have changed its position.

No. 80.

Mr. Bayard to Mr. Gresham.

EMBASSY OF THE UNITED STATES,
London, April 13, 1894. (Received April 23, 1894.)

SIR: I have now the honor to acknowledge the receipt of your telegraphic instruction of to day.

The inclosed report * of the proceedings in the House of Lords yesterday will show you that the bill to put in operation the award and regulations of the Paris Tribunal of Arbitration, having passed the House of Commons, had its second reading in the Lords, and will, as I suppose, be finally acted upon by that body next Monday.

Their methods of legislative procedure are not in formal accord with those of Congress, and there is no reference whatever in the debate in either house to the suggested discrimination from forfeiture of the sealers, who have sought by anticipation to violate the regulations imposed by the tribunal (and to the obedience to which national faith was internationally and mutually pledged). I am unable to state the exact provisions of the measure.

I will at once telegraph you the text of the act when it has been finally acted upon, and meanwhile,

1 have, etc.,   T. F. BAYARD.

No. 81.

Mr. White to Mr. Gresham.

LEGATION OF THE UNITED STATES,
St. Petersburg, April 16, 1894. (Received May 2.)

SIR: I have the honor to acknowledge your instructions relative to the arrangement initiated between yourself and the Russian minister at Washington.

I have submitted the same to the foreign office here and find there a strong preference for their original proposal, namely, the adoption of the Russo-British modus vivendi by the United States and Russia, on the ground that this new form of proposal requires time for consideration by the various departments of the Russian Government interested, and therefore a delay, perhaps too long a delay, in notifying sealers would be necessitated.

I showed Count Kapnist, director of Asiatic affairs at the foreign office, with whom I had the interview, that the delays and difficulties in the matter had not been of our seeking, and gave him the reasons, as I conceive them, why you naturally desire the matter settled at Washington, as proposed in your dispatch above referred to.

I also showed him that with promptitude and expedition on the part of the Imperial Government very little delay would be caused, and I assured him that our Government simply desired a fair and speedy settlement of the question.

I am, etc.,   AND. D. WHITE..

---

* Not printed.

No. 82.

[Note verbale.]

Sir Julian Pauncefote to Mr. Gresham.

BRITISH EMBASSY,
Washington, April 17, 1894. (Received April 17, 1894.)

The undersigned has the honor to inform the Secretary of State that he has received a telegram from the Earl of Kimberley to the effect that amendments have been made in articles 2 and 7 of the Bering Sea bill during its passage through the House of Lords which it is believed will entirely remove the objections raised by the United States Government.

As regards article 1, which relates to penalties, Lord Kimberley states that Her Majesty's Government have given their most careful consideration to the objections raised thereto.

The undersigned is instructed to assure the Secretary of State that Her Majesty's Government yield in no respect to the United States Government in their desire to carry out the award effectually, and they are satisfied that the provision in question is framed in the manner which will best secure that object.

JULIAN PAUNCEFOTE.

No. 83.

Mr. Gresham to Sir Julian Pauncefote.

DEPARTMENT OF STATE,
Washington, April 18, 1894.

The Secretary of State has read with satisfaction the note verbale of the British ambassador of yesterday saying that he has received a telegram from the Earl of Kimberley to the effect that amendments have been made in articles 2 and 7 of the Bering Sea bill during its passage through the House of Lords which it is believed will entirely remove the objections raised by the United States Government; that Her Majesty's Government have given their most careful consideration to the objections raised by the United States to article 1 of the bill, and that he is instructed to assure the undersigned that Her Majesty's Government yield in no respect to the United States Government in their desire to carry out the award effectually, and they are satisfied the provision in question is framed in a manner which will best secure that object.

No. 84.

Mr. Gresham to Sir Julian Pauncefote.

DEPARTMENT OF STATE,
Washington, April 18, 1894.

EXCELLENCY: There is a palpable error in the act of Congress entitled "An act to give effect to the award rendered by the Tribunal of Arbitration at Paris, under the treaty between the United States and Great Britain, concluded at Washington February 29, 1892, for the purpose of submitting to arbitration certain questions concerning the preservation of the fur seals," approved April 6, 1894.

The first regulation or article of the award provides that fur seal shall not be pursued or captured at any time within a zone of 60 geographical miles around the Pribilof Islands "inclusive of the territorial waters," plainly meaning 60 miles from the shore and not 60 miles beyond the 3-mile limit. In describing the zone in the first section of the act, however, the word exclusive was used instead of inclusive.

While the mistake is regretable it can lead to no embarrassment, as this Government construes section 1 as meaning precisely the same as article 1 of the award, and instructions to our naval commanders will be framed accordingly.

I have, etc.,   W. Q. GRESHAM.

No. 85.

Mr. Gresham to Sir Julian Pauncefote.

DEPARTMENT OF STATE,
Washington, April 18, 1894.

The Secretary of State presents his compliments to his excellency the British ambassador, and has the honor to hand him herewith a list of the vessels which are to compose the United States naval force in Bering Sea during the coming season, which has been sent him by the Secretary of the Navy in compliance with the request made him by Sir Julian Pauncefote.

[Inclosure in No. 85—List.]

U. S. S. *Mohican*, U. S. S. *Concord*, U. S. S. *Yorktown*, U. S. S. *Bennington*, U. S. S. *Ranger*, U. S. S. *Alert*, U. S. S. *Adams*, U. S. S. *Petrel*, U. S. S. *Albatross*, Revenue cutter *Bear*, Revenue cutter *Rush*, Revenue cutter *Corwin*.

No. 86.

Mr. Bayard to Mr. Gresham.

[Telegram.]

LONDON, *April 18, 1894.*

Act passed both houses; second section substitutes word "shall" for "may." Paragraph 3 of section 3 is verbatim: An order in council under this act may provide that such officers of the United States of America as are specified in the order may, in respect of offenses under this act, exercise the like powers under this act as may be exercised by a commissioned officer of Her Majesty in relation to a British ship and the equipment and certificate thereof, or such of those powers as appear to Her Majesty in council to be exercisable under the law of the United States of America against ships of the United States; and that such British officers as are specified in the order may exercise *the powers* conferred by this act, with any necessary modifications specified in the order, in relation to a ship of the United States of America and the equipment and certificate thereof. Order in council, regulating seizure of British sealing vessels by United States officers, now in preparation by admiralty. Copy promised in a day or two.

Second paragraph of section 7 is verbatim: Where, on any proceeding in any court against a person or a ship in respect of any offense under this act, it is proved that the ship sailed from its port of departure before the provisions of the award, mentioned in the first schedule of this act, were known there, and that such person or the master of the ship did not, after such sailing and before the alleged offense, become aware of those provisions, such persons shall be acquitted, and the ship shall be released and not forfeited.

No. 87.

Mr. Gresham to Sir Julian Pauncefote.

DEPARTMENT OF STATE,
Washington, April 20, 1894.

EXCELLENCY: I have had the honor to receive your note of the 11th instant, in response to mine of the 10th, relating partly to the inability of the two Governments to agree upon a reasonable and mutually satisfactory modus vivendi for the protection of seal life in Bering Sea and the North Pacific, and partly to certain details of the pending British bill to give effect to the award of the Paris Tribunal of Arbitration.

I note your expression of a desire to correct what you regard as a misapprehension touching the abandonment of the proposals for a modus vivendi, and your statement that you have no recollection of Her Majesty's Government having refused to assent to any reasonable proposal on the subject.

Now that the timely enactment by the United States of a statute to execute, on its part, the terms of the Paris award, and the adoption by Her Majesty's Government to the same end of legislation which I trust will be equally effective to give due force to the joint obligations of that award, have gone far toward removing the occasion for the proposed modus vivendi, consideration of the causes which led to the abandonment of negotiations for that object becomes retrospective and important only as affording a clearer appreciation of what has taken place. In this sense I understand your present statements, and am happy to contribute my share, so far as I may, to that desirable result.

Up to the time it was dropped, the negotiations for a modus had passed through various successive stages. Several proposals put forward by me, in conference, and which you regarded as reasonable and fair, when referred to your Government, were met by objections or counter proposals necessitating renewed efforts on our part to seek a basis for common agreement.

You will recall that on March 23, and in view of the dilatory causes which even then appeared to tend to defeat an agreement for the renewal of last year's modus vivendi with such amendment as was made necessary by the Paris award, I suggested that it might be better to cease efforts to reach a temporary understanding and proceed at once with all dispatch in obtaining needed legislation. Your instructions, communicated to me the same day, contemplated the continuance

of negotiations for a modus, coincidently with the adoption of concurrent legislation, and to this I consented, but not without misgivings
as to the outcome.   Under these circumstances we proceeded to draw
up the arrangement of March 24, providing:

1. That Her Britannic Majesty's Government should establish and
enforce the close season in the North Pacific, including Bering Sea,
which is prescribed by the Paris award, viz, during the months of
May, June, and July, but not further south than the forty-second
parallel.

2. That similar steps should be taken by the United States Government, under the then existing act of Congress.

3. That the two Governments should proceed forthwith with the
necessary legislation to carry out the whole of the award, and that
such legislation should be put in force immediately on the expiration of
the close season—that is to say, on the 1st of August.

4. That if, owing to any unexpected delay, such legislation should
not be completed so as to be put in force on the 1st of August, the close
season should continue for such further period as the two Governments
might think necessary for effecting that purpose.

5. That, as soon as the necessary legislation for carrying out of the
whole of the award should be completed, a convention should be entered
into by the two powers for the settlement of the Bering Sea claims.

6. That the two powers should immediately invite Russia and Japan
to negotiate with them a quadruple convention for the adoption of
international regulations for the preservation of the fur-seal species,
and applicable within the sovereignty of the four powers as well as on
the high seas.

You will recall the importance I attached to the insertion of the
fourth proviso of the foregoing proposal, and your acquiescence therein,
in our conference on the morning of March 24.   You then stated that
you saw no objection to such a provision; indeed, you thought it would
be fair, and you said you had reason to believe that Lord Kimberley
would agree to it.

Upon this understanding you reduced the arrangement to writing,
including my amendment, and the same afternoon, upon learning the
President's acquiescence in its terms, you telegraphed its text to Lord
Kimberley.

The proposal so accepted by us in the name of our respective Governments, and which we justly regarded as a final disposition of the
matter, proved to be no exception to the general dilatory course of the
negotiation theretofore, inasmuch as a day or two later you submitted
a counter proposition on the part of Her Majesty's Government, modifying the essential terms suggested by me and which you had been
pleased to regard as reasonable and fair.   Your present note recites
that counter proposition, being to the effect that "if the British legislation should be completed by the 1st of August the seas should be open
to British sealers whether, at that date, the legislation of the United
States were completed or not."

The President's objection to the counter proposition lay, not so much,
as you understand, on the ground that it implied a possible tardiness
on the part of the United States in perfecting their legislation (a needless, gratuitous implication, be it observed, in view of the interest no
less than the good faith which prompted immediate legislation on our
part) as because it was one-sided and tantamount to a rejection of the
stipulation which I had advanced as indispensable.

Thereupon you brought forward another proposition similarly one-sided, in that it provided for the continuance of the modus only as regards the vessels, subjects, or citizens of the power which might not by the 31st of July have carried out by legislation its obligations under the Paris award.

All efforts in this direction having so far proved abortive, my reasonable proposal of March 24 having been refused and the opening of the sealing season being close at hand, immediate action was forced upon the President, and I was directed by him to acquaint you with the purpcse of the Government to proceed at once with legislation which, on its part, would fully meet the obligations of the Paris award. How abundantly able this Government was to carry out those obligations is shown by the passage through both Houses of Congless of the bill which was introduced in the Senate on April 2, and became a law by the President's approval only four days later.

The amended British bill for the enforcement of the Paris award, which this Government is pleased to learn has passed both Houses of Parliament, and the explicit and gratifying assurances of the course to be pursued by Her Majesty's Government, have allayed the apprehensions which I expressed to you touching the efficiency of the measure as it was originally prepared and submitted to this Government for its consideration.

I have, etc.,

W. Q. GRESHAM.

No. 88.

Mr. Bayard to Mr. Gresham.

[Telegram.]

LONDON, *April 21, 1894.*

Draft of naval instructions forwarded by the dispatch bag to day. Please send names of the United States vessels, and if possible their commanders, designated to police North Pacific Ocean and Bering Sea.

No. 89.

Sir Julian Pauncefote to Mr. Gresham.

WASHINGTON, *April 23, 1894.*   (Received April 24, 1894.)

SIR: I have the honor to acknowledge the receipt of your note of the 20th instant, in which you are good enough to enter at some length into the reasons which led to the abandonment of the modus vivendi proposed on the 24th of March, and the acceptance of which by my Government was communicated to you on the 28th of that month.

I am unable to modify the views expressed in my note of the 11th instant, regarding the statement to which I ventured to take exception, namely, that it was after Her Majesty's Government had refused its assent to one or more offers of your Government to enter into a modus vivendi that the arrangement, which is set out at length in your note, was abandoned.

I have no desire to prolong the correspondence on this subject, but I think it my duty to point out that the stipulation made by my Government in accepting the arrangement, that the close season should only continue as regards the subjects or citizens of the power whose legislation should not be completed before the 1st of August, was in no manner inconsistent with the substance or spirit of the arrangement, but was merely designed to meet a contingency, which had been left unprovided for.

The Earl of Kimberley, in instructing me to make that stipulation, informed me that he had mentioned it to Mr. Bayard, who seemed to think it reasonable.

I regret that it should have been viewed by your Government in any other light, and that any difference of opinion should have arisen on this point, but it gives me pleasure to think that, owing to the liberal and conciliatory spirit in which our negotiations have been conducted on your side, they have given rise to so little disagreement.

I have the honor to be, etc.,

JULIAN PAUNCEFOTE.

No. 90.

Mr. Uhl to Mr. Bayard.

DEPARTMENT OF STATE,
Washington, April 25, 1894.

SIR: I inclose herewith copy of communication addressed by Secretary Herbert to the British ambassador at this capital on the 19th instant, giving a complete list of the officers who will have charge of our cruisers in Bering Sea and the North Pacific Ocean during the present season.

I am, etc., EDWIN F. UHL,
Acting Secretary.

[Inclosure in No. 90.]

Mr. Herbert to Mr. Gresham.

NAVY DEPARTMENT,
Washington, April 21, 1894.

SIR: I have the honor to transmit herewith a copy of a letter, and inclosures, addressed to his excellency the British ambassador, under date of the 19th instant, transmitting a list of the officers attached to vessels of the Bering Sea fleet.

Very respectfully, H. A. HERBERT,
Secretary of the Navy.

A.

NAVY DEPARTMENT,
Washington, April 19, 1894.

SIR: Reading carefully the section of the British act you had the kindness to send me on yesterday, it occurs to me that it may be construed to mean that each officer who is to take part in the execution of the award of the acts of Congress and the Parliament of Great Britain should be named by orders in council. I therefore have the honor to transmit to you a complete list of all the officers, including naval cadets, who, in case of emergency, are sometimes put, as officers, in charge of detachments of men, that your Government may have these names before it, if it be deemed desirable *to insert them in* orders.

Under the instructions issued by this Department, a copy of which is herewith transmitted to you, it will be seen that the American act contemplates the sending of British vessels seized, under a sufficient force to secure their safe delivery, to British authorities.

I have the honor to be, very respectfully, your obedient servant,

H. A. HERBERT,
Secretary of the Navy.

His Excellency THE BRITISH AMBASSADOR,
Washington, D. C.

LINE OFFICERS OF THE NAVY ATTACHED TO THE BERING SEA FLEET.

U. S. S. MOHICAN.

Commander Charles E. Clark; Lieuts. Albion V. Wadhams, John B. Collins, and Bernard O. Scott; Lieut. J. G. James H. Hetherington, and Ensigns Charles F. Hughes, William K. Harrison, and Thomas J. Senn.

U. S. S. CONCORD.

Commander Caspar F. Goodrich, Lieuts. Ebenezer S. Prime, Greenleaf A. Merriam, and William S. Hogg; Lieut. J. G., Edwards F. Leiper, Ensigns Marbury Johnston, Nathan C. Twining, and Lay H. Everhart, and naval cadets, line division, Chester Wells, James B. Potter, Alfred A. Pratt, and André M. Proctor.

U. S. S. YORKTOWN.

Commander William M. Folger, Lieuts. Arthur B. Speyers, Herman F. Fitchbohm, William G. Cutler, and Clifford J. Boush; Lieut. J. G., William A. Gill, and Ensigns Harry A. Field and Richard H. Jackson.

U. S. S. BENNINGTON.

Commander Charles M. Thomas, Lieut. Commander Robert T. Jasper, Lieuts. James C. Cresap, Frederick W. Coffin, Thomas S. Rodgers; Lieuts. J. G., Harry Phelps and Theodore G. Dewey; Ensigns Charles B. McVay and Renwick J. Hartung, and naval cadets, line division, Edwin A. Elder, Henry A. Pearson, Frank L. Chadwick, and John L. Sticht.

U. S. S. RANGER.

Commander Edwin Longnecker, Lieuts. William C. Strong, Francis E. Greene, and Edward D. Bostick; Lieut. J. G., Thomas Snowden, and Ensigns William C. Cole, DeWitt Blamer, and Henry H. Hough.

U. S. S. ALERT.

Commander William A. Morgan, Lieuts. John H. C. Coffin, Asher C. Baker, and Charles F. Pond; Lieut. J. G., William E. Safford, and Ensigns Carlo B. Brittain, Lucius A. Bostwick, and Harry H. Caldwell.

U. S. S. ADAMS.

Commander John J. Brice, Lieuts. Charles F. Norton, William P. Elliott, Fidelio S. Carter, and William G. Hannum, and Ensigns George R. Marvell, Henry J. Ziegemeier, and Charles T. Vogelgesang.

U. S. S. PETREL.

Lieut. Commander William H. Emory, Lieuts. Nathan Sargent and Oren E. Lasher, and Ensigns Guy W. Brown, Mark L. Bristol, Benjamin F. Hutchison, William V. Pratt, and George B. Bradshaw.

U. S. S. ALBATROSS.

Lieut. Commander Franklin J. Drake, Lieut. Augustus F. Fechteler, and Ensigns Houston Eldredge, William R. Shoemaker, Charles M. Fahs, and Philip Williams.

LIST OF OFFICERS ON BOARD THE REVENUE CUTTERS THAT WILL CRUISE IN
BERING SEA DURING THE COMING SEASON.

REVENUE CUTTER BEAR.

Capt. M. A. Healy, First Lieut. F. G. Wadsworth, Second Lieut. Jno. L. Davis, Second Lieut. Jno. E. Reinburg.

REVENUE CUTTER RUSH.

Capt. C. L. Hooper, First Lieut. H. B. Rodgers, Second Lieut. F. M. Dunwoody.

REVENUE CUTTER CORWIN.

Capt. F. M. Munger, First Lieut. Albert Buhner, Second Lieut. W. V. E. Jacobs, Third Lieut. G. C. Carmine, Third Lieut. G. M. Daniels.

It is the intention to assign another lieutenant to the *Rush.*

No. 91.

Mr. Uhl to Mr. Bayard.

DEPARTMENT OF STATE,
Washington, April 25, 1894.

SIR: I inclose herewith copy of a letter of the 19th instant from the Acting Secretary of the Navy covering an order issued to Commander C. E. Clark, United States Navy, who has been detailed to command a force of naval vessels and revenue cutters in Bering Sea.

I am, etc.,

EDWIN F. UHL, *Acting Secretary.*

[Inclosure in No. 91.]

ORDER TO COMMANDER CLARK.

[Transmitted by the Navy Department April 19, 1894.]

NAVY DEPARTMENT,
Washington, April 18, 1894.

SIR: 1. Having been detailed to command a force of naval vessels and revenue cutters to carry out the provisions of an act of Congress, approved April 6, 1894, "to give effect to the award rendered by the Tribunal of Arbitration at Paris, under the treaty between the United States and Great Britain, concluded at Washington, February twenty-ninth, eighteen hundred and ninety-two, for the purpose of submitting to arbitration certain questions concerning the preservation of fur seals," and of the President's proclamation of the same, dated Washington, D. C., April 9, 1894, you will order the vessels under your command to warn all American and British vessels they may meet outside of the waters prohibited by this act not to enter these waters for the purpose of sealing during the periods of time in which fur-seal fishing is so prohibited, and you will deliver to the commanding officer of each vessel so warned a copy of the President's proclamation, of the British act, and of these instructions.

2. An entry, showing the notice of warning, shall be made upon the register of all vessels of the United States and Great Britain that have been warned.

3. In accordance with the provisions of the above-mentioned act, as appears by reference to section 1 thereof, fur seal fishing is forbidden to the persons mentioned therein, and to all subjects of Great Britain, to persons owing the duty of obedience to the laws or the treaties of Great Britain, and to all persons belonging to or on board of a vessel of Great Britain, at any time or in any manner whatever, outside of territorial waters, in the waters surrounding the Pribilof Islands within a zone of 60 geographical miles thereof (60 to a degree of latitude) around said islands, *inclusive* of the territorial waters.

You will observe that the act of Congress extends the zone referred to in this paragraph 60 (geographical) miles around said islands, *exclusive* of the territorial waters, but you are hereby instructed to treat the limit as extending only 60 (geographical) miles around said islands, *inclusive* of the territorial waters. The word *exclusive* was inadvertently inserted in the act of Congress instead of the word *inclusive*, which appears in the award, and which it is the purpose of the act to enforce.

4. During the season extending from May 1 to July 31, both inclusive in each year, fur-seal fishing is forbidden to all persons mentioned in the first section of the act, and to all subjects of Great Britain, to persons owing the duty of obedience to the laws or the treaties of Great Britain, and to all persons belonging to or on board of a vessel of Great Britain, not only in the zone mentioned in the third paragraph of these instructions, but in that part of the Pacific Ocean, including Bering Sea, which is situated to the north of the thirty-fifth degree of North latitude and to the east of the one hundred and eightieth degree of longitude from Greenwich, till it strikes the water boundary between the United States and Russia. This boundary line passes through a point in Bering's straits on the parallel of 65° 30′, north latitude, at its intersection by the meridian which passes midway between the islands of Krusenstern, or Ingalook, and the island of Ratmanoff, or Noonarbook, and proceeds due north, without limitation, into the same frozen ocean. The same western limit, beginning at the same initial point, proceeds thence in a course nearly southwest through Bering's straits and Bering Sea, so as to pass midway between the northwest point of the Island of St. Lawrence and the southeast point of Cape Choukotski, to the meridian of one hundred and seventy-two west longitude; thence, from the intersection of that meridian, in a southwesterly direction until it strikes the one hundred and eightieth degree of longitude from Greenwich.

5. The regulations respecting the "special license" for sailing vessels, and the "distinguishing flag" to be worn by the same during the open season, mentioned in sections 3 and 7 of the act, are hereafter to be prescribed and promulgated by the Governments of the United States and Great Britain.

6. Any vessel or person described in the first section of this act, or any subject of Great Britain, or person owing obedience to the laws or the treaties of Great Britain, or any person belonging to or on board of any vessel of Great Britain, unauthorized by this act, found to be or to have been employed in sealing during the period of time and in the waters therein prohibited, whether with or without warning, and any of such vessels or persons found therein, whether warned or not, having on board or in their possession apparatus or implements suitable for taking seal, or seal skins, or bodies of seals, you will order seized.

7. The commanding officer making the seizure will, at the time thereof, draw up a declaration in writing stating the condition of the seized

vessel, the date and place of seizure, giving-latitude and longitude and circumstances showing guilt. The seized vessel will be brought or sent, as soon as practicable, with all persons on board thereof, in charge of a sufficient force to insure delivery, together with witnesses and proofs, and the declaration of the officer making the seizure, if American, to the most convenient port of Alaska, California, Oregon, or Washington, and there delivered to the officers of the United States court having jurisdiction to try the offense and impose penalties for the same; and, if British, to Unalaska, and there delivered to the senior British naval officer present, or to the most convenient port in British Columbia, and delivered to the proper authorities of Great Britain, or delivered to the commanding officer of any British vessel charged with the execution of the award herein referred to.

8. A signed and certified list of the papers of the seized vessel will be delivered to the master thereof, and a duplicate copy will be transmitted with the declaration.

9. Copies of the act of the British Parliament are herewith inclosed.

Very respectfuly,

H. A. HERBERT,
Secretary of the Navy.

Commander CHARLES E. CLARK, U. S. N.,
Commanding U. S. Naval Force in Bering Sea,
U. S. S. Mohican, Port Townsend, Washington.

No. 92.

Mr. Uhl to Mr. Bayard.

DEPARTMENT OF STATE,
Washington, April 27, 1894.

SIR: I have received your dispatch of the 11th instant, concerning the enforcement of the Bering Sea regulations and calling attention to the use of the word "exclusive" in section 1 of the act approved April 6, 1894.

For your information, I inclose copy of the Department's note of the 18th instant[*] on this subject to the British ambassador at the capital, together with six copies of an act of Congress, approved April 24, 1894, wherein the error referred to is corrected.

I am, etc.,

EDWIN F. UHL,
Acting Secretary.

No. 93.

Mr. Webb to Mr. Gresham.

[Telegram.]

LEGATION OF THE UNITED STATES,
St. Petersburg, April 27, 1894. (Received April 27.)

Russian minister, Washington, authorized to sign arrangement annexed to your instruction of March 30. Russian Government ready to enter into negotiations.

---

*See No. 84.

No. 94.

Mr. Webb to Mr. Gresham.

LEGATION OF THE UNITED STATES,
St. Petersburg, April 16–28, 1894. (Received May 12.)

SIR: Upon a request from Count Kapnist, the head of the Asiatic department of the foreign office, I called upon the gentleman yesterday afternoon. He imparted to me the following information.

Prince Cantacuzene has received authority to sign the agreement annexed to your instruction of March 30. He is further authorized to state that Russia is ready to enter into negotiations at any time tending to extend the terms fixed by the Paris Tribunal of Arbitration to the Pacific Ocean as far as the thirty-ninth degree of latitude.

The first portion of this I have telegraphed to you at the earnest request of Count Kapnist. The matter that concerns the extending of the terms fixed by the Paris Tribunal to the thirty-ninth degree of latitude I did not cable, as the count said that he had cabled himself to Count Cantacuzene.

I am, etc., G. CREIGHTON WEBB.

No. 95.

Sir Julian Pauncefote to Mr. Gresham.

WASHINGTON, *April 30, 1894.* (Received April 30, 1894.)

SIR: In accordance with the arrangement made when I had the honor of an interview with you and the Secretary of the Navy at the State Department, Mr. Herbert was good enough to send me on the 19th instant the draft of the instructions which it was proposed to issue to the officer commanding the United States naval force in Bering Sea, for his guidance in carrying out the provisions of the act of Congress passed to give effect to the award of the Bering Sea Tribunal of Arbitration.

On the following day I transmitted the draft instructions to my Government for their observations, and I am now in receipt of a telegram from Her Majesty's principal secretary of state for foreign affairs, in which I am directed to draw your attention to paragraph 6 of the draft instructions, so far as it relates to British vessels. That paragraph requires modification in order to bring, it as regards the powers to be exercised by United States cruisers over British vessels, within the limits prescribed by the British order in council conferring such powers.

The Earl of Kimberley desires me to state to you that the order in council which is about to be issued to empower United States cruisers to seize British vessels will only authorize them to make seizures of vessels contravening the provisions of the British act of Parliament, or, in other words, the provisions of the award.

There is no clause in the British act corresponding with section 10 of the United States act of Congress. United States cruisers can not therefore seize British vessels merely for having on board, while within the area of the award and during the close season, implements suitable for taking seal. The mode in which such vessels should be dealt with is indicated in the instructions issued on that point to the British naval officers, and of which I have the honor to inclose a copy, and Lord

Kimberley suggests that the instructions to the United States cruisers should coincide with the British instructions so far as regards the seizure of British vessels. The Secretary of the Navy was good enough to furnish me, in addition to the draft of the proposed instructions to the United States cruisers, with a map intended to accompany them and purporting to show the delimitation of the waters embraced in the award. As regards this map Lord Kimberley points out that the red line drawn thereon is not quite correct. It makes the meridian 180 strike the Russian water boundary north of the sixtieth degree of latitude, instead of reaching it south of that degree, as it should do according to the award.

I have the honor, etc.,   JULIAN PAUNCEFOTE.

[Inclosure in No. 95.]

Instructions to British cruisers as to seizure.

If a vessel which appears to be a sealing vessel is found in any waters in which, at the time, hunting is prohibited, you will ascertain whether she is there for the purpose of hunting, or whether she has hunted, or whether she was carried there by stress of weather, or by mistake, during fog, or is there in the ordinary course of navigation on her passage to any place.

If you are satisfied that the vessel has hunted contrary to the act, you will seize her and order her to proceed to the British port hereinafter mentioned; but if you are of opinion that no offense has been committed you should warn her and keep her, as far as you think necessary and as is practicable, under supervision.

Whether this vessel has been engaged in hunting you must judge from the presence of sealskins or bodies of seals on board and other circumstances and indications. If the vessel is found outside the specified limits and it is evident that she has been hunting within those limits, and that thus an offense has been committed, you will seize her and send her to port.

A vessel, though herself not within the prohibited limits, may violate the act by her boats hunting within such limits.

No. 96.

Mr. Bayard to Mr. Gresham.

[Telegram.]

EMBASSY OF THE UNITED STATES,
London, April 30, 1894.

British minister for foreign affairs asks me to inform him exact terms President's instructions authorizing British officers to arrest the United States vessels contravening act of Congress as proclaimed.

No. 97.

Mr. Gresham to Mr. Bayard.

[Telegram.]

WASHINGTON, *May 1, 1894.*

After several conferences Secretary Carlisle, the British ambassador, and Dr. Dawson, agent for Canada, reached the conclusion that the following regulations would meet the present situation and avoid embarrassment this season:

REGULATIONS GOVERNING VESSELS EMPLOYED IN FUR SEAL FISHING.

ARTICLE I.—*Fitness of crews to use arms.*

Before the issuance of a special license, the master of any sailing vessel proposing to engage in fur-seal fishing shall produce satisfactory evidence to the collector of customs that the hunters employed by him are competent to use the weapons authorized by law.

ART. II.—*The use of firearms, when prohibited.*

Firearms, nets, or explosives shall not be used for taking or killing fur seals in that portion of Bering Sea described in the act approved April 6, 1894, entitled "An act to give effect to the award rendered by the Tribunal of Arbitration at Paris, under the treaty between the United States and Great Britain, concluded at Washington, February 29, 1892, for the purpose of submitting to arbitration certain questions concerning the preservation of fur seals."

ART. III.—*Vessels now sealing in the North Pacific east of 180° longitude; how to secure safe conduct to home port, or to Bering Sea.*

Any vessel having license to hunt fur seal in the North Pacific and Bering Sea east of 180° longitude shall, before entering Bering Sea, or at Unalaska, report to a customs officer of the United States, or an officer of the United States Navy, and have all arms and ammunition therefor on board secured under seal; such seal shall not be broken except by a customs officer of the United States, or an officer of the United States Navy. The breaking of this seal, otherwise than above described, shall forfeit the license. The United States officer breaking the seal shall make a note of the fact on the margin of the license over his signature, showing the date. Any sealing vessel found in the prohibited waters of the North Pacific between May 1 and July 31, both inclusive, by any vessel or customs officer of the United States, shall be seized, as provided above, if there be evidence that she has violated the law. Otherwise her sealing outfit shall be secured under seal by the commander of any cruising vessel or customs officer upon declaration by her master that she wishes to proceed to a home port, and the officer placing this seal shall enter the date of same upon her register with the number of seal skins, given under oath, then on board. Said seal shall be broken by a customs officer upon her arrival at a home port. In the case of a sealing vessel wishing to proceed direct from the North Pacific to Bering Sea without touching at a home port, any officer authorized as above to seal her arms and ammunition shall, upon application of the master, enter upon her register his permission to do so, subject to the restrictions contained in the President's proclamation. This permission shall confer upon the vessel all the privileges and subject it to all the penalties of a regular license.

ART. IV.—*Vessels now in the North Pacific west of 180° longitude; how to secure safe conduct to home port or to Bering Sea.*

Vessels now in Japanese waters, on the Siberian coast west of 180° longitude, wishing to return to a home port, may enter the port of Attou, and there have their sealing outfits secured under seal and the fact entered on their registers. Such seal and entry shall be considered as sufficient protection against seizure whilst in prohibited water on their direct passage to a home port.

In case a sealing vessel, as described above, shall before leaving a Japanese port declare her intention of returning to a port of the United States, the United States consular officers of the port shall secure her sealing outfit as described above.

Any vessel, as described above, may obtain special license to hunt fur seals in Bering Sea upon application to the United States consular office of any port in Japan, or from the customs officer at Attou, after furnishing the evidence required in Art. I, but in no case shall such vessel enter the prohibited waters of Bering Sea until the arms and ammunition therefor on board have been secured under seal.

Any customs officer of the United States, or officer of the United States Navy, cruising to the westward of 180° longitude, may grant permission to enter Bering Sea as described in Art. III of these regulations.

ART. V.—*Vessels wishing to hunt for seals in Bering Sea on and after August 1; sealing of outfit, etc.*

Any vessel in a home or foreign port wishing to engage in fur-seal fishing in Bering Sea shall obtain special license for the same from a customs officer of the United States, if in a home port, and from a consular officer if in a foreign port. Before sailing the sealing outfit of such vessel shall be secured under seal and the fact noted on her license. Before entering Bering Sea such seal must be broken by a customs officer of the United States or an officer of the United States Navy. The breaking of this seal otherwise than as above will forfeit the special license and render the vessel liable to seizure.

ART. VI.—*Vessels at sea without special license and distinctive flag.*

Vessels now at sea in the pursuit of fur seals and found not to have violated the law in reference to the taking of fur seals, and which have not cleared from port on or after May 1, 1894, will not be molested on account of not having special license or distinctive flag, but may continue their cruise without either if they have complied, or shall comply, with the requirements of Articles IV and V of these regulations.

ART. VII.

Every vessel employed in fur-seal fishing as above described shall have, in addition to the papers now required by law, a special license for fur-seal fishing.

ART. VIII.

Every sealing vessel provided with special license shall show under her national colors a flag not less than 4 feet square, composed of two equal pieces, yellow and black, joined from the right-hand upper corner of the fly to the left-hand lower corner of the luff, the part above and to the left to be black, and the part to the right and below to be yellow.

ART. IX.

The authority hereinbefore granted to United States consular officers, customs officers, and officers of the United States Navy may be exercised by like officers in the service of the Government of Great Britain, except in the ports of the United States.

NOTICE.

Officers herein authorized to carry out the provisions of the act approved April 6, 1894, entitled "An act to give effect to the award rendered by the Tribunal of Arbitration at Paris, under the treaty between the United States and Great Britain, concluded at Washington, February 29, 1892, for the purpose of submitting to arbitration certain questions concerning the preservation of fur seals," will observe that the objects of the foregoing articles are to prevent the unlawful destruction of seals and to protect from unnecessary seizure or loss sealing vessels already at sea in ignorance of the provisions of the act or unable to comply strictly with its requirements. Should cases occur which are not here definitely provided for, they must be dealt with by the officers with the above-mentioned objects in view, and as nearly in accordance with the law and regulations as possible.

Having sent a copy to Canada, and, I presume, to London, Sir Julian yesterday informed us that Canada strenuously opposed regulations as unfair and not in accordance with Paris award. President thinks that under the circumstances the two Governments should put these regulations or something substantially like them into force at once. Disagreement at this time very unfortunate, and if understanding is not reached in a day or two instructions will be sent to our officers to enforce award on our part.

No. 98.

Mr. Gresham to Prince Cantacuzene.

DEPARTMENT OF STATE,
Washington, May 3, 1894.

The Secretary of State presents his compliments to the minister of Russia, and has the honor to request that Prince Cantacuzene will have the kindness to call at the Department of State to-morrow morning, at 10.30 o'clock, for the purpose of signing with the Secretary of State the proposed agreement for a modus vivendi between the United States and Russia in relation to the fur-seal fisheries in Bering Sea and the North Pacific Ocean.

No. 99.

Mr. Gresham to Mr. Bayard.

[Telegram.]

DEPARTMENT OF STATE,
Washington, May 4, 1894.

Following special instructions relative to sealing vessels lawfully navigating area of award, approved to-day:

I. No sealing vessel shall be seized or detained, by reason of the absence of a license or of a distinctive flag or merely on account of seals, seal-skins or fishery implements being found on board, but unless there be evidence of unlawful seal hunting the commander of the cruiser visiting such sealing vessel shall deliver to the master a certificate of the number of seals and seal skins found on board on that date (keeping a copy of such certificate), and allow the vessel to proceed on her way.

II. Any sealing vessel lawfully traversing or intending to traverse the said waters during the close season for the purpose of returning to her home port or of proceeding to any other port or to or from the sealing grounds, or for any other legitimate purpose, may, on the application of the master, have her fishery implements sealed up and an entry thereof made on her clearance or log book, and such sealing up and entry, shall be a protection to the vessel against interference by any cruiser in the said waters during the close season, so long as the seals so affixed shall remain unbroken, unless there shall be evidence of seal hunting notwithstanding.

III. The sealing up of fishing implements and the entry thereof may be effected by any naval officer, or customs officer, or (in Japan) by any consul of the nation to which the vessel belongs. It may be also effected at sea, as regards United States vessels by the commander of a British cruiser, and as regards British vessels by the commander of a United States cruiser.

No. 100.

Prince Cantacuzene to Mr. Gresham.

[Translation.]

WASHINGTON, *April 22–May 4, 1894.*

Mr. SECRETARY OF STATE: On the 8–20th of April last you were pleased, in pursuance of the instructions of the President of the United States, to inform me that if the Imperial Government assented thereto, the Federal Government was prepared to conclude with Russia, England and Japan—in lieu of any provisional arrangement—a treaty regulating and establishing the conditions of fur-seal hunting in the Pacific Ocean on bases identical for all and in conformity with the decisions and regulations of the Paris Tribunal of Arbitration. You expressed, at the same time, the opinion that this object would be best attained by extending from one continent to the other the prohibited and protected zone, the southern boundary of which should be the thirty-fifth parallel of north latitude.

I immediately communicated to my Goverment these propositions which furnish evidence conclusive of the principles of equity and jus' tice that actuate the Federal Government in this matter, and I have already had the honor verbally to inform'you of the satisfaction with which these overtures have been received by the Emperor's Government.

As the season is now too far advanced to permit us to negotiate such a treaty without adopting temporary measures for the protection of our waters, it has been thought necessary to conclude in the meantime a modus vivendi, which may at any time be superseded by a more complete treaty.

In signing to-day this essentially provisional arrangement, I hereby reiterate to you. in writing, the declaration that the Imperial Government is, for its part, prepared to negotiate and sign with the United States, England, and Japan a treaty in virtue of which the principles and regulations of the Paris Tribunal of Arbitration shall be applicable, indifferently, to all the waters of the Pacific Ocean situated north of the thirty-fifth parallel of north latitude.

Be pleased to accept, etc., CANTACUZENE.

No. 101.

Mr. Gresham to Sir Julian Pauncefote.

DEPARTMENT OF STATE,
Washington, May 7, 1894.

EXCELLENCY: The two Governments having provided by legislation and regulations for the enforcement of the award of the Paris Tribunal under the treaty of February 29, 1892, the time appears to have arrived for carrying out the stipulation of article 7 of the convention.

I am therefore directed by the President to invite the attention of Her Majesty's Government to the matter, to the end that with all convenient speed the two Governments may cooperate in securing the adhesion to the award of other powers, especially Russia and Japan.

I have the honor to be, etc.,

W. Q. GRESHAM.

No. 102.

Mr. Gresham to Mr. Bayard.

DEPARTMENT. OF STATE,
Washington, May 8, 1894.

SIR: I inclose herewith copy of a note* which I have this day addressed to the British ambassador at this capital, suggesting that the time has arrived for the Governments of the United States and Great Britain to cooperate in securing the adhesion of other powers, especially Russia and Japan, to the award of the Paris Tribunal.

I am, etc.,

W. Q. GRESHAM.

----

*No. 101.

No. 103.

Sir Julian Pauncefote to Mr. Gresham.

WASHINGTON, *May 8, 1894.*

SIR: In accordance with a request made to me by the governor-general of Canada, acting under instructions from Her Majesty's Government, I have the honor to transmit herewith, for the information of the United States Government, a copy of a minute of his excellency's council, dated the 16th ultimo, to which is appended a complete list of such British vessels as have cleared from Canadian ports for the sealing grounds during the present season.

Of these vessels it appears that 34 have cleared for the coast of Japan and 24 for the American coast, making in all 58.

I have, etc., JULIAN PAUNCEFOTE.

[Inclosure in No. 103 —Extract from a report of the committee of the honorable the privy council, approved by his excellency on the 16th of April, 1894.—In triplicate.]

On a report dated 12th April, 1894, from the minister of marine and fisheries stating that he has received the appended letter from the collector of customs at Victoria, British Columbia, forwarding complete lists of the sealing vessels which have cleared and sailed for the Japan coast and west coast of British Columbia, respectively, on sealing voyages for the season of 1894.

The minister observes that of these vessels 34 have cleared for the Japan coast and 24 for the American coast, making in all 58 Canadian sealing vessels engaged in the industry this year.

That, of the vessels which sailed for the Japan coast, the earliest clearance was made on the 14th December, 1893, 2 vessels having cleared on that date, and between the 18th and 30th of that month 11 cleared, while between the 2d and 10th January, 1894, 18 cleared.

All of these vessels cleared from Victoria. The date of clearance of the schooner *Beatrice* of Vancouver is not given, while the *Maud S.* and the *Aurora* winter in Yokahama.

The minister further observes that of the vessels which cleared for the North America coast, 2 cleared on the 6th January, 1894, 2 on the 11th, 5 on the 13th, and 7 between the 15th and 29th of that month.

During February, 3 cleared, and during March, 3. All of these vessels cleared from Victoria. The date of clearance of the *C. D. Rand* of Victoria is not given. The *Kilmeny* is reported as "still in port; will clear in a few days."

The committee on the recommendation of the minister of marine and fisheries, advise that a certified copy of this minute, if approved, be forwarded to the right honorable the principal secretary of state for the colonies.

All of which is respectfully submitted for your excellency's approval.

JOHN J. McGEE,
Clerk of the Privy Council.

[Annex A to P. C. 1147, 16th April, 1894.]

CUSTOMS CANADA.

VICTORIA, B. C., *31st March, 1894.*

SIR: I beg to transmit herewith for the information of the honorable the minister of marine and fisheries, a complete list of vessels that have cleared and sailed for Japan this season; also, a complete list of all those who are sealing on the west coast of British Columbia this year.

I have the honor to be, sir, your obedient servant,

A. R. MILNE, *Collector.*

WM. SMITH, Esq.,
Deputy Minister of Marine and Fisheries, Ottawa.

[Annex *b* to P. C. 1147, 16th April, 1894.]

List of Canadian vessels sealing on east side of North Pacific Ocean. Season, 1894.

Vessels.*	Tons.	Masters.	Date of clearing.	Port sailed from.
Triumph	98	C. N. Cox	Jan. 6, 1894	Victoria, British Columbia.
Sapphire	109	Wm. Cox	....do	Do.
Beatrice	66	D. Macauley	Jan. 11, 1894	Do.
Mascot	40	H. F. Sieward	Jan. 13, 1894	
Favourite	80	L. McLean	....do	
Annie C. Moore	115	J. Daley	....do	
Labrador	25	J. J. Whiteley	....do	
Wanderer	25	H. Paxton	....do	
Pioneer	66	W. E. Baker	Jan. 15, 1894	
Saucy Lass	38	R. E. Crowell	Jan. 16, 1894	
Borealis	37	G. Meyer	Jan. 19, 1894	
Katharine	82	J. Gould	Jan. 20, 1894	
Ainoko	75	G. Heater	Jan. 22, 1894	
Kate	58	N. Moos	Jan. 27, 1894	
Shelby Hr	16	F. Jones	Jan. 29, 1894	
Venture	48	J. Mohrhouse	Feb. 2, 1894	
Walter L. Rich	76	S. Balcom	Feb. 6, 1894	
South Bend	21	C. F. Dillon	Mar. 15, 1894	
Minnie	46	V. Jackobson	Mar. 27, 1894	
San Jose	31	M. Foley	Mar. 28, 1894	
Mountain Chief	23	Jamieson	Jan. 11, 1894 (coasting).	
Fisher Maid	21	C. Chipps	Feb. 3. 1894 (coasting).	
C. D. Rand	51			Vancouver, British Columbia.
Kilmeny	19	L. Olsen	Still in port, will clear in a few days.	

* Total, 24.

CUSTOMS, CANADA, VICTORIA, B. C., *31st March, 1894.*

[Annex to P. C. 1147, 16th April, 1894.]

List of Canadian vessels sealing on the Japan Coast. Season, 1894.

Vessels.*	Tons.	Masters.	Date of clearing.	Port of sailing.
Enterprise	69	Oscar Scarf	Dec. 14, 1893	Victoria, British Columbia.
Rosie Olsen	39	A. B. Whidden	....do	Do.
Umbrinia	99	C. Campbell	Dec. 18, 1893	Do.
Oscar and Hattie	81	T. Magnesen	Dec. 19, 1893	Do.
Diana	50	A. Nelson	Dec. 20, 1893	Do.
Brenda	100	C. E. Locke	Dec. 21, 1893	Do.
Arietis	86	A. Douglas	Dec. 23, 1893	Do.
Casco	63	O. Buchholz	Dec. 26, 1893	Do.
Dora Sieward	94	F Cole	Dec. 27, 1893	Do.
Walter A. Earle	68	L. Magnesen	Dec. 28, 1893	Do.
Fawn	59	M. Keefe	Dec. 29, 1893	Do.
Agnes McDonald	107	M. Cutler	Dec. 30, 1893	Do.
Walter P. Hall	99	J. B. Brown	....do	Do.
Mermaid	73	W. H. Whiteley	Jan. 2, 1894	Do.
City of San Diego	46	M. Pike	Jan. 3, 1894	Do.
Mary Taylor	43	E. F. Robbins	....do	Do.
Libbie	93	F. Hackett	....do	Do.
May Belle	58	E. Shields	Jan. 4, 1894	Do.
Mary. Ellen	63	W. O. Hughes	....do	Do.
Viva	92	J. Anderson	....do	Do.
W. P. Sayward	60	G. A. Ferey	Jan. 5, 1894	Do.
Penelope	70	L. McGrath	....do	Do.
Vera	60	W. Shields	....do	Do.
Carlotta G. Cox	76	W. D. Byers	....do	Do.
Otto	86	J. McLeod	Jan. 6, 1894	Do.
E. B. Marvin	96	C. J. Harris	....do	Do.
Annie E. Paint	82	A. Bissett	....do	Do.
Geneva	92	W. A. Leary	Jan. 9, 1894	Do.
Teresa	63	F. Gilbert	....do	Do.
Ocean Belle	83	T. O'Leary	Jan. 10, 1894	Do.
Sadie Turpel	56	C. Le Blanc	....do	Do.
Beatrice, of Vancouver	49			Vancouver, British Columbia.
Maud S	97	R. McKeil		Yokahama, Japan.
Aurora	41			Do.

* Total, 34.

31st MARCH, 1894.

No. 104.

Sir Julian Pauncefote to Mr. Gresham.

WASHINGTON, *May 8, 1894.*

SIR: By direction of Her Majesty's principal secretary of state for foreign affairs I have the honor to inform you that instructions will be sent to the officers in command of Her Majesty's cruisers in Bering Sea to distribute copies of the Bering Sea award act and of an explanatory map to all British sealers which they may meet in those waters.

As, however, the United States cruisers patrolling in those waters may meet with British sealers which have not been spoken by one of Her Majesty's ships, Lord Kimberley requests me to ask you whether your Government would instruct United States naval officers to give copies of these documents to any British vessels which they may find to be without them.

In case your Government accede to this request, I shall have the honor to inclose copies of the act and map for the purpose above mentioned.

I have, etc.,   JULIAN PAUNCEFOTE.

_____

No. 105.

Mr. Gresham to Sir Julian Pauncefote.

DEPARTMENT OF STATE,
Washington, May 9, 1894.

EXCELLENCY: I have the honor to acknowledge the receipt of your note of yesterday's date, in which, referring to the steps taken to warn sealing vessels in Bering Sea, you ask whether the naval officers of the United States would be instructed to give to British sealers they may speak copies of the Bering Sea award act and of an explanatory map thereto annexed, of which you offer to furnish copies for that purpose.

By the second paragraph of the amended instructions issued by the Secretary of the Navy to the commanding officers of the United States fleet in Bering Sea, under date of 4th instant, in place of the previous instructions of April 18, the British act is among the papers to be delivered to the masters of sealing vessels so warned.

It will give me much pleasure to receive and communicate to the Secretary of the Navy for appropriate distribution the copies of the British act and the annexed map which you offer to supply.

I inclose for your information copies of the above-mentioned naval instructions and of the regulations governing vessels employed in fur-seal fishing.

I have, etc.,   W. Q. GRESHAM.

_____

[Inclosure in No. 105.]

NAVY DEPARTMENT,
Washington, May 4, 1894.

SIR: Congress having passed acts which were approved April 6, 1894, and April 24, 1894, and the Government of the United States having made arrangements with Great Britain to give effect to the award rendered by the Tribunal of Arbitration at Paris, under the treaty between the United States and Great Britain, concluded at Washington, February 29, 1892, for the purpose of submitting to arbitration certain questions concerning the preservation of fur seals, you are detailed to command a force of naval and revenue vessels to carry out the provisions of the award, of the acts of Congress, and of the President's proclamation dated Washington, D. C., April 9, 1894.

You will order the vessels under your command to warn all American and British vessels they may meet not to engage in fur-seal fishing within the area of the award, during the periods of time in which fur-seal fishing is forbidden, and to deliver to the master of each of such vessels a copy of the President's proclamation, of the act of Congress, approved April 24, 1894, of the President's regulations governing vessels employed in fur-seal fishing, of the British act, and of these instructions.

Whenever a vessel may be warned, the commander of the cruiser, or the customs officer, as the case may be, shall, after making an examination of the vessel, leave with the master of said vessel a certificate showing the date and place of examination, the number of seal skins, and the number of bodies of seals then on board, and shall preserve a duplicate of said certificate. And no officer, subsequently boarding such vessel, shall seize the same, unless he shall be satisfied, as herein provided, that it has committed a violation of law by killing fur seal within the area of the award subsequent to the 30th day of April, 1894.

Fur-seal fishing is forbidden to all persons mentioned in section 1 of said act of Congress, to all subjects of Great Britain, to persons owing the duty of obedience to the laws or the treaties of Great Britain, and to all persons belonging to or on board of a vessel of Great Britain, at any time, or in any manner whatever, outside of territorial waters, in the waters surrounding the Pribilof Islands within a zone of 60 geographical miles thereof (60 to a degree of latitude) around said islands, inclusive of the territorial waters.

Fur-seal fishing is forbidden during the season extending from May 1, to July 31, both inclusive, in each year, to all persons mentioned in the first section of said act of Congress, and to all subjects of Great Britain, to persons owing the duty of obedience to the laws or the treaties of Great Britain, and to all persons belonging to or on board of a vessel of Great Britain, not only in the zone mentioned in the fourth paragraph of these instructions, but in that part of the Pacific Ocean, including Bering Sea, which is situated to the north of the thirty-fifth degree of north latitude and to the east of the one hundred and eightieth degree of longitude from Greenwich, till it strikes the water boundary between the United States and Russia. This boundary line passes through a point in Bering Straits on the parallel of 65° 30′ north latitude, at its intersection by the meridian which passes midway between the islands of Krusenstern or Ignalook, and the island of Ratmanoff or Noonarbook, and proceeds due north, without limitation, into the same frozen ocean. The same western limit, beginning at the same initial point, proceeds thence in a course nearly southwest, through Bering Straits and Bering Sea, so as to pass midway between the northwest point of the island of St. Lawrence and the southeast point of Cape Choukotski to the meridian of one hundred and seventy-two west longitude; thence, from the intersection of that meridian, in a southwesterly direction, until it strikes the one hundred and eightieth degree of longitude from Greenwich.

Any vessel or person described in the first section of said act of Congress, or any vessel or subject of Great Britain, or person owing obedience to the laws or the treaties of Great Britain, or any person belonging to or on board of any vessel of Great Britain, unauthorized by this act, found to be or to have been engaged in fur-seal fishing within the area of the award, during the periods of time in which fur-seal fishing is forbidden, you will order seized.

If a vessel which appears to be a sealing vessel is found within the area of the award, during the periods of time in which fur-seal fishing is forbidden, you will ascertain whether she is there for the purpose of fur-seal fishing, whether she has been engaged in fur-seal fishing, whether she was carried there by stress of weather, by a mistake during foggy or thick weather, or is there in the ordinary course of navigation, making the best of her way to any place. You must judge whether such vessel has been engaged in fur-seal fishing from the presence of seal skins or bodies of seals on board, and from other circumstances and indications. If such vessel is found outside of the area of the award, and it is evident that she has been engaged in fur-seal fishing within said area, and has thus committed an offense, you will order her seized. A vessel may violate the law by her boats fur-seal fishing within said area, while the vessel, herself, is outside of said area.

The commanding officer making the seizure will, at the time thereof, draw up a declaration in writing, stating the condition of the seized vessel, the date and place of seizure, giving latitude and longitude and circumstances showing guilt. The seized vessel will be brought or sent, as soon as practicable, with all persons on board thereof, in charge of a sufficient force to insure delivery, together with witnesses and proofs, and the declaration of the officer making the seizure, if American, to the most convenient port of Alaska, California, Oregon, or Washington, and there delivered to the officers of the United States court having jurisdiction to try the offense and impose penalties for the same; and if British, to Unalaska, and there delivered to the senior British naval officer present, or carried to the most convenient port in British Columbia, and delivered to the proper authorities of Great Britain, or delivered to the commanding officer of any British vessel charged with the execution of the award herein referred to.

A signed and certified list of the papers of the seized vessel will be delivered to the master thereof, and a duplicate copy will be transmitted with the declaration.

You will arrange with the commanders of the British vessels engaged in carrying out the provisions of the award for the mutual delivery of vessels of the one country seized by officers of the other.

These instructions will remain in force only during the present season.

Very respectfully,

H. A. HERBERT,
Secretary of the Navy.

Commander CHARLES E. CLARK, U. S. N.,
Commanding U. S. Naval Force in Bering Sea,
U. S. S. Mohican, Port Townsend, Wash.

Regulations governing vessels employed in fur-seal fishing.

ARTICLE I.

FITNESS OF CREWS TO USE ARMS.

Before the issuance of a special license the master of any sailing vessel proposing to engage in fur-seal fishing shall produce satisfactory evidence to the collector of customs that the hunters employed by him are competent to use the weapons authorized by law.

ARTICLE II.

THE USE OF FIREARMS—WHEN PROHIBITED.

Firearms, nets, or explosives shall not be used for taking or killing fur seals in that portion of Bering Sea described in the act approved April 6, 1894, entitled "An act to give effect to the award rendered by the Tribunal of Arbitration at Paris, under the treaty between the United States and Great Britain, concluded at Washington, February 29, 1892, for the purpose of submitting to arbitration certain questions concerning the preservation of fur seals."

ARTICLE III.

VESSELS NOW SEALING IN THE NORTH PACIFIC EAST OF 180° LONGI- TUDE—HOW TO SECURE SAFE CONDUCT TO HOME PORT OR TO BERING SEA.

Any vessel having license to hunt fur seals in the North Pacific and Bering Sea east of 180° longitude may, before entering Bering Sea, or at Unalaska, report to a customs officer of the United States, or an officer of the United States Navy, and have all arms and ammunition therefor on board secured under seal; such seal shall not be broken during the time fur-seal fishing is prohibited. In order to protect vessels found within the area of the award between April thirtieth and August first, but which have not violated the law, from improper seizure or detention, the masters thereof may, by applying to the commander of any cruiser or to a customs officer and declaring that she intends to proceed to a home port, have her sealing outfit secured under seal, and the officer placing this seal shall enter the date of the same upon her log book, with the number of seal skins and bodies of seals then on board, and said seal shall not be broken during the time fur-seal fishing is prohibited, except at the home port.

ARTICLE IV.

VESSELS NOW IN THE NORTH PACIFIC WEST OF 180° LONGITUDE— HOW TO SECURE SAFE CONDUCT TO HOME PORT OR TO BERING SEA.

Vessels now in Japanese waters or on the Siberian coast west of 180° longitude, wishing to return to a home port, may enter the port of Attou and there have their sealing outfits secured under seal and the fact entered on their log books. Such seal shall not be broken except at her home port, and such seal and entry shall constitute a sufficient protection against *seizure* whilst within the area of the award on their direct passage to such port.

In case a sealing vessel, as described above, shall before leaving a Japanese port declare her intention of returning to a port of the United States, the United States consular officers of the port may, upon application of her master, secure her sealing outfit as described above.

Any vessel, as described above, may obtain special license to hunt fur seals in Bering Sea upon application to the United States consular office of any port in Japan or from the customs officer of Attou, after furnishing the evidence required in Article I.

ARTICLE V.

VESSELS WISHING TO HUNT FUR SEALS IN BERING SEA ON AND AFTER AUGUST 1—SEALING OF OUTFIT, ETC.

Any vessel in a home or foreign port wishing to engage in fur-seal fishing in Bering Sea shall obtain special license for the same from a customs officer of the United States, if in a home port, and from a consular officer, if in a foreign port. Before sailing the sealing outfit of such vessel may be secured under seal, upon application, as hereinbefore provided, and the fact noted on her license. Such seal shall not be broken during the time fur-seal fishing is prohibited.

ARTICLE VI.

VESSELS AT SEA WITHOUT SPECIAL LICENSE AND DISTINCTIVE FLAG.

Vessels now at sea in the pursuit of fur seals and found not to have violated the law in reference to the taking of fur seals, and which have not cleared from any port on or after May 1, 1894, will not be seized solely on account of not having special license or distinctive flag.

ARTICLE VII.

Every vessel employed in fur-seal fishing, as above described, shall have, in addition to the papers now required by law, a special license for fur-seal fishing.

ARTICLE VIII.

Every sealing vessel provided with special license shall show under her national colors a flag not less than four feet square, composed of two equal pieces, yellow and black, joined from the right-hand upper corner of the fly to the left-hand lower corner of the luff, the part above and to the left to be black, and the part to the right and below to be yellow.

ARTICLE IX.

The authority hereinbefore granted to United States consular officers, customs officers, and officers of the United States Navy may be exercised by like officers in the service of the Government of Great Britain, except in the ports of the United States.

NOTICE.

Officers herein authorized to carry out the provisions of the act approved April 6, 1894, entitled "An act to give effect to the award rendered by the Tribunal of Arbitration at Paris, under the treaty between the United States and Great Britain, concluded at Washington February 29, 1892, for the purpose of submitting to arbitration certain questions concerning the preservation of fur seals," will observe that the objects of the foregoing articles are to prevent the unlawful destruction of seals and to protect from unnecessary seizure or loss sealing vessels already at sea in ignorance of the provisions of the act or unable to comply strictly with its requirements. Should cases occur which are not here definitely provided for, they must be dealt with by the officers with the above-mentioned objects in view and as nearly in accordance with the law and regulations as possible.

These regulations are intended to apply only to the closed season of 1894, and are not to be regarded as a complete execution of the authority conferred upon the Executive by the act of Congress.

Approved May 4, 1894.

GROVER CLEVELAND.

No. 106.

Sir Julian Pauncefote to Mr. Gresham.

WASHINGTON, *May 10, 1894.*

SIR: In accordance with the agreement arrived at during the recent negotiations in relation to the means of giving effect for the present year to the fishery regulations prescribed by the award of the Bering Sea Tribunal of Arbitration, I have the honor to inclose for your approval a memorandum recording the arrangements concluded on that subject and accepted by both Governments, and I shall feel obliged if you will be good enough to inform me whether the memorandum meets with your approval.

I have, etc.,   JULIAN PAUNCEFOTE.

[Inclosure in No. 106.]

Memorandum of the arrangements agreed upon between the Governments of Great Britain and the United States for giving effect during the year 1894 to the fur-seal fishery regulations prescribed by the award of the Bering Sea Tribunal of Arbitration.

LICENSES.

The special license to be issued to sealing vessels under article 4 of the regulations of the award shall declare that the licensee has given satisfactory evidence of the fitness of the hunters to be employed by him, as required by article 7.

It shall be issued subject to the observance of the said regulations and to the penalties imposed by law for the violation thereof.

It shall be in such form as each Government shall determine for itself.

DISTINCTIVE FLAG.

Every sealing vessel provided with a special license shall show, under her national colors, a flag, not less than 4 feet square, composed of two equal pieces, yellow and black, joined from the right-hand upper corner of the fly to the left-hand lower corner of the luff, the part above and to the left to be black and the part to the right and below to be yellow.

REGULATIONS RESPECTING SEALING VESSELS LAWFULLY NAVIGATING THE MARITIME AREA OF THE AWARD DURING THE CLOSE SEASON.

1. No sealing vessel shall be seized or detained by reason of the absence of a license or of a distinctive flag, or merely on account of seals, seal skins, or fishery implements being found on board; but, unless there be evidence of unlawful sealing, the commander of the cruiser ivsiting such vessel shall deliver to the master a certificate of the num-

ber of seals and seal skins found on board on that date (keeping a copy
of such certificate) and allow the vessel to proceed on her way.

2. Any sealing vessel lawfully traversing, or intending to traverse,
the said waters during the close season, for the purpose of returning to
her home port, or of proceeding to any other port, or to or from the
sealing grounds, or for any other legitimate purpose, may, on the application of the master, have her fishery implements sealed up and an
entry thereof made on her clearing and log book, and such sealing up
and entry shall be a protection to the vessel against interference by any
cruiser in the said waters during the close season so long as the seals
so affixed shall remain unbroken, unless there shall be evidence of
seal hunting notwithstanding.

3. The sealing up of fishery implements and the entry thereof may
be effected by any naval officer or customs officer, or (in Japan) by any
consul of the nation to which the vessel belongs. It may also be
effected at sea, as regards United States vessels, by the commander of
a British cruiser, and, as regards British vessels, by the commander of
a United States cruiser.

No. 107.

Sir Julian Pauncefote to Mr. Gresham.

WASHINGTON, *May 10, 1894.*

SIR: With reference to my note of the 8th instant and to your reply
thereto of the 9th instant, I have the honor to inclose copies of the
British Bering Sea award act and of the explanatory map therein mentioned, which you are good enough to state will be distributed by the
United States cruisers among British sealers in the manner requested
by Her Majesty's Government.

I have also the honor to acknowledge the receipt of the amended
naval instructions issued by the Secretary of the Navy on the 4th
instant to the commanding officers of the United States fleet in Bering
Sea, and of the regulations attached thereto, which I shall lose no time
in transmitting to my Government.

I have, etc.,   JULIAN PAUNCEFOTE.

No. 108.

Mr. Gresham to Sir Julian Pauncefote.

DEPARTMENT OF STATE,
Washington, May 11, 1894.

EXCELLENCY: In reply to your excellency's note of the 10th instant
inclosing a memorandum of certain arrangements agreed upon between
our respective Governments for giving effect during the year 1894 to
the fur-seal fishery regulations prescribed by the award of the Bering
Sea Tribunal of Arbitration, I have the honor to state that I approve of
the memorandum as containing a correct record of the arrangements
agreed upon.

I have the honor to be, etc.,   W. Q. GRESHAM.

No. 109.

Mr. Gresham to Mr. Bayard.

DEPARTMENT OF STATE,
Washington, May 12, 1894.

SIR: Yours of the 27th ultimo* has been received. I note your citation of the reply, made in the House of Commons on the 26th ultimo by Sir E. Grey to an inquiry of Sir G. Baden-Powell, wherein the important announcement is made that the provisions of the award of the Tribunal of Arbitration, which Great Britain and the United States were bound to carry out, were matters of common knowledge in August last, and that " every possible means will be taken to give to sealers now at sea specific warning that the regulations will be enforced." Sir E. Grey added the equally positive statement that "any British or United States vessel contravening the provisions of the Bering Sea award act, 1894, will be liable to be arrested and sent to a British court for trial," the last phrase, of course, relating to the jurisdiction of the courts of the two countries over vessels of the respective nationalities seized under the provisions of the concurrent acts of Parliament and Congress.

In this relation I may properly mention a conversation I had on the 12th ultimo with Mr. Goschen, Secretary of the British embassy, who called upon me in behalf of Sir Julian Pauncefote, then confined to his house by indisposition.

Mr. Goschen stated that Sir Julian had received an instruction from Lord Kimberley interpreting subclause 2 of section 7 of the British bill then pending, and read from a written memorandum as follows:

In clause 7, subclause 2, of the British bill the following phrase occurs: "Where * * * it is proved that the ship sailed from its port of departure before the scheduled provisions were published there," etc. The publication referred to is that of the provisions of the award, not that of the bill.

Mr. Goschen added that it would please Sir Julian if I would make this statement to the Senate Committee on Foreign Affairs, in order that the position of Great Britain might be correctly understood.

After some conversation as to whether the "scheduled provisions" so referred to in the British bill were those of the Paris award itself, or of the regulations reported by the tribunal, I said to Mr. Goschen that it would be for the courts to decide what the words "scheduled provisions" mean; and that, in construing statutes and for the purpose of ascertaining the legislative intention, courts sometimes have recourse to the debates or discussions which occurred while the measure was under consideration, but that mere verbal communications from one government to another—such as that now made—would not be considered by a court. I preferred that any communication the British Government might desire to make on this subject should be official and in writing. I added that if I should inform the Senate committee of the interpretation which Lord Kimberley placed upon subclause 2, and British courts should subsequently give it another and different construction, Her Majesty's Government might feel somewhat embarrassed.

I subsequently received from the ambassador under date of the same day, a personal note, of which a copy is inclosed herewith,† conveying Lord Kimberley's interpretation of the clause in question.

---

* Not printed.   † See inclosure in No. 78.

Not the least gratifying incident of the protrated negotiations was the subsequent amendment of subclause 2, section 7, of the bill, so that as finally passed it provides for proof that "the ship sailed from its port of departure before the provisons of the award mentioned in the first schedule of the act were known there, and that such person or the master of the ship did not, after such sailing and before the alleged offense, become aware of such provisions" in order to exonerate them.

I am, etc.,

W. Q. GRESHAM.

No. 110.

Mr. Uhl to Prince Cantacuzene.

DEPARTMENT OF STATE,
Washington, May 12, 1894.

SIR: I have the honor to acknowledge the receipt of your note of the 4th instant, and to express to you the gratification with which this Government accepts your declaration that the Imperial Government is prepared to negotiate and sign with the United States, England, and Japan a treaty in virtue of which the principles and regulations of the Paris Tribunal of Arbitration shall be applicable, indifferently, to all the waters of the Pacific Ocean north of the thirty-fifth parallel of north latitude.

Accept, etc.,   EDWIN F. UHL, *Acting Secretary.*

No. 111.

Mr. Uhl to Mr. Bayard.

DEPARTMENT OF STATE,
Washington, May 14, 1894.

SIR: I inclose herewith for your information copy of an agreement* between the Government of the United States and the Imperial Government of Russia for a modus vivendi in relation to the fur-seal fisheries in Bering Sea and the North Pacific Ocean, concluded on May 4, 1894.

I also inclose translation of a note of the 4th instant † from the Russian minister in this capital, wherein he declares that the Imperial Government is prepared to negotiate and sign with the United States, England, and Japan a treaty, in virtue of which the principles and regulations of the Paris Tribunal of Arbitration shall be applicable, indifferently, to all the waters of the Pacific Ocean situated north of the thirty-fifth parallel of north latitude.

I am, etc.,

E. F. UHL, *Acting Secretary.*

---

*See No. 57.   † See No. 100.

No. 112.

Mr. Gresham to Sir Julian Pauncefote.

DEPARTMENT OF STATE,
Washington, May 28, 1894.

EXCELLENCY: Referring to my note to you of the 7th instant regarding the joint invitation of foreign powers to adhere to the award of the Bering Sea Tribunal, I beg to inquire whether you have received instructions from your Government on the subject.

In the judgment of the President prompt action is very desirable.

I have, etc.,

W. Q. GRESHAM.

No. 113.

Mr. Bayard to Mr. Gresham.

EMBASSY OF THE UNITED STATES,
London, May 30, 1894.

SIR: I have the honor to acknowledge your instructions dated May 12, with certain inclosures, all having relation to the international arrangements to carry into effect the award and regulations by the Paris Tribunal of fur sealing in the waters of the North Pacific and Bering Sea.

Your expressions of appreciation and approval of my official action here, in assisting your efforts to make this resort to arbitration successful, are naturally gratifying and are fully appreciated by me.

As the transaction has been conducted on both sides with honorable candor, and with the single purpose of performing a clearly stipulated class of international duties and obligations, it may reasonably be expected that the progressive execution of the treaty and the award, under the cooperative laws and regulations of the two high contracting powers, will be complete and satisfactory.

I beg now to inclose copies of two notes, dated respectively April 30 and May 3, addressed by me to Lord Kimberley, in relation to the orders in council requisite to execute the British statutes, and prevent violation of the interdictions against pelagic sealing within the award area.

These documents complete, I believe, the correspondence which has thus far taken place touching the arrangements between the United States and Great Britain for the policing of the award area recited in the regulations established by the Paris Tribunal.

I have also the honor to acknowledge your instruction, dated May 14, transmitting a copy of an agreement between the United States and Russia for a modus vivendi, in relation to fur sealing in the waters of Bering Sea and the North Pacific Ocean.

This instrument runs upon the identical lines of the British arrangement with Russia, which was in force in 1893, and is renewed for the present year.

The announcement in the note of the Russian minister at Washington of the readiness of Russia to join in a quadripartite convention with the United States, Great Britain, and Japan, to regulate sealing in all the waters of the Pacific Ocean north of the thirty-fifth parallel of north longitude is very satisfactory, and I can not doubt that Japan will be equally willing to lend her aid in putting an end to pelagic sealing.

The interdiction of the use of firearms, nets, and explosives, in the capture of seals, can not fail, if obeyed, to make pelagic sealing almost profitless, and one or two seasons of rigid enforcement of the regulations by active marine police will suffice, I trust, to. put an end to the wasteful and cruel slaughter of the seal in the sea.

I have, etc.,

T. F. BAYARD.

[Inclosure 1 in No. 113.]

EMBASSY OF THE UNITED STATES,
London, April 30, 1894.

DEAR LORD KIMBERLEY: Let me thank you for your note of Saturday last, which came to my residence that night.

I am glad to have copies of the British Bering Sea act as finally approved, and also of the explanatory maps of the award area in these waters.

The questions of the form of license and the distinguishing flag for the fur-sealing vessels will no doubt be easily and satisfactorily agreed upon at the State Department at Washington by the representatives mutually in charge.

While it does not occur to me that there will probably be any objection to the United States officers of the marine patrol distributing copies of any of the documents of either Government to the sealing vessels, yet the protecting value or condoning force of such papers to vessels found flagrante delicto is not quite obvious, i. e., pursuing seals in contravention of the provisions of the award at Paris, which, in the words of the instructions of the admiralty issued to Her Majesty's vessels, were "matters of common knowledge before the sealers started."

Although the telegraph newspaper reports allege the delivery several days ago to Sir Julian Pauncefote in Washington of (confidential) copies of the President's instructions to United States cruisers in which authority is given to Her Majesty's officers in command of the patrolling vessels to make seizure of United States sealing vessels contravening the act of Congress, yet I have telegraphed to Washington for the information requested in your note, and so soon as I receive the exact terms by which the President will confer on commanders of Her Majesty's cruisers, authority to arrest United States vessels I will communicate with you.

Believe me, etc.,

T. F. BAYARD.

[Inclosure 2 in No. 113.]

EMBASSY OF THE UNITED STATES,
London, May 3, 1894.

DEAR LORD KIMBERLEY: The mail of last night did not bring me the documents I expected, relating to the United States ships and officers detailed for service in the patrol of the Bering Sea award area, nor the precise terms of the President's instructions including therein authority to the commanders of Her Majesty's cruisers.

Impressed with our conversation yesterday afternoon, I felt very desirous of conveying reassurances to my Government of the fulfillment uberimma fide of the British share of duty in carrying out the results of the arbitration, and. I have to-day telegraphed Secretary Gresham to the effect that, in my interview with your lordship, I became fully impressed with the belief that the reported objections or interference by the Canadian officials would not be allowed by the Government of Her Majesty to prevent the consummation of the agreement to execute the letter and spirit of the award, by competent regulations under the authority of the order in council.

Believe me, etc.,   T. F. BAYARD.

No. 114.

Mr. Gresham to Sir Julian Pauncefote.

DEPARTMENT OF STATE,
Washington, June 2, 1894.

EXCELLENCY: I have the honor to inclose herewith for your information copy of a modus vivendi between the United States and Russia* for the protection of fur seals in and near the Russian waters of the Bering Sea and in a zone of 30 miles around the Commander and Robben Islands.

I have, etc.,   W. Q. GRESHAM.

No. 115.

Mr. Gresham to Sir Julian Pauncefote.

DEPARTMENT OF STATE,
Washington, June 2, 1894.

EXCELLENCY: I have the honor to inclose herewith copy of a bill which has passed both Houses of Congress and been approved by the President, entitled "A bill supplementary to an act approved April 6, 1894, for the execution of the award rendered at Paris, August 15, 1893, by the Tribunal of Arbitration constituted under the treaty between the United States and Great Britain, concluded at Washington, February 29, 1892, in relation to the preservation of the fur seal."

I have, etc.,   W. Q. GRESHAM.

[Inclosure in No. 115.]

A BILL supplementary to an act approved April sixth, eighteen hundred and ninety-four, for the execution of the award rendered at Paris, August fifteenth, eighteen hundred and ninety-three, by the Tribunal of Arbitration constituted under the treaty between the United States and Great Britain, concluded at Washington, February twenty-ninth, eighteen hundred and ninety-two, in relation to the preservation of the fur seal.

Whereas by the seventh article of the treaty between the United States and Great Britain, concluded at Washington, February twenty-ninth, eighteen hundred and ninety-two, in relation to the preservation

---

*See inclosure in No. 57.

of the fur seal, the high contracting parties agree to cooperate in securing the adhesion of other powers to such regulations as the arbitrators under said treaty might determine upon for that purpose; and

Whereas by an act of Congress, approved April sixth, eighteen hundred and ninety-four, provision has been made by the United States for the execution of the regulations so determined upon and for the punishment of any infractions of said regulations: Therefore,

Be it enacted by the Senate and House of Representatives of the United States of America in Congress assembled, That the procedure and penalties provided by said act, in case of the violation of the provisions of said regulations, are hereby made applicable to and shall be enforced against any citizen of the United States, or person owing the duty of obedience to the laws or the treaties of the United States, or person belonging to or on board of a vessel of the United States who shall kill, capture, or pursue, at any time or in any manner whatever, as well as to and against any vessel of the United States used or employed in killing, capturing, or pursuing, at any time or in any manner whatever, any fur seal or other marine fur-bearing animal, in violation of the provisions of any treaty or convention into which the United States may have entered or may hereafter enter with any other power for the purpose of protecting fur seals or other marine fur-bearing animals, or in violation of any regulations which the President may make for the due execution of such treaty or convention.

No. 116.

Sir Julian Pauncefote to Mr. Gresham.

WASHINGTON, *June 7, 1894.*

SIR: Adverting to the verbal communications which have passed between us respecting the best mode of verifying and adjusting the British claims for compensation for the seizure of British sealing vessels in Bering Sea, I have now the honor to transmit herewith, by direction of Her Majesty's principal secretary of state for foreign affairs, a complete list and summary of those claims, together with memoranda of the additions and amendments made since their original presentation. I am at the same time to make the following suggestion, with a view to adjustment of those claims with the least possible labor, expense, and delay:

The whole of the claims, excepting that of the *Henrietta* and that of the *Black Diamond* (1886), were laid before the Tribunal of Arbitration at Paris, together with the evidence in support of them. The facts on which they rest were found by the arbitrators, as provided by Article VIII of the Treaty of Arbitration, and form part of the award. In view of the decision of the Tribunal on the questions of law submitted to them, it only now remains to assess the damages. I am accordingly authorized by the Earl of Kimberley to propose that, for the purpose of such assessment, each Government should appoint a duly qualified commissioner, who should be a lawyer and, if possible, possess some knowledge of the conditions of the sealing industry.

That the two commissioners should sit together at Victoria, British Columbia, where all the evidence in verification of the claims can be obtained on the spot. That they should make a joint report on all the claims in which they have agreed as to the amount of damages, and separate reports in the cases in which they have failed to agree, fully stating the grounds of such disagreement.

That the assessment of damages by the two commissioners, where they have been able to agree, shall be final.

That in cases where they have been unabled to agree the differences shall be settled by the two Governments within a fixed period, failing which such differences shall be referred for final adjustment to an umpire to be appointed by the two Governments jointly, or, in case of disagreement, to be nominated by a foreign Government.

You informed me some time ago that, in the view of your Government, a convention would be necessary for the adjustment of the claims, and the Earl of Kimberley, to whom I did not fail to communicate that opinion, has instructed me to proceed at once with the negotiation of such a convention, on the basis of the arrangement above proposed, should it be favorably entertained by your Government.

I have, etc.,

JULIAN PAUNCEFOTE.

[Inclosure in No. 116.]

Memoranda of additions and amendments made since original presentation of list of British claims for compensation for the seizure of British sailing vessels in Bering Sea.

ADA.

Claim of the master, Captain Gaudin, for personal loss and damage......... $3,000

This claim was, by a mistake on the part of the agent of the owner of the *Ada*, not included when the other claims in connection with this vessel were entered. Captain Gaudin thought that it had been so included, and it was only on seeing the printed list of the British claims that he discovered that such was not the case. He at once requested that the omission might be rectified and his claim added to the list, and Her Majesty's Government, after causing an inquiry to be made into the circumstances of the case, decided that his application should be granted.

Captain Gaudin's claim has accordingly been added to the schedule of the claims entered with respect to the schooner *Ada*.

HENRIETTA.

[Seized by the U. S. war ship *Yorktown* on September 4, 1892.]

Value of vessel	$4,000
Value of outfit and equipment	3,000
Value of 420 seal skins, at $18	7,560
Value of balance of estimated full catch for season in Bering Sea for three boats and three canoes, viz, 561 skins, at $18	10,098
Legal and personal expenses in defending action against vessel and cargo at Sitka, and in preparing and forwarding this claim	2,000
Claim of owner, with interest at 7 per cent, to date of payment	26,658

In his note, dated 13th of March last, Mr. Gresham stated that from the date on which the *Henrietta* was handed over to her captain, the United States Government ceased to bear any responsibility or to exercise any control with regard to that vessel, and that therefore they were unable to comply with the request of Her Majesty's Government that she should be sent to a British port for trial; but he added that the claim of her owner for compensation would receive due consideration when presented.

The claim in question has, therefore, been added to the general list of British claims.

BLACK DIAMOND,

[Additional claim submitted by the master, Mr. Henry Paxton, for damages alleged to have been sustained by reason of the above schooner having been ordered out of Bering Sea in 1886 by the United States authorities.]

Estimated catch for August, 1886, 1,000 skins at $7.50 each (the price of skins at Victoria during the fall of 1886)... $7,500,

This claim was sent in too late for insertion in the general list of British claims. In view of the length of time that had elapsed since the occurrence of the action complained of, Her Majesty's Government deemed it advisable to cause an inquiry to be made as to the reason for the delay in presenting the claim. The reason given was that at the time of the seizure of the vessel, the coowners, who were three in number, were doubtful as to how far an appeal to the United States Government for redress would be entertained. In the following year one of the owners was lost at sea and another left the country, and it was only after the publication of the award that the surviving owner consulted his solicitor and was informed that he had a good and equitable claim for compensation. The claim was then drawn up and presented at once.

Her Majesty's Government also ascertained from the solicitors in question that the fact of the *Black Diamond* being boarded by the revenue officers of the United States and ordered out of Bering Sea in 1886 is entered in the records of the custom-house of Unalaska, and that due protest was made by the master of the vessel on the arrival of the schooner at Victoria.

Under the circumstances Her Majesty's Government considered that the reasons alleged for the delay were reasonable, and gave instructions that the claim should be presented to the United States Government, together with the other similar claims.

JUANITA.

It will be noticed that the original claim of the owner of the *Juanita*, which was stated at $14,695, has been amended so as to amount to $17,697.66.

The ground upon which this claim was amended was that the owner made his original statement on the basis of $8 per skin, whereas it was ascertained afterwards that the skins had been sold at San Francisco at an average of $9.67 per skin.

List and summary of the claims for compensation in respect of the seizures of British vessels in Bering Sea by the authorities of the United States.

CAROLENA.

[Seized by U. S. S. *Corwin* August 1, 1886.]

For—	Amount of claim as put forward by owner.
Value of vessel, 32 tons	$4,000.00
Value of outfit (inconsumable)	3,002.89
Insurance	352.50
Wages of crew up to date of seizure	1,832.22
Passage of crew from San Francisco to Victoria	71.72
Passage of mate, Sitka to Victoria, after release from prison	100.00
Personal expenses of owner	250.00
Legal expenses	1,250.00
Estimated seal catch for 1886	16,667.00
	27,526.33
Deduct value consumed during a full voyage	3,213.32
Claim by owner, with interest at 7 per cent to date of payment	24,313.01

List and summary of the claims for compensation, etc.—Continued.

THORNTON.

[Seized by U. S. S. *Corwin* August 1, 1886.]

For—	Amount of claim as put forward by owner.
Value of vessel, 78 tons	$6,000.00
Value of outfit (inconsumable)	2,941.68
Insurance	591.40
Wages paid to date of seizure to crew, etc	1,370.04
Passage money of crew from San Francisco to Victoria	177.16
Passage money of crew and expense of captain and mate after release, Sitka to Victoria	200.00
Personal expenses of owners	1,000.00
Legal expenses	1,250.00
Estimated catch of seals for 1886	16,667.00
	30,197.23
Deduct value consumed on a full voyage	3,379.58
Claim by owners, with interest at 7 per cent to date of payment	26,817.65

ONWARD.

[Seized by U. S. S. *Corwin* August 2, 1886.]

Value of vessel, 94 tons	$4,000.00
Value of outfit (inconsumable)	1,778.89
Insurance	260.00
Wages paid for voyage	1,820.00
Passage, etc., of master and mate	200.00
Personal expenses of owner	250.00
Legal expenses	1,250.00
Estimated catch	16,667.00
	26,225.69
Deduct value consumed during full voyage	2,955.98
Claimed by owner, with interest at 7 per cent to date of payment	23,269.71

FAVOURITE.

[Warned out of Bering Sea by U. S. S. *Corwin* August 2, 1886.]

Estimated loss of catch of 1,000 seals	$7,000.00
Claim by owner, with interest at 7 per cent to date of payment	7,000.00

W. P. SAYWARD.

[Seized by U. S. S. *Richard Rush* July 9, 1887.]

Passage of crew, etc	$255.00
Passage of officers	250.00
Legal expenses of owners	850.00
Probable seal catch, 1887, 3,500 seals, at $5.50	19,250.00
Loss by detention, October 1, 1887, to February 1, 1888	1,200.00
Loss of profit in season 1888 (February 1 to October 1)	6,000.00
Personal expenses of owners	250.00
Claim by owner, with interest at 7 per cent to date of payment	28,055.00
Cost of suit before Supreme Court United States, in reseizure of *W. P. Sayward*	62,847.12
Total	118,957.12

GRACE.

[Seized by U. S. S. *Richard Rush* July 17, 1887.]

Value of vessel, 182 tons	$12,000.00
Nonconsumable outfit	1,742.57
Passage of master and crew	200.00
Personal expenses of owners	250.00
Legal expenses	850.00
Probable catch, 1887, 4,200 seals, at $5.50	23,100.00
Claim of owner, with interest at 7 per cent to date of payment	38,142.57

List and summary of the claims for compensation, etc.—Continued.

ANNA BECK.
[Seized by U. S. S. *Richard Rush* June 28, 1887.]

For—	Amount of claim as put forward by owner.
Value of vessel	$8,000.00
Nonconsumable outfit	977.50
Passage of master and crew	460.54
Personal expenses of owner	250.00
Legal expenses	850.00
Probable seal catch, 1887, 3,150, at $5.50	17,325.00
Claim of owner, with interest at 7 per cent to date of payment	27,863.04

DOLPHIN.
[Seized by U. S. S. *Richard Rush* July 12, 1887.]

For—	
Value of vessel, 174 tons	$12,000.00
Value of nonconsumable outfit	2,051.50
Passage of master and crew	300.00
Personal expenses of owner	250.00
Legal expenses	850.00
Probable catch, 1887, 4,500, at $5.50	24,750.00
Claim of owner, with interest at 7 per cent to date of payment	40,201.50

ALFRED ADAMS.
[Seized by U. S. S. *Richard Rush* July 10, 1887.]

For—	
Value of outfit seized	$683.00
Personal expenses	200.00
Legal expenses	300.00
Probable catch, 3,500, at $5.50	19,250.00
Claim of owner, with interest at 7 per cent to date of payment	20,433.00

ADA.
[Seized by U. S. S. *Bear* August 25, 1887.]

For—	
Value of vessel, 68 tons	$7,000.00
Value of nonconsumable outfit	2,500.00
Passage, etc., of master	100.00
Personal expenses	250.00
Legal expenses	850.00
Probable catch, 1887, 2,876, at $5.50	15,818.00
Claim of owner, with interest at 7 per cent to date of payment	26,518.00

TRIUMPH.
[Ordered not to enter Bering Sea by U. S. S. *Richard Rush* August 4, 1887.]

For—	
Illegal boarding and searching of *Triumph*, as set forth in affidavit	$2,000.00
1,000 seal skins	8,000.00
Legal and other expenses	250.00
Claim of owner, with interest at 7 per cent to date of payment	10,250.00

JUANITA.
[Seized by U. S. S. *Richard Rush* July 31, 1889.]

For—	
620 seal skins, at $8	$4,960.00
Balance of estimated catch for 1889, at $8	9,424.00
Spears, etc.	36.00
New ship's papers	25.00
Legal and other expenses	250.00
Claim of owner, with interest at 7 per cent to date of payment	14,695.00
For amended claim, see colonial office to foreign office, November 23, 1893	17,697.66

List and summary of the claims for compensation, etc.—Continued.

PATHFINDER.

[Seized by U. S. S. *Richard Rush* July 29, 1889.]

For—	Amount of claim as put forward by owner.
854 skins seized, and estimated balance of catch (1,246), at $12.25 a skin	$25,725.00
Guns, etc., seized	765.00
New papers	25.00
Legal expenses	250.00
Claim of owner, with interest at 7 per cent to date of payment	26,765.00

TRIUMPH.

[Ordered out of Bering Sea by U. S. S. *Richard Rush* July 11, 1889.]

Balance of estimated catch of 2,500, at $8 a skin	$19,424.00
Legal and other expenses	250.00
Claim by owner, with interest at 7 per cent to date of payment	19,674.00

BLACK DIAMOND.

[Seized by U. S. S. *Richard Rush* July 11, 1889.]

76 skins seized, at $8	$608.00
2,024 skins, balance of estimated catch, at $8	16,192.00
Rifles, spears, etc., seized	110.00
New ship's papers	25.00
Legal and other expenses	250.00
Claim of owner, with interest at 7 per cent to date of payment	17,185.00

LILY.

[Seized by U. S. S. *Richard Rush* August 6, 1889.]

333 skins seized, at $8	$2,664.00
Balance of catch, 1,767, at $8	14,136.00
Spears and salt seized	101.00
New ship's papers	25.00
Legal and other expenses	250.00
Claim of owner, with interest at 7 per cent to date of payment	17,176.00

ARIEL.

[Ordered out of Bering Sea by U. S. S. *Richard Rush* July 30, 1889.]

Balance of estimated catch of 2,000 (1,156), at $8	$9,248.00
Legal and other expenses	250.00
Claim of owner, with interest at 7 per cent to date of payment	9,498.00

KATE.

[Ordered out of Bering Sea by U. S. S. *Richard Rush* August 13, 1889.]

Balance of catch	$10,960.00
Legal and other expenses	250.00
Claim of owner, with interest at 7 per cent to date of payment	11,210.00

List and summary of the claims for compensation, etc.—Continued.

MINNIE.

[Seized by U. S. S. *Richard Rush* July 5, 1889.]

For—	Amount of claim as put forward by owner.
420 skins seized	$3,360.00
Balance of catch	12,752.00
Guns and spears seized	98.00
Legal and other expenses	250.00
Claim of owner, with interest at 7 per cent to date of payment	16,460.00

PATHFINDER.

[Seized by U. S. S. *Thomas Corwin* March 27, 1890.]

Seizure and detention from March 27, 1890, to March 29, 1890	$2,000.00
Claim of owner, with interest at 7 per cent to date of payment	2,000.00

CLAIMS FOR 1886.

Claimed by—		Amount claimed.
David Moore, master of Onward	Illegal arrest and imprisonment	$4,000
Margotich, mate of Onward	do	2,500
Hans Guttornaseu, master of Thornton	do	4,000
Harry Norman, mate of Thornton	do	2,500
Jas. Ogilvie, master of Carolena	do	2,500
Jas. Black, mate of Carolena	do	2,500
Total for 1886		18,000

CLAIMS FOR 1887.

Warren, master of Dolphin	Sufferings and losses navigating four vessels from Unalaska to Sitka.	$2,635
John Riely, mate of Dolphin	do	1,000
George P. Ferey, master of W. P. Sayward	do	2,000
A. B. Laing, mate of W. P. Sayward	do	1,000
Louis Olsen, master of Anna Beck	do	2,000
Michael Keefe, mate of Anna Beck	do	1,000
W. Petit, master of Grace	do	2,000
C. A. Lundberg, mate of Ada	do	2,000
Total for 1887		13,635
Total for 1886 and 1887		31,635
To be added to 1886, personal claims Captain Gaudin, of Ada.		3,000
Amended total 1886 and 1887		34,635

*List and summary of the claims for compensation, etc.—*Continued.

RECAPITULATION.

Year.	Vessel.	Amount claimed.	Total.
1886	Carolena	$24,313.01	
	Thornton	26,817.65	
	Onward	23,269.71	
	Favourite	7,000.00	
	Personal claims	18,000.00	
			$99,400.37
1887	W. P. Sayward	28,055.00	
	Grace	38,142.57	
	Anna Beck	27,863.04	
	Dolphin	40,201.50	
	Ada	26,518.00	
	Alfred Adams	20,433.00	
	Triumph	10,250.00	
	Personal claims	13,635.00	
			205,098.11
1889	Juanita	14,695.00	
	Pathfinder	26,765.00	
	Triumph	19,674.00	
	Black Diamond	17,185.00	
	Lily	17,176.00	
	Ariel	9,498.00	
	Minnie	16,460.00	
	Kate	11,210.00	
			132,663.00
1890	Pathfinder		2,000.00
	Total claims without interest		439,161.48
	Costs of suit before Supreme Court, United States, in reseizure of W. P. Sayward		62,847.12

TOTAL.

1886.	Vessels	$81,400.37
	Personal claims	18,000.00
1887.	Vessels	191,463.11
	Personal claims	13,635.00
1889.	Vessels	132,663.00
1890.	Vessels	2,000.00
		439,161.48
W. P. Sayward costs		62,847.12
Total		502,008.60
Extra for Juanita		3,002.66
Extra for Black Diamond (1886)		7,500.00
Extra for Ada		3,000.00
Total		515,511.26
Henrietta		26,658.00
Amended total		542,169.26

No. 117.

Mr. Uhl to Sir Julian Pauncefote.

DEPARTMENT OF STATE,
Washington, June 8, 1894.

EXCELLENCY: Referring to the Department's note of the 2d instant, transmitting copy of a bill which had passed both Houses of Congress, and which was inadvertently stated to have been approved by the President, entitled "A bill supplementary to an act approved April 6, 1894, for the execution of the award rendered at Paris, August 15, 1893, by the Tribunal of Arbitration constituted under the treaty between the United States and Great Britain, concluded at Washington, February 29, 1892, in relation to the preservation of the fur seal," I have now the honor to inclose, three copies of the act as approved by the President on June 5, 1894. It will be observed that the words "securing the adhesion of such power to the regulations aforesaid," occurring in the sixteenth and seventeenth lines of the bill sent you (second page), were not in the bill as passed, and do not appear in the approved act.

I have, etc.,   EDWIN F. UHL,
                                          Acting Secretary.

[Inclosure in No. 117.]

[PUBLIC—No. 76.]

An act supplementary to an act approved April sixth, eighteen hundred and ninety-four, for the execution of the award rendered at Paris, August fifteenth, eighteen hundred and ninety-three, by the Tribunal of Arbitration constituted under the treaty between the United States and Great Britain, concluded at Washington, February twenty-ninth, eighteen hundred and ninety-two, in relation to the preservation of the fur seal.

Whereas by the seventh article of the treaty between the United States and Great Britain, concluded at Washington, February twenty-ninth, eighteen hundred and ninety-two, in relation to the preservation of the fur seal, the high contracting parties agree to cooperate in securing the adhesion of other powers to such regulations as the arbitrators under said treaty might determine upon for that purpose; and

Whereas by an act of Congress approved April sixth, eighteen hundred and ninety-four, provision has been made by the United States for the execution of the regulations so determined upon and for the punishment of any infractions of said regulations: Therefore,

Be it enacted by the Senate and House of Representatives of the United States of America in Congress assembled, That the procedure and penalties provided by said act, in case of the violation of the provisions of said regulations, are hereby made applicable to and shall be enforced against any citizen of the United States, or person owing the duty of obedience to the laws or the treaties of the United States, or person belonging to or on board of a vessel of the United States who shall kill, capture, or pursue, at any time or in any manner whatever, as well as to and against any vessel of the United States used or employed in killing, capturing, or pursuing, at any time or in any manner whatever, any fur seal or other marine fur-bearing animal, in violation of the provisions of any treaty or convention into which the United States may have entered or may hereafter enter with any other power for the purpose of protecting fur seals or other marine fur-bearing animals, or in violation of any regulations which the President may make for the due execution of such treaty or convention.

Approved, June 5, 1894.

No. 118.

Mr. Gresham to Sir Julian Pauncefote.

DEPARTMENT OF STATE,
Washington, July 21, 1894.

EXCELLENCY: Referring to your interview in June last with the Secretary of the Treasury, relative to the request of the Makah Indians for permission to use their schooners as places of refuge while fishing

in Bering Sea and the waters thereof, I have the honor to inclose herewith copy of Mr. Carlisle's letter of the 19th instant, transmitting for
your information copy of a letter from the Secretary of the Interior,
dated June 27, 1894, and of its inclosure regarding this matter.
I have, etc.,

W. Q. GRESHAM.

No. 119.

Sir Julian Pauncefote to Mr. Gresham.

WASHINGTON, *July 30, 1894.*

SIR: With reference to the identic note which it is proposed that the
Governments of Great Britain and of the United States should address
to the maritime powers inviting their adhesion to the Bering Sea regulations, I have the honor to submit for your consideration the accompanying list of powers to whom it is suggested by my Government that
the identic note should be addressed. I should be glad to be informed
whether the list meets with the approval of your Government, and, if so,
of the date on which you would propose that the identic note should
be issued.
I have, etc.,   JULIAN PAUNCEFOTE.

[Inclosure in No. 119.]

Argentine Republic, Austria-Hungary, Belgium, Brazil, Chile, China,
Colombia, Costa Rica, Denmark, Dominican Republic, Ecuador, France,
Germany, Greece, Guatemala, Hawaii, Haiti, Honduras, Italy, Japan,
Mexico, Netherlands, Nicaragua, Peru, Portugal, Russia, San Salvador,
Spain, Sweden and Norway, Turkey, Uruguay, Venezuela.

KIMBERLEY.

DRAFT IDENTIC NOTE TO THE MARITIME POWERS.

SIR: I have the honor to address you, under instructions from my
Government, on the subject of the regulations established on the eastern side of the North Pacific Ocean, from the twenty-fifth degree of
north latitude to the Bering Straits, for the proper protection and preservation of the fur-seal species.
Those regulations which are at present applicable only to the subjects or citizens of Great Britain and of the United States are prescribed by the award of the Tribunal of Arbitration constituted under
Article I of the treaty concluded between those two powers at Washington on the 29th day of February, 1892. The preservation of the fur-
seal species, however, being an object of interest and concern to the
whole of the civilized world, the high contracting parties agreed, by
Article VII of the above-mentioned treaty, to cooperate in securing
the adhesion of other powers to such regulations as the arbitrators
should deem necessary to carry out the purpose in view, having regard
to the particular conditions of fur-seal hunting in the waters referred to.
The Governments of Great Britain and the United States of America have given effect by suitable legislation to the regulations prescribed by the award, and the time has therefore now arrived for inviting the adhesion of the other powers thereto. Accordingly, I have the

honor to transmit herewith a copy of the award setting out in substance the provisions of the treaty and prescribing the regulations in question. I have also the honor to transmit a copy of the $\frac{\text{British}}{\text{United States}}$ act of $\frac{\text{Parliament}}{\text{Congress}}$ passed to give effect to those regulations as regards $\frac{\text{British}}{\text{United States}}$ vessels and $\frac{\text{subjects}}{\text{citizens}}$.

It only remains to me, on behalf of my Government and in execution of my instructions, to invite the adhesion of your Government to the regulations prescribed by the award with a view to their application to the vessels and $\frac{\text{subjects}}{\text{citizens}}$ of your country and to their enforcement by appropriate national legislation.

My Government will be much gratified to learn that your nation is willing to support the efforts made by $\frac{\text{Great Britain}}{\text{United States}}$ and the $\frac{\text{United States}}{\text{Great Britain}}$ in so beneficent a cause.

No. 120.

Sir Julian Pauncefote to Mr. Gresham.

WASHINGTON, *July 31, 1894.*

SIR: I have the honor to acknowledge the receipt of your note of the 21st instant, in which you were good enough to transmit for my information copies of communications from Mr. Secretary Carlisle and the Secretary of the Interior with regard to the request of the Makah Indians for permission to use their schooners as places of refuge while fishing in Bering Sea and the waters thereof.

I lost no time in forwarding copies of these communications to Her Majesty's principal secretary of state for foreign affairs, and as soon as I receive a reply from his Lordship I will inform you of the views entertained on this subject by Her Majesty's Government.

I have, etc.,

JULIAN PAUNCEFOTE.

No. 121.

Sir Julian Pauncefote to Mr. Gresham.

WASHINGTON, *August 1, 1894.*

SIR: In accordance with instructions which I have received from the Earl of Kimberley, I have the honor to inclose herewith copy of an Order in Council of the 27th ultimo, providing for the special form of license to be granted to sealing vessels in the Bering Sea, and describing the distinctive flag to be flown by them.

I have etc.,

JULIAN PAUNCEFOTE.

[Inclosure in No. 121.—Extract from the London Gazette of Friday, June 29, 1894.]

ORDER IN COUNCIL.

Bering Sea Award (No. 2), 1894.

WINDSOR, *26th June, 1894.*

At the Court at Windsor, the 27th day of June, 1894. Present: The Queen's Most Excellent Majesty, Earl Spencer, Lord Chamberlain, Lord Kensington.

Whereas by "the Bering Sea award act, 1894," it is enacted that Her Majesty the Queen in council may make orders for carrying into effect the provisions of the Bering Sea arbitration award set out in the first schedule to that act, and therein referred to as the scheduled provisions.

And whereas by Article three of "The Bering Sea award order in council, 1894," Her Majesty ordered that until arrangements for giving further effect to Articles four and seven of the said scheduled provisions should have been made between Her Majesty and the Government of the United States, the provisions contained in that article should have effect;

And whereas arrangements have been made for giving further effect to the said articles, and for regulating during the present year the fishing for fur seals in accordance with the said scheduled provisions; and it is expedient that effect should be given to those arrangements by an order in council under the said act:

Now, therefore, Her Majesty, in virtue of the powers vested in her by the said recited act, and of all other powers enabling her in that behalf, is hereby pleased by and with the advice of her privy council, to order, and it is hereby ordered, as follows:

1. On the application of the owner of any British sailing vessel intended to be employed in fur-seal fishing under the provisions of the recited act, a secretary of state may, if satisfactory evidence as required by the said article seven has been given by such owner of the fitness of the men to be employed by him on the said vessel in the said fishing, grant a special licence in the form in the schedule hereto, authorizing that vessel for the present year to fish for fur seals during the period in the manner and in the waters in which fur-seal fishing is allowed by the recited act, and the said special licence, when so granted, shall be carried on board the said vessel at all times while so employed.

2. Every British sailing vessel provided with a special licence under this order or the recited order, or which, under the recited order, is deemed to have been so provided, shall show under her national colours a flag, not less than four feet square, of two equal triangular pieces, yellow and black, joined from the right hand upper corner of the fly to the left hand lower corner of the luff, the part above and to the left to be black, and the part to the right and below to be yellow.

3. If, in the case of any vessel, there is any contravention of these regulations, the Secretary of State, whether any penalty has been recovered under the recited act or not, may revoke the special licence.

4. Article three of the recited order is hereby repealed, without prejudice, however, to any authorization given thereunder.

5. This order may be cited as "The Bering Sea award order in council (No. 2), 1894," and the recited order and this order may together be cited as "The Bering Sea award orders in council, 1894."

And the right honorable the Earl of Kimberley, K. G., and the most honorable the Marquess of Ripon, K. G., two of Her Majesty's principal secretaries of state, and the Lords of the Admiralty, are to give the necessary directions herein as to them respectively appertain.

C. L. PEEL.

SCHEDULE.

Form of special licence.

["The Bering Sea award act, 1894;" "The Bering Sea award orders in council, 1894."]

Special licence.

Whereas the British sailing-vessel —— is intended to be employed during the present year in fishing for fur seals under the provisions of "The Bering Sea award act, 1894:"

And whereas A. B., the owner [or A. B. and others, owners] of the said vessel, have given satisfactory evidence of the fitness of the men who are to be employed on board the said vessel in the said fishing:

Now, therefore, in pursuance of the above-mentioned act and orders in council, I hereby authorize the said vessel for the present year to be employed in fur-seal fishing during the period of time in the manner and in the waters in which fur-seal fishing is allowed by the above-mentioned act.

This special licence is subject to revocation in case of any contravention of the above-mentioned act or orders in council.

Given under my hand this —— day of ——, one thousand eight hundred and ninety-four.

——— ———,
Secretary of State.

No. 122.

Mr. Gresham to Sir Julian Pauncefote.

DEPARTMENT OF STATE,
Washington, August 6, 1894.

EXCELLENCY: I have the honor to say, in reply to your note of the 30th ultimo, that the list therewith submitted of the maritime powers proposed to be concurrently invited to adhere to the Bering Sea regulations meets with the approval of this Government.

In response to your further inquiry, I would suggest the 20th instant as a convenient date for the dispatch of the identic note to the enumerated powers.

I have, etc.

W. Q. GRESHAM.

No. 123.

Mr. Gresham to Sir Julian Pauncefote.

DEPARTMENT OF STATE,
Washington, August 16, 1894.

DEAR SIR JULIAN: I have your note of the 15th instant in relation to the proposed convention for the settlement of the Bering Sea claims. Referring to the doubts raised by Her Majesty's Government as to the restrictive effect of the words "British subjects," in the fourth recital of Article I of my counterdraft, you state that you mentioned to Lord Kimberley I had given you the assurance that the Government of the United States "desired to satisfy all claims, the payment of which was justly due by international law;" and you then say that you have received a reply from His Lordship "to the effect that Her Majesty's Government take note of that assurance and waive their objection to the words in question.".

While I am not of opinion that the language of your note is ambiguous, it is perhaps advisable, in order to avoid any possible misunderstanding hereafter, to say that in referring to international law it was not my intention either to enlarge or restrict the language of the proposed convention, but it was my intention to convey the idea that the Commissioners would, in construing its terms, be governed by the principles of international law. Such I understand to be your interpretation of my meaning, as expressed in your note; but out of abundant caution, I desire to avoid any possible ground for the inference that anything may have been said by me with the intention of modifying or controlling the convention by assurances given outside of it.

If convenient to you I shall be pleased to meet you at this Department at 11 o'clock a. m. to-morrow, for the purpose of signing the convention.

I remain, etc.,   W. Q. GRESHAM.

No. 124.

Mr. Gresham to Mr. Zeballos.

DEPARTMENT OF STATE,
Washington, August 20, 1894.

SIR: I have the honor to address you on the subject of the regulations established on the eastern side of the North Pacific Ocean from the thirty-fifth degree of north latitude to the Bering Straits for the proper protection and preservation of the fur-seal species.

Those regulations, which are at present applicable only to the subjects or citizens of the United States and of Great Britain, are prescribed by the award of the Tribunal of Arbitration constituted under Article I of the treaty concluded between the two powers at Washington on the 29th of February, 1892. The preservation of the fur-seal species, however, being an object of interest and concern to the whole of the civilized world, the high contracting parties agreed, by Article VII of the above-mentioned treaty, to cooperate in securing the adhesion of other powers to such regulations as the arbitrators should deem necessary to carry out the purpose in view, having regard to the particular conditions of fur-seal hunting in the waters referred to.

The Government of the United States has given effect by suitable legislation to the regulations prescribed by the award, and the time has therefore now arrived for inviting the adhesion of the other powers thereto. Accordingly, I have the honor to transmit herewith a copy of the award, setting out in substance the provisions of the treaty and prescribing the regulations in question. I have also the honor to transmit a copy of the acts of Congress passed to give effect to those regulations as regards United States vessels and citizens.

It only remains for me to invite the adhesion of your Government to the regulations prescribed by the award, with a view to their application to the vessels and citizens of your country and to their enforcement by appropriate national legislation.

This Government will be much gratified to learn that the Government of the Argentine Republic is willing to support the efforts made by the United States and Great Britain in so beneficent a cause.

Accept, sir, etc.,

W. Q. GRESHAM.

[Inclosures.]

Identic note sent to—	Acknowledged.	Identic note sent to—	Acknowledged.
Argentine legation	Sept. 4. 1894.	Japanese legation	Aug. 23, 1894.
Austro-Hungarian legation	Aug. 22, 1894.	Mexican legation	Aug. 21, 1894.
Belgian legation	Dec. 23, 1894.	Netherlands consulate-general.	Sept. 17, 1894.
Brazilian legation	Aug. 24, 1894.	Peruvian legation	Aug. 21, 1894.
Chilean legation	Aug. 21. 1894.	Portuguese legation	Oct. 15, 1894.
French embassy	Oct. 5, 1894.	Russian legation	Aug. 10–22, 1894.
German embassy	Oct. 29, 1894.	Spanish legation	Aug. 24, 1894.
Hawaiian legation	Aug. 22, 1894.	Swedish legation	
Italian embassy	Nov. 5, 1894.	Turkish legation	

Acknowledgments of receipt of identic note are as follows:

Mr. Zeballos to Mr. Gresham.

[Translation.]

ARGENTINE LEGATION,
Washington, September 4, 1894.

MR. SECRETARY OF STATE: I have had the honor to receive your excellency's communication of the 20th ultimo relative to the rule established on the east coast of the North Pacific Ocean, from parallel 35 north latitude to Bering Strait, for the protection and preservation of fur seals. Your excellency calls attention to Article VII of the treaty concluded between the United States of America and Great Britain on the 29th of February, 1892, whereby the high contracting parties agreed to endeavor to secure the adhesion of the other powers to the rules established by the arbitrators for the aforesaid purpose. Your excellency inclosed two copies of the decision and the declarations of the tribunal, and two copies of the law of Congress approved April 6, 1894. Your excellency concludes by courteously inviting the Government of the Argentine Republic to adhere to the rules established by the national legislation on the subject.

I shall be very happy to submit the note and the documents with which your excellency has honored me to the consideration of the Argentine Government.

It is proper for me to inform your excellency that the Argentine Congress will terminate its ordinary sessions, according to the national constitution, on the 30th day of the present month of September, so that if my Government decides to lay the matter before that body, as I do not doubt that it will, it can not be acted upon before the first session of 1895.

I renew to your excellency, Mr. Secretary of State, the assurances of my highest consideration.

ESTANISLAO S. ZEBALLOS.

Mr. Mezey to Mr. Gresham.

IMPERIAL AND ROYAL AUSTRO-HUNGARIAN LEGATION,
Washington, August 22, 1894. (Received August 22.)

SIR: I have the honor to acknowledge the receipt of your note of the 20th instant on the subject of the regulations established on the eastern side of the North Pacific Ocean from the thirty-fifth degree of north latitude to the Bering Straits, for the protection and preservation of the fur-seal species.

In reply to it I have the honor to inform you, sir, that, in compliance with your desire, I have referred the matter to the Imperial and Royal Government for its adhesion to the regulations prescribed by the award of the Tribunal of Arbitration constituted under Article I of the treaty concluded between the United States and Great Britain the 29th of February, 1892.

I avail, etc., MEZEY.

M. de Buisseret to Mr. Gresham.

[Translation.]

LEGATION OF BELGIUM,
Washington, December 23, 1894.

MR. MINISTER: Your excellency did me the honor to address to me, under date of the 20th of August last, the regulations for the protection of fur seals in Bering Sea, adding that the United States Government invited the Belgian Government to adhere thereto.

As no Belgian vessel ever visits the regions in question, my Government thinks—and it has instructed me so to inform your excellency—that there is no reason for proposing any special measure to the legislative body of Belgium.

It adds that it nevertheless renders sincere homage to the efforts that are made by the United States, together with Great Britain, in behalf of a cause which interests the entire world.

I beg your excellency to accept, etc., for the minister,

CONRAD DE BUISSERET.

Mr. Mendonca to Mr. Gresham.

LEGATION OF THE UNITED STATES OF BRAZIL,
New York, August 24, 1894. (Received August 28).

SIR: I have the honor to acknowledge the receipt of your excellency's note and inclosures of the 20th instant, on the subject of the regulations established for the protection and preservation of the fur-seal species and inviting the adhesion of my Government to said regulations.

I will transmit to my Government the aforesaid documents for its action.

Accept, etc., SALVADORO MENDONCA.

Mr. Gana to Mr. Gresham.

LEGATION OF CHILE,
Washington, August 21, 1894. (Received August 22.)

SIR: I have the honor to acknowledge the communication of your excellency, of yesterday's date, in which your excellency is pleased to express to me the wish that the Government of Chile should adhere to the provisions for the preservation of the fur seal made by the Arbitration Tribunal created by the treaty of February 29, 1892, and that it should adopt the legislative measures requisite to that end.

In reply I hasten to inform your excellency that I forward without delay to my Government both your excellency's communication and the accompanying documents.

I avail, etc.,   DOMINGO GANA.

Mr. Patenôtre to Mr. Gresham.

[Translation.]

EMBASSY OF THE FRENCH REPUBLIC
IN THE UNITED STATES,
Washington, October 5, 1894.

MR. SECRETARY OF STATE: In advising me, as you did by your note of August 20, of the enforcement of the new regulations adopted by the Washington and London cabinets in order to secure, in conformity with the decisions of the Paris Tribunal of Arbitration, the protection of fur seals in Bering Sea, you were pleased to inform me of the wish entertained by the Federal Government that the Government of the Republic should render these regulations obligatory upon French citizens. The minister of foreign affairs, to whom I transmitted your communication, informs me that the question has just been submitted to the competent authorities for examination. As soon as a decision shall have been reached in the matter, I shall have the honor to communicate it to you.

Be pleased to accept, Mr. Secretary of State the assurance of my very high consideration.

PATENÔTRE.

Baron Saurma to Mr. Gresham.

[Translation.]

IMPERIAL GERMAN EMBASSY,
Washington, October 29, 1894.

MR. SECRETARY OF STATE: Pursuant to instructions, I have the honor to inform your excellency, in reply to your note of the 20th of August last, that, upon investigation, it is shown that German shipping has never taken part in seal hunting in Bering Sea, and that under these circumstances the Imperial Government does not consider it sufficiently important to resort to imperial legislation for the protection of the seals in the manner proposed.

The Imperial Government, however, will gladly take occasion, through public notices, and by executive means, to issue warnings to its people interested in shipping, in conformity with the laws enacted by Great Britain and the United States.

Accept, etc.,

SAURMA.

Mr. Hastings to Mr. Gresham.

HAWAIIAN LEGATION,
Washington, August 22, 1894.

SIR: I have the honor to acknowledge the receipt of your communication of the 20th instant, on the subject of the regulations established on the eastern side of the North Pacific Ocean from the thirty-fifth degree of north latitude to the Bering's Straits for the protection and preservation of the fur seal, and inviting the adhesion of the Government of Hawaii to the regulations prescribed by the award of the Tribunal of Arbitration concluded at Paris on August 15, 1893, between the Government of the United States and that of Great Britain.

In reply thereto, I beg to inform you that a copy of your communication, and the, inclosures therewith, will at once be forwarded to my Government, and I venture to predict that the earliest possible action will be taken by the authorities at Honolulu in issuing the necessary orders to the masters of Hawaiian vessels and to citizens of the Hawaiian Republic to observe the regulations prescribed, and that every aid will be given the high contracting parties by legislation and otherwise, looking to the protection of the fur seal in the territory described.

With renewed assurances, etc.

FRANK P. HASTINGS.

Baron Fava to Mr. Gresham.

[Translation.]

EMBASSY OF H. M., THE KING OF ITALY,
Washington, November 5, 1894.

MR. SECRETARY OF STATE: His Majesty's minister of foreign affairs, to whom I hastened to communicate the contents of the note of your honorable Department of the 30th of August last, instructs me to thank your excellency for this communication, and at the same time to announce the adhesion of the King's Government to the rules established by agreement between the Federal Government and that of Her Britannic Majesty for the regulation of seal fishing in Bering Sea.

I therefore have the honor, in obedience to the instructions which I have received, to communicate the foregoing to your excellency, and I avail myself, at the same time, of this occasion to renew to you, Mr. Secretary of State, the assurances of my highest consideration.

FAVA.

Mr. Miyaoka to Mr. Gresham.

LEGATION OF JAPAN,
Washington, August 23, 1894. (Received August 24.)

SIR: I have the honor to acknowledge the receipt of your communication dated the 20th instant and having reference to the regulations for the preservation of the fur-seal species agreed to by the Governments of the United States and Great Britain in conformity with the award of the Tribunal of Arbitration between those two powers held at Paris. I have also the honor to acknowledge the receipt of the copies of the award and of the acts of Congress passed to give effect to the regulations embodied in it, which you have been good enough to transmit with your communication.

With reference to the invitation which you convey to the Imperial Government to give its adhesion to these regulations for the protection and preservation of fur seal, I beg to say that I shall hasten to take advantage of the earliest opportunity to inform my Government of the contents of your communication, in order that a formal reply may be given as soon as possible.

Be pleased to accept, etc.,

TSUNEJIRO MIYAOKA.

Mr. Romero to Mr. Gresham.

[Translation.]

LEGATION OF MEXICO,
White Plains, N. Y., August 21, 1894. (Received August 23.)

Mr. SECRETARY: I have the honor to acknowledge the receipt of your note of the 20th instant, with the inclosed documents, in which you request, in virtue of the treaty signed at Washington February 29, 1892, between the United States of America and Great Britain, the adhesion of the Government of Mexico to the regulations prescribed by the Tribunal of Arbitration organized in virtue of Article I of said treaty, applicable to the eastern side of the North Pacific Ocean from the thirty-fifth degree of north latitude to Bering Straits, for the protection and preservation of the fur seals, and to prevent their extermination by hunters in that region.

The signatory powers to this treaty propose to obtain the adhesion of the other nations to the regulations prescribed by the Tribunal of Arbitration, which have hitherto been binding upon the two contracting nations only, in order to prevent the extermination of the seals, a matter which concerns the civilized world, and to this end you request the adhesion of the Government of Mexico.

I have the honor to inform you in reply that I have transmitted to my Government a copy of your note, and of each of the inclosed documents, in order that, being informed of them and of the circumstances of the case, they may decide as they may deem convenient.

Accept, etc.,

M. ROMERO.

Mr. Planten to Mr. Gresham.

CONSULATE-GENERAL OF THE NETHERLANDS,
New York, September 17, 1894. (Received September 19.)

SIR: In reply to your letter of August 20 last, on the subject of the regulations established on the eastern side of the North Pacific Ocean from the thirty-fifth degree of north latitude to the Bering Straits for the proper protection and preservation of the fur-seal species, I am instructed to inform your excellency that Her Majesty's Government is taking the matter in consideration and will inform your Government as soon as possible of the result of its consideration.

Accept, etc.,

J. R. PLANTEN.

Mr. Yrigoyen to Mr. Gresham.

LEGATION OF PERU,
Washington, August 21, 1894. (Received August 21.)

SIR: I have the honor to acknowledge the receipt of your favor of yesterday's date, and the documents to which you refer.

In your favor you are pleased to inform me that agreeably to the provision of Article VII of the treaty of arbitration concluded between the United States and Great Britain, February 29, 1892, the United

States seek to obtain the adhesion of the other powers to the regulations which the arbitrators consider necessary for the preservation of the fur seal on the east side of the North Pacific Ocean from the thirty-fifth degree of north latitude to Bering Straits.

For that purpose you are pleased to express to me the desire that my Government should adhere to said regulations, by means of adequate legislation.

In reply, I have the pleasure to inform you that I will forward to my Government by the next steamer your highly esteemed note and the documents inclosed, and that as soon as I shall receive his reply I will communicate it to your Department.

I avail, etc.,

JOSE M. YRIGOYEN.

Mr. Da Costa Duarte to Mr. Gresham.

[Translation.]

LEGATION OF PORTUGAL,
Washington, October 15, 1894.

MR. SECRETARY: The Government of his very faithful majesty having decided to give its adherence to the regulations prescribed by the Tribunal of Arbitration of Paris which, for the effective protection and preservation of the fur seal must be applied to the eastern side of the North Pacific Ocean from the thirty-fifth degree of north latitude to Bering Straits, agreeably to the wishes expressed in the note which your excellency did the honor to address to me on the 20th of last August, has instructed me to notify your excellency thereof.

The Government of His Majesty, however, desires that it be distinctly and clearly established that its adherence is restrictive simply as regards the taking of the fur seal, and in the waters comprised within the limits traced by the Tribunal of Arbitration of Paris, this act of the Government implying no recognition on its part of any principle tending to regulate fishing outside of the territorial waters of each nation.

Be pleased to accept, etc., IGNACIO DA COSTA DUARTE.

Prince Cantacuzene to Mr. Gresham.

[Translation.]

NEW LONDON, CONN., *August 10–22, 1894.*

MR. SECRETARY OF STATE: I have had the honor to receive the note which you were pleased to address me on the 20th of August instant, transmitting to me the declarations and the award of the Tribunal of Arbitration in the matter of the preservation of fur seal as well as the legislative measures taken by the United States to the end of assuring the efficacy of the Paris regulations.

Resting on the seventh article of your treaty with England of February 29, 1892, you are pleased to address to me at the same time the invitation of the Federal Government to the Imperial Government to adhere to the arbitral decisions of Paris, and to cause them to be respected by Russian subjects and vessels, by taking to such end the necessary legislative steps.

I will make it my prompt duty to transmit to my Government the communication you have addressed to me on this subject, and I reserve informing you of the reply of the Imperial Government when it shall reach me.

I think that I can, however, at once inform you that Russia, having to the same degree as the United States an interest and an imperative duty to equally assure in her waters the preservation of fur seal, the Imperial Government could not give its adhesion to the Paris regulations and to the legislative measures adopted in consequence thereof at Washington and at London unless the totality of those measures be applied likewise to all the waters of the Pacific situated to the north of the thirty-fifth degree of north latitude.

Be pleased, etc.,   CANTACUZENE.

Mr. Muruaga to Mr. Gresham.

LEGATION OF SPAIN,
Washington, August 24, 1894.   (Received August 25.)

The undersigned, envoy extraordinary and minister plenipotentiary of Spain, has the honor to inform the honorable Secretary of State that he has received his note of the 20th instant, relative to the judgments pronounced by the Tribunal of Arbitration at Paris in the question submitted to it by the Government of the United States and that of Great Britain, concerning the taking and preservation of fur seals in Bering Sea, and to the invitation addressed to the Government of Spain to adhere to the decisions of said tribunal.

The undersigned minister has informed the Government of His Majesty of the desire expressed in the said note, and has transmitted to it at the same time the documents inclosed therein, and as soon as an answer shall be received he will hasten to transmit it to the honorable Secretary of State.

The undersigned avails, etc.,   E. DE MURUAGA.

No. 125.

Mr. Gresham to Sir Julian Pauncefote.

DEPARTMENT OF STATE,
Washington, August 21, 1894.

EXCELLENCY: Referring to our verbal communications of a recent date, I have now the honor formally to acknowledge the receipt of your note of the 7th of June last, in which you propose in behalf of Her Majesty's Government the establishment of a mixed commission for the purpose of " verifying and adjusting the claims for compensation for the seizure of British sealing vessels in Bering Sea."

While no serious difficulty is anticipated in settling and determining the claims by means of a mixed commission, it is a matter of interest to both Governments that they should, if possible, be disposed of in a simpler and less expensive way.   Proceedings by a mixed commission, while always more or less formal and cumbersome, are, like all other processes of litigation, necessarily attended with expense, not infrequently considerable in amount, as well as with delay.

In the present case the award and findings of the Tribunal of Arbitration at Paris have, to a great extent, determined the facts and the principles on which the claims should be adjusted, and in the course of the negotiations for a mixed commission, they have been subjécted by both Governments to a thorough examination, both upon the principles and the facts which they involve.

Under these circumstances the President, after full consideration of the whole subject, has reached the conclusion that it may be practicable as well as advantageous to effect a direct settlement of the claims by the payment of a lump sum in full satisfaction of all demands for damages against the United States growing out of the controversy between the two Governments as to the fur seals in Bering Sea; and to this end I am instructed by the President to propose the sum of $425,000.

This propositon, if it should prove to be acceptable to Her Majesty's Government, is to be understood as having been made subject to the action of Congress on the question of appropriating the money. The President can only undertake to submit the matter to Congress at the beginning of its session in December next, with a recommendation that the money be appropriated and made immediately available for the purpose above expressed; and if at any time before the appropriation is made your Government shall desire, it is understood that the negotiations on which we have for some time been engaged for the establishment of a mixed commission will be renewed.

I have, etc.   W. Q. GRESHAM.

No. 126.

Sir Julian Pauncefote to Mr. Gresham.

WASHINGTON, *August 21, 1894.*

SIR: I have the honor to acknowledge the receipt of your note of this date on the subject of our recent negotiations for the adjustment, by means of a mixed commission, of the claims of Great Britain against the United States in respect of the seizure of British sealing vessels by United States cruisers in Bering Sea.

You state that the President, after full consideration, is of opinion that it would be in the interest of both Governments to effect the direct settlement of the claims by the payment of a lump sum, in order to avoid the delay and expense of a mixed commission, and that you have been instructed to propose the sum of $425,000.

You also state that the proposal is made subject to the necessary appropriation by Congress, to which it would be submitted at the beginning of its session in December next, with a recommendation that the money be made immediately available for the purpose above mentioned.

You add that if at any time before the appropriation is made Her Majesty's Government shall desire it the negotiations for the establishment of a mixed commission shall be resumed.

I have the honor to state in reply that Her Majesty's Government concur in the views of the President as to the expediency of effecting a settlement by the method proposed, and that they are indeed so fully sensible of the great advantages presented to both Governments by that course that they are willing to accept the sum offered, coupled with the assurance of prompt payment, although the amount is much below their estimate of the compensation, which might fairly be awarded by a mixed commission.

It should be understood, therefore, that if the negotiations for a mixed commission should be resumed the acceptance of your proposal shall in no way prejudice the claimants in the further prosecution of their demands.

It only remains for me to express my gratification at this amicable solution of the last subject of discussion in the long Bering Sea controversy.

I have, etc.   JULIAN PAUNCEFOTE.

No. 127.

Mr. Gresham to Sir Julian Pauncefote.

DEPARTMENT OF STATE,
Washington, January 23, 1895.

EXCELLENCY: I have the honor to transmit to you an official statement of the American pelagic fur-seal catch of 1894, taken from the records of the custom-houses at the ports of San Francisco, Port Townsend, and Astoria, for transmission to your Government in compliance with Article V of the Bering Sea arbitration award.

It will be observed by reference to this statement that in many instances the latitude and longitude have been omitted. In explanation of this omission I am informed by the Secretary of the Treasury that the collector of customs at San Francisco has reported the masters of the vessels deposed under oath, that they cleared without notice of the pending award, and consequently were ignorant of this requirement.

In addition to the number of seals officially entered as mentioned in the statement above referred to, namely, 26,095, information obtained from the annual sales of fur-seal skins in London indicates that there were, in fact, sent to London about 139,000 skins, Asiatic and American, taken in the North Pacific Ocean and Bering Sea. Adding to this the skins estimated as retained in the United States, about 3,000, the total catch would appear to be about 142,000. The number of skins entered at Victoria, according to a report transmitted by the United States consul, is 95,048. The total of the American and British entries therefore is 121,143, being about 20,000 skins less than the total catch as appears from the statistics of the London sales and estimates of skins retained in this country.

Presumably these 20,000 skins were transshipped by American or British vessels at Yokohama, reaching London via Suez Canal. The Secretary of the Treasury reports that there is no record of any transshipments received in the United States ports, except as regards 6,760 skins which arrived in the port of San Francisco and appear in our official returns herewith transmitted. These skins were presumably taken off the Japanese and Russian coasts. All of the skins of which the sex is indicated in the accompanying statement were carefully examined by an inspector at the time of their entry.

I have the honor to request the following official information from your Government as to the pelagic catch of fur seals for the years 1893 and 1894:

1. The total number of seals taken by British vessels in the North Pacific Ocean and Bering Sea, both on the Asiatic and American sides.

2. The total number of skins landed at British ports by said vessels.

3. The total number transshipped in Japanese or Russian ports, including any that may have been ultimately entered at Victoria.

4. The total number of skins landed as entered at Victoria by American vessels.

5. A report as to the sex of all skins taken in Bering Sea and the North Pacific Ocean.

6. Location of the place of catch by latitude and longitude.

7. The names of all vessels employed, tonnage, number of the crew, and number of seal hunters, indicating whether whites or Indians.

I have the honor to further request that your Government inform me whether the pelagic skins taken by its vessels were examined as to sex by expert inspectors, as was done in the case of skins entered in United States ports.

I have, etc.,

W. Q. GRESHAM.

Summary of pelagic seal catches for 1893 and 1894, based on the official returns from ports of entry.

Year.	Nationality.	British Columbia and Northwest coasts.	Bering Sea.	Japan coast.	Russian coast.	Locality undetermined.	Total.	Grand total.
1893..	American		(Modus vi-vendi in operation.)	29,173	11,955	8,432	8,342	....
	Canadian	28,613				....	69,741	* 78,083
1894..	American	12,398	5,160	1,500	201	6,836	† 26,095	....
	Canadian	11,703	26,425	49,483	7,437	....	95,048	† 121,143
	Total ...	24,101	31,585	50,983	7,638	6,836	....	....

* Notes concerning catch for 1893. † Notes concerning catch for 1894.

The United States consul at Victoria states (Consular Reports No. 161, p. 279) that American schooners in 1893 transshipped at Yokohama and Hakodadi between 17,000 and 18,000 skins. These skins, added to those which in all probability were transshipped by British Columbia vessels on the Asiatic coast, and including the estimated number retained in America for treatment, would swell the total catch to about 109,000. The accuracy of these figures is corroborated by the fact that the trade sales of London (all seal skins are sold there) account for the disposition of 109,669 skins in 1893.

The catch of 6,836, noted in column headed "Locality undetermined," were skins, 76 of which were landed at Astoria without statement as to place of capture; 641 were transshipped at Unalaska, and the remaining 619 were transshipped from Yokohama. All were entered and recorded in American ports of entry, and they are quite certainly a mixture of Northwest coast and Japan skins.

It has been ascertained from the sales of seal skins in London that about 125,000 skins were actually sold and about 14,000 withheld for future sale in 1894. In addition thereto it is estimated that about 3,000 skins were retained in this country and elsewhere for treatment. It thus appears that about 142,000 is a figure much more closely representing the number of skins taken in 1894 than the official returns of 121,143. The balance, about 20,000 skins, was probably shipped to London via Suez Canal from the Asiatic Coast.

Number of schooners reported as having taken skins.

Year.	American.	Canadian.	Total.
1893	28	* 56	84
1894	35	* 60	95

* Indian canoe catch counted as one vessel. In destructive effects the canoe catch is about equal to three average schooner catches.

Number of schooners reported as having made catches in Bering Sea.

Year.	American.	Canadian.	Total.
1893 *			
1894	10	27	37

* Modus vivendi was in operation.

No. 128.

·Mr. Gresham to Sir Julian Pauncefote.

DEPARTMENT OF STATE,
Washington, January 23, 1895.

EXCELLENCY: I have the honor to inform you for communication to your Government, of the deep feeling of solicitude on the part of the President of the United States with regard to the future of the Alaskan seal herd as disclosed by the official returns of seals killed at sea during the present season in the North Pacific Ocean, filed in the respective custom-houses of the United States and British Columbia, and by reliable estimates of skins shipped to London from the Asiatic coast by way of the Suez Canal.

It would appear that there were landed in the United States and Victoria 121,143 skins, and that the total pelagic catch, as shown by the London trade sales and careful estimates of skins transshipped in Japanese and Russian ports, amounts to about 142,000, a result unprecedented in the history of pelagic sealing. It would further appear that the vessels engaged in Bering Sea, although only one-third of the total number employed in the North Pacific, in four or five weeks killed 31,585 seals, not only over 8,000 more than were killed in Bering Sea in 1891 (the last year the sea was open) but even more than the total number killed during the four months on the American side of the North Pacific this season.

This startling increase in the pelagic slaughter of both the American and Asiatic herds has convinced the President, and it is respectfully submitted can not fail to convince Her Majesty's Government, that the regulations enacted by the Paris Tribunal have not operated to protect the seal herd from that destruction which they were designed to prevent, and that, unless a speedy change in the regulations be brought about, extermination of the herd must follow. Such a deplorable result should if possible be averted.

The experience of the past year under the regulations has demonstrated that not alone are the United States and Great Britain deeply interested in the preservation of the seal herd; Russia and Japan have interests commercially almost as important. Any new system of regulations of necessity should embrace the whole North Pacific Ocean from the Asiatic side to the American side, and should be binding upon the citizens and subjects alike of all of these countries.

In order to add to our scientific knowledge upon this question as to the habits of the seal, its feeding grounds, and the effect of pelagic sealing upon the herd, and other similar questions, the President deems it advisable to suggest to Her Majesty's Government, and to the Governments of Russia and Japan, that a commission be appointed, consisting of one or more men from each country, eminent for scientific knowledge and practical acquaintance with the fur trade. This commission should visit the Asiatic side of the North Pacific as well as the American, and also the islands which the seals frequent, and report to their respective Governments as to the effects of pelagic sealing on the herd and the proper measures needed to regulate such sealing so as to protect the herd from destruction and permit it to increase in such numbers as to permanently furnish an annual supply of skins.

I am directed by the President to propose for the consideration of your Government, and the Governments of Russia and Japan, the appointment of such a commission, and I am further directed to suggest that during its deliberations the respective Governments agree upon a modus vivendi, as follows:

That the regulations now in force be extended along the line of the thirty-fifth degree of north latitude from the American to the Asiatic shore, and be enforced during the coming season in the whole of the Pacific Ocean and waters north of that line. Furthermore, that sealing in Bering Sea be absolutely prohibited pending the report of such commission.

Inasmuch as the sealing season will shortly commence, and the fleet will leave the western coast for the sealing grounds, I beg to suggest the necessity of speedy action in regard to this proposition.

I have, etc.,

W. Q. GRESHAM.

No. 129.

Mr. Foster to Mr. Gresham.

AGENCY OF THE UNITED STATES,
Paris, August 17, 1893.

SIR: In fulfillment of what I regard as my duty before terminating my services as agent, to wit, to place my Government in possession of all information I have acquired which may be useful in future negotiations or action connected with the fur-seal arbitration, I direct attention to the subject of the British claims for damages on account of the seizure of certain vessels in Bering Sea in 1886, 1887, and 1889.

It will be seen from the decision of the tribunal that a finding of facts, agreed upon by counsel, was rendered in accordance with Article VIII of the treaty. This finding will be found to relate entirely to the facts of the seizures and, as agreed to by counsel, did not in any manner involve the question of liability or the value or ownership of the vessels. By reference to Protocol XXX, of May 31, it will be seen that the British Government has withdrawn all claim for damages under Article V of the modus vivendi of 1892. In further confirmation of this I inclose the statement of the British counsel before the tribunal on the subject.

S. Ex. 67——11

In view of these facts it would seem that the only question of damages open for the consideration of the two Governments was that arising out of the seizure of vessels in Bering Sea. The claims on this account as presented by the British Government will be found in the Schedule of Claims annexed to and bound with the British Case, and on page 315 of the British Counter Case.

The defense of the United States, so far as it was thought necessary to make one under Article VIII of the treaty, will be found in the United States Counter Case, pages 129 to 135, and the evidence there cited, contained in the appendix thereto, as also in the printed United States Argument, pages 215 to 227.

The total amount of the British claim, as presented at page 60 of the Schedule of Claims, is $439,171, of which $357,353 consist of a claim for prospective earnings, which I suggest can not be properly asserted, for the reasons set forth in the United States Argument.

It will appear from an examination of the evidence in the Case and Counter Case of the United States that most of the vessels appear in reality to be the property of American citizens. Further and more searching investigation may show that others of the vessels were the property of our citizens. In this connection, I refer to a correspondence at Paris had by me with the British agent in reference to the citizenship of Boscowitz, owner or mortgagee of several of these vessels.

I also inclose a memorandum in regard to the value of several of the seized vessels, which may be of service in the further examination of these claims.

Mr. Robert Lansing, associate counsel in the arbitration, made a visit in 1892 to Victoria and San Francisco for the purpose of collecting evidence in relation to this branch of the case, and I have no doubt he would cheerfully go to Washington at any time, if you or the person having charge of the Government's interests in this matter should think it desirable to confer with him.

I am, etc.,   JOHN W. FOSTER.

[Inclosure 1 in No. 129.—Extract from British report of proceedings of Tribunal of Arbitration, May 31, 1893, pp. 1197-1198.]

Sir CHARLES RUSSELL: * * * I wish to relieve, and am glad to relieve, the tribunal of one question at all events, and that is the question of damages under Article V of the modus vivendi of 1892, which is also remitted to this tribunal. This, sir, will not need any troublesome reference, because it is an admission I am going to make. At page 216 of the printed argument of the United States (you need not, sir, trouble to refer to it, if I may be permitted to say so, because it is not a point of difference between us—it is a matter I am clearing out of the way) the United States give up any claim to damages under that treaty; and I have to say, on the part of Great Britain, and speaking with authority in the matter, that although they had under the earlier modus vivendi to pay a very large sum for damages to their Canadian sealers—a sum, I think, exceeding $100,000—looking to the fact, nevertheless, that under the modus vivendi in question a great many, at least, if not all of the sealers who would have resorted to the eastern part of Bering Sea had made catches of seals in other parts of the ocean, and although I think it might be argued that this tribunal is required by Article V to give damages on the basis of a limited catch or catches which might have been taken in Bering Sea—in all the circumstances of the case Great Britain does not desire to press that view upon the tribunal, and, therefore, will ask for no finding for damages upon and under that fifth article of the modus vivendi; but it probably will be convenient in the award which the arbitrators may think proper to make, to state upon its face that both the United States and Great Britain have abandoned any claim for damages under that head.

The PRESIDENT. You are agreed also as to that, Mr. Phelps?

Mr. PHELPS. Yes.

[Inclosure 2 in No. 129.]

Mr. Tupper to Mr. Foster.

PARIS, *May 26, 1893.*

DEAR MR. FOSTER: Referring to the suggestion advanced on page 130 of the United States counter case, that some of the vessels for the seizure of which damages were claimed by Her Majesty's Government were owned by citizens of the United States, and to the promise made to the tribunal by the Attorney-General on the 11th of May, that, if possible, the arbitrators should not be troubled with the consideration of the subject, I now write to inquire whether we can agree upon the facts in dispute in order that the Attorney-General's suggestion should be made effective.

As regards Mr. Franks, I have not yet complete evidence. As regards Mr. Boscowitz, this gentleman denies that he is the owner of the vessels, and further denies that he is an American citizen. And, as at present advised, I shall have to ask the tribunal so to hold, unless, of course, it is possible, as I hope it may be, for me to come to an arrangement with you upon this matter.

Your suggestion being first made in your counter case, it was not possible to produce in court evidence on the point in the ordinary way; but Mr. Boscowitz happens at the present moment to be in Paris, and I would suggest that a fair way of eliciting the actual facts would be that we should examine and that you should cross-examine Mr. Boscowitz in the presence of a shorthand writer. His evidence might then be laid before the arbitrators as material for a decision, if this should be thought necessary by either side.

Yours, very truly, CHARLES H. TUPPER.

Mr. Foster to Mr. Tupper.

AGENCY OF THE UNITED STATES,
Paris, May 27, 1893.

DEAR MR. TUPPER: I have the honor to acknowledge the receipt of your communication of the 26th instant, in which you inform me that a Mr. Boscowitz "happens at the present moment to be in Paris," and, in view of certain proofs adduced in behalf of the United States respecting him, you suggest that he be examined and cross-examined here for the purpose of submitting his evidence to the arbitrators as material for a decision on their part.

An examination of the treaty under which the pending arbitration is constituted must satisfy you that I have no power or authority to accede to your request. The manner in which evidence is to be submitted to the arbitrators is precisely fixed by the terms of the treaty, and no opportunity or method for such submission is therein afforded to either party, except through its respective case and counter case.

Besides, it would hardly seem reasonable to allow one party, after the case, counter case, and printed argument had been submitted, and while the oral argument was in progress and near its close, to examine an important witness on its behalf, when the witnesses of the other party, whose testimony might be material to refute his statements, were 6,000 miles away, and who could not be reached in time to submit their testimony to the tribunal.

Referring to your inquiry as to whether we can agree upon the facts in dispute in order that the suggestion of Sir Charles Russell might be made effective, I have pleasure in saying that I am prepared to concur with you in any statement of facts proper to be considered by the tribunal and warranted by the evidence now legitimately before that body.

In closing I beg to remind you that "the suggestion * * * that some of the vessels for the seizure of which damages were claimed by Her Majesty's Government were owned by citizens of the United States" was not for the first time advanced by the United States in its counter case, as will be seen by references to the case of the United States, App., Vol. II, p. 505.

I am, etc.,   JOHN W. FOSTER.

[Inclosure 3 in No. 36.]

Memoranda as to ownership and value of vessels for which damages are claimed by the British Government, with accompanying envelope.

Carolena (p. 1 of Schedule to Claims, British case).—Was owned by A. J. Bechtel, American citizen (United States Argument, p. 219). Upon the question of American ownership of vessels, see, generally, United States case, Vol. II, p. 497. Mortgaged to A. J. Bechtel for $1,000 (U. S. C. C., p. 261).

British Government claims $125 per ton for this vessel (Schedule of Claims, p. 1).

That this is excessive, see United States Counter Case, pp. 247 and 248, where it appears that the *Marvin,* a fine boat, sold in 1892 for $58 per ton. A survey in 1885 shows her value to have been $3,000. (See report on survey on *Carolena,* envelope A.

As to value of sealing vessels and equipments, generally, see, report of United States Special Agent Henry, United States Counter Case, p. 245.

Thornton (p. 6).—Owned one-half by Boscowitz, American (United States Argument (p. 218), and in addition to references there given see also United States Counter Case, p. 314).

Value: British Government alleges 78 tons burden and value of $6,000, or $76.92 per ton. Her actual registered tonnage was 29.36 (U. S. C. C., pp. 339, 258).

NOTE.—That all calculations for value are made on net registered tonnage. See ibid., p. 350, per Turner.

Mortgaged to Boscowitz for $4,000 (U. S. C. C., p. 261). Actual value, at $76.92 per ton (which is probably excessive), $2,258.37.

Onward, (p. 10).—Maj. Wm. H. Williams says that Capt. Alexander

McLean, sealing captain of San Francisco, has stated to him that he, McLean, was part owner of this vessel. Major Williams believes that Captain McLean would be willing to make an affidavit to this effect.

Value: Alleged tonnage, 94; value claimed, $4,000; i. e., $42.55 per ton; actual tonnage, 32.20 (U. S. C. C., p. 339); actual value, at $42.55 per ton, $1,497.76.

W. P. Sayward (p. 17).—Owned by Boscowitz (see mem. for Thornton). Mortgaged in 1887 to Boscowitz for $2,500 (U. S. C. C., p. 261).

Grace (p. 20).—Owned by Boscowitz (see mem. for Thornton). Mortgaged to Boscowitz in 1886 for $6,000 (U. S. C. C., p. 261).

Value: Alleged tonnage, 182; alleged value, $12,000; i. e., value per ton, $65.93; actual tonnage, 76.87; actual value (at $65.93 per ton), $5,068.03 (U. S. C. C., p. 339); appraised value, $10,404 (U. S. C. C., p. 339); amount realized at sale, $1,525 (U. S. C. C., p. 339). The *Grace* was a steamer (U. S. C. C., p. 258). That the appraised value was considered too high at the time, see Senate Ex. Doc. No. 106, Fiftieth Congress, second session, p. 72. That no steps were taken by owners of *Grace, Anna Beck, Dolphin,* or *Ada,* to obtain their release, see ibid., p. 80.

Anna Beck (p. 24).—Owned by Boscowitz (see mem. for Thornton). Mortgaged in 1886 to Boscowitz for $6,000 (U. S. C. C., p. 261).

Value: Appraised value, $2,600; sold for $907; value claimed, $8,000 (U. S. C. C., p. 339); registered tonnage (U. S. C. C., p. 258), 40.38.

(In confirmation of the actual tonnage given by the United States, and hereinafter mentioned, of *Grace, Anna Beck, Dolphin,* and *Ada,* see Senate Ex. Doc. No. 106, Fiftieth Congress, second session, p. 72, where it is stated from a wholly independent source that the total tonnage of these four vessels is 249; this tallies closely with that now alleged by the United States.)

As to appraised value, see under *Grace.* Her appraised value was accepted by owner for purposes of bonding (Senate Ex. Doc. No. 106, Fiftieth Congress, second session, p. 76). She was built in 1865 (see certificate of enrollment). Now called the *James G. Swan* (envelope A).

Dolphin (p. 28).—Owned by Boscowitz (see mem. for Thornton).

Value: Mortgaged in 1886 to Boscowitz for $6,000 (U. S. C. C., p. 261); alleged tonnage, 174 tons; alleged value, $12,000; i. e., $68.96 per ton; actual tonnage, 60.10; actual value, at $68.96 per ton, $4,144.49 (U. S. C. C., p. 339); a steamer (U. S. C. C., p. 258); appraised value, $7,750 (U. S. C. C., p. 339); sold for $1,225 (ibid). (See remarks under *Grace* as to appraised value.)

Alfred Adams (p. 32).—Owned by A. Frank, American (United States) Argument, p. 219.)

Ada (p. 34).—Value: Tonnage alleged, 68; value alleged, $7,000, i. e., $103 per ton. This valuation is excessive (see value of *Marvin,* U. S. C. C., pp. 248 and 257.) Actual tonnage, 56.95 (U. S. C. C., p. 339); appraised value, $2,900; sold for $1,900 (U. S. C. C., p. 339).

(See remarks under *Grace* as to appraised value.)

That her appraisement was generally accepted, see Senate Ex. Doc. No. 106, Fiftieth Congress, second session, p. 78. Became in 1888 the *James Hamilton Lewis;* was seized by Russia for raiding Copper Island in 1891.

Lily (p. 50).—Owned by A. Frank, American (United States Argument, p. 219).

Black Diamond (p. 48).—Owned by A. Frank, American (United States Argument, p. 219).

Pathfinder (pp. 40 and 57).—Owned by A. J. Bechtel, American (United States Argument, p. 219).

CPSIA information can be obtained
at www.ICGtesting.com
Printed in the USA
BVHW08s1022210918
528173BV00022B/1465/P